Navigating New Cyber Risks

Ganna Pogrebna · Mark Skilton

Navigating New Cyber Risks

How Businesses Can Plan, Build and Manage Safe Spaces in the Digital Age

Ganna Pogrebna
University of Birmingham
Birmingham, UK

The Alan Turing Institute
London, UK

Mark Skilton
Warwick Business School
University of Warwick
Coventry, UK

ISBN 978-3-030-13526-3   ISBN 978-3-030-13527-0   (eBook)
https://doi.org/10.1007/978-3-030-13527-0

Library of Congress Control Number: 2019933311

Cover design by Alexander Kharlamov

This Palgrave Macmillan imprint is published by the registered company Springer Nature Switzerland AG
The registered company address is: Gewerbestrasse 11, 6330 Cham, Switzerland

"If I had a world of my own, everything would be nonsense. Nothing would be what it is, because everything would be what it isn't. And contrary wise, what is, it wouldn't be. And what it wouldn't be, it would. You see?"
Lewis Carroll "Alice in Wonderland"

*For my son Madoc, my husband Alex, and all those wonderful people
who didn't find my quest to beat cybersecurity with a measuring stick
to be positively hysterical*
—Ganna Pogrebna

For my mother Angela
—Mark Skilton

Foreword

Cybercrime is the fastest-growing industry in the world and cybersecurity is the hottest topic on the planet. The one aspect of this topic that has the industry in a quandary is how to identify, protect, contain, and mitigate against cyberattacks on your business, customers, partners, estate, systems, and infrastructure. The variety, complexity, sophistication, and velocity continue to increase and expand at scale; and the threats are endless. While globally organized cybercriminal groups continue to launch increasingly sophisticated attacks against our networks, suppliers, and clients for monetary gain, it appears that some of the oldest and more simplistic techniques have proven to be highly effective and lucrative for these miscreants. For those of us engaged in cyberdefense on a daily basis, social media has become a major enemy, as it is used by cybercriminals to get to unsuspecting citizens as these citizens complain on Twitter, Facebook and other platforms when systems of a particular bank or financial institution are down or not working properly. Adversaries seize the moment to offer assistance, use social engineering to trick innocent victims into giving them private logins and credentials and wipe out their lifetime savings. Due to the scale and velocity with which such malicious activities propagate, the impact of these crimes is devastating. For more than 20 years we have been educating end users about the danger of clicking on a link in an email and, later on, on their smartphone. Yet, phishing attacks based on user-activation of malicious links are still widely used and continue to be extremely effective and profitable. While the largest and most widely known cybersecurity events held each year worldwide fill their floors with suppliers promoting their products and services and claiming to offer "silver bullet" solutions to protect and save you against cyberthreats; in reality, there is no silver bullet, and the hacks, compromises, and losses continue to increase. Not only financial, but also industrial espionage, counterfeit goods, theft of intellectual property, stealing trade secrets and compromising propriety research and development (just to name a few) continue to grow and threaten the very core of the economic health of our countries and society. Perhaps it is simple: technology alone is not the answer. It is simply a tool; and in the modern digital world the only thing that distinguishes cybercriminal from an honest individual is "opportunity", or the way in which we take or not take advantage of opportunities which are coming our way. Therefore, cybersecurity is not just a technical science, it is a behavioral science. It is now clear that we keep doing the same thing over and over again (i.e., trying to beat cybersecurity problems with a technological stick), expecting a different result—that is the definition of insanity. Yet, the problems we are facing in cybersecurity not only require a new and different approach, but most certainly a paradigm shift in our thinking. In order to successfully alleviate the risk of cyberattacks, we need to focus on people behind the keyboard or on the other side of the phoneline. We need to understand how they behave, think, act, and react—only by doing this we will be able to predict and, possibly, prevent their criminal actions. The human element of cybersecurity lies at the heart of this book's analysis, which is based on the real-world examples of how behavioral science can be effective and critical for enhancing our ability to address cybersecurity gaps. Obviously, there does not exist one simple answer to cybersecurity problems. Cybersecurity is constantly evolving, as are the people and minds behind cybercrime. Therefore, we need to be agile and understand that we too must innovate and evolve our thinking, technology, processes, education, and skills, while making full use of the recent breakthroughs in behavioral science.

If you have been working in cybersecurity for decades, or are making your first steps and want to feed your curiosity about this field not only from a risk, compliance, or technology perspective, but also from a behavioral science perspective, then I would say you have already opened your mind to the art of the possible, a new and different approach to the problem. I would then tell you to read on, as this book is the best place for you to start. It will most definitely expand your mind. It challenges the thinking of the most experienced and brightest cybersecurity practitioners as well as offers a nice guideline to cybersecurity as a behavioral science for beginners. It will take you back in time and give you a very thorough overview of where it all started, charting the course of the evolution of cybersecurity and, even more fascinatingly, the evolution of cybercriminal, the criminality, and the conscience of these nefarious actors. The authors approach this as behavioral scientists, from the viewpoint of someone who was trying to make sense of the field. They adopt the perspective of a typical practitioner (not a technical specialist), someone who is trying to understand the true risks and simply navigate this complex field, by considering alternative cybersecurity solutions and enhancements as well as leveraging the people aspect to improve outcomes and achieve more effective results in building safe digital spaces for business and beyond. The first chapters of the book provide a general summary of the field and systematize the threats. The second part of the book describes how behavioral science (both conceptual and algorithmic) could contribute to solving the majority of cybersecurity issues. Something we can all embrace.

This book offers a different view on cybersecurity and cyberdefense—a behavioral (human) view. Its purpose is to consider how to frame the new threats in the digital and physical world, understand their nature, and formulate cybersecurity responses, which, in the face of the contemporary threats, need to combine both technical and behavioral strategies beyond compliance certification and standards. Security and compliance are not the same; we have to get beyond thinking that being compliant is being secure. The authors call upon recent evidence from leading practitioners and academics and offer new methods which will help organizations to plan, build, and manage cyber risks.

In this book, leading business thinkers and experts came together, combining contemporary visions from cybersecurity, behavioral science, human–data and human–computer interactions, and artificial intelligence (AI) fields, to provide practical insights for businesses and help them anticipate new risks and vulnerabilities, which they have never encountered earlier in digital environments. The authors analyse practical evidence-based cyberthreats and organize expert responses into a practical toolbox on how to consider risks and vulnerabilities across different dimensions, as well as suggesting ways to discover new risks and vulnerabilities. After reading this book, you will gain a better understanding of predictive analysis as well as learn how to anticipate what is coming next (e.g., future threats and vulnerabilities).

This book focuses not only on how new risks and vulnerabilities could be identified but also on human interpretations of these risks and, ultimately, on how the actual threats could be overlooked by humans. It delivers a piece of the puzzle that meets a critical gap in helping to identify ways to embed human behavior into the design of safe human-cyber spaces so these systems operate in the service of making human-centered digital ecosystems more secure. These ideas help us get closer to security-by-design and must be considered when thinking about the future of security and proactive network defense.

The authors explore whether and to what extend human psychology is prone to different social-engineering tricks, which cybercriminals play on us. Knowing this allows us to use cutting-edge behavioral measures and tools in order to complement the technical solutions which already exist.

This book will help everyone who reads it, no matter how much or how little experience you have in this field. It will give you insights, ideas, and stimulate thoughts, challenging the norm and your usual way of thinking about the problem of cybersecurity. Make no doubt about it: cybersecurity is a systemic and global problem, an arms race complemented by the looming feeling that the criminals are outpacing us in every way. The authors suggest alternative ways to close the existing gap. By treating cybersecurity as a behavioral issue, we can open the door to incredible critical and problem-solving thinking and innovation in this area. Just imagine the exciting possibilities, which behavioral approach can offer! We can algorithmically predict attacks using the behavioral topology of cybercriminals and their business models. This will enable us to design smart active cyberdefense mechanisms by anticipating attacks and collecting forensic evidence "on the fly" when attacks are still in progress. In this book, you will receive practical tips about incorporating behavioral approaches for understanding and improving cybersecurity within your organization and learn how to integrate it into your environment to enhance your holistic approach to building safe digital spaces. There are a number of new ideas regarding the psychology of cybersecurity—behavioral segmentation of users and cybercriminals, new "positive" approaches to cybersecurity campaigns, multilayered cybersecurity systems tailored to different types of cybercriminals, etc.

It is a fascinating read and makes tremendous sense. The authors provide us with well-defined ways of thinking about security and get us one step closer to uncovering the anatomy of the criminal activities and business models and, ultimately, advance us towards finding that silver bullet, which would give us tangible advantages over cybercriminals in the future. Taking human behavior into account when thinking about cybersecurity is extremely important and should not just be a factor we consider after the design of security systems is complete. The reality dictates that we should have a human (and our propensity to make errors, show bias, etc.) in mind when we build secure environments and when we are trying to defend against threats. As I said at the beginning—the problem often boils down to understanding who is behind the keyboard. After all, cybercriminals are only human: they are just people who exploit those endless opportunities which come their way in the digital age and pray on the innocent without a conscience.

This is a thought-provoking, compelling book that adds a whole new dimension to how we address cybersecurity and cyberdefense from the perspective of human behavior. It is a must-read for cybersecurity practitioners, cybersecurity professionals, researchers, behavioral scientists, and people who are simply interested in this field or worried about their personal security in cyber spaces.

London, UK

Maria Vello
CEO of the Cyber Defence Alliance

Preface

This book brings together leading experts and builds on the latest exciting research advances from cybersecurity, behavioral science, human–data interaction, human–computer interaction, as well as artificial intelligence (AI) fields, in order to offer new practical insights for businesses and help them to identify and address new vulnerabilities in human-cyber spaces. We are particularly focusing on threats and vulnerabilities, which businesses otherwise would not be able to identify in the modern complex digital environments. We consider cyberthreats, most recently and frequently observed in practice, and, organize expert views and opinions into a practical toolkit. This toolkit is intended to help practitioners and business owners to anticipate, consider, and tackle risks and vulnerabilities across different dimensions. It also suggests ways in which new (previously unobserved) risks and vulnerabilities can be discovered by looking at the wider ecosystem of issues beyond data and technology.

Our attention goes beyond traditional detection of risks and vulnerabilities. We pay particular attention to how humans perceive these risks and vulnerabilities and how those perceptions can misrepresent the actual threats, leading to under- or overreaction when responses to threats are formulated. We also look at how the ability to anticipate new risks and vulnerabilities can influence business models and business model innovation. Our goal is to empower businesses to be able to apply a new human-centered vision to cybersecurity problems in order to detect risks which they have not encountered or have not anticipated before. Furthermore, these risks and vulnerabilities do not only have to be detected, but also effectively communicated.

We aim to demonstrate how understanding and effective communication of risk-related issues can help build secure and safe human-cyber spaces in the new digital economy.

This book provides a detailed gap-bridging guide, which explains how to embed human behavior into the design of safe human-cyber spaces. It shows that cybersecurity should not be viewed as a *fixed cost* factor by businesses, which can only be addressed through technological upgrades. It is important to understand, that cybersecurity in many ways depend on humans and there is a need to design and build security systems with humans in mind. While there is a plethora of cybersecurity books, the existing book market offers little guidance on how to anticipate and diagnose new threats related to advanced AI cyberattacks and criminal social engineering, even though these threats are discussed by governments and international forums, requiring the development of new theoretical methodology, empirical tools, as well as policy. What seems to be missing is a way for current business practitioners to understand these new threats and risks and bring these together into an integrated toolkit. The new approach developed in this book helps us to address these issues as it draws upon the ideas and thoughts of leading experts, supported by the practical evidence.

Warwick, UK
January 2019

Ganna Pogrebna
Mark Skilton

Acknowledgements

The development of this book has involved many hours of research and interviews with leading practitioners and academics in the fields of cyber-security, behavioral science, machine learning, artificial intelligence (AI), economics, and business. We are extremely grateful to **Ms. Maria Vello**, CEO of the Cyber Defence Alliance, who wrote the foreword for this book. Maria's contribution to cybersecurity in the UK and internationally continues to inspire the authors of this book as well as many cybersecurity scholars and practitioners globally. We would like to recognize and sin-cerely thank the following people who gave their time in discussions, shar-ing thoughts and ideas that have helped us craft this book: **Debi Ashenden**, Professor of Cyber Security, School of Computing, and Programme Director for Protective Security and Risk at the Centre for Research and Evidence for Security Threats (CREST), University of Portsmouth; **Jon Crowcroft**, Marconi Professor of Communications Systems, Computer Laboratory at the University of Cambridge, Associate Fellow at the Centre for Science and Policy, and Fellow of the Alan Turing Institute; **Anthony Phipps**, cybersecurity expert and Senior Manager leading the Digital Cyber Research team at one of the largest financial institutions in Europe; **Haydn Povey**, CEO and Founder of Secure Thingz and board member of the IoT Security Foundation; **Karen Renaud**, Professor of Cybersecurity at Abertay University, Professor Extraordinarius at the University of South Africa, Fullbright Scholar, Honorary Research Fellow (Computing Science) at the University of Glasgow; **Boris Taratine**, cybersecurity expert, passionate visionary, and an influential ambassador of cybersecurity and cyberdefense; **Tim Watson**, Professor of Cybersecurity and Director of the Cyber Security

Centre at Warwick Manufacturing Group (WMG) at the University of Warwick; **Sir Alan Wilson**, Executive Chair of the Ada Lovelace Institute, Professor of Urban and Regional Systems at University College London, and former CEO of the Alan Turing Institute; **Karen Yeung**, Professorial Fellow in Law, Ethics and Informatics, University of Birmingham, member of the European Union (EU) High Level Expert Group on Artificial Intelligence, and member and rapporteur for the Council of Europe's Expert Committee on human rights dimensions of automated data processing and different forms of artificial intelligence (MSI-AUT). We also thank many cybersecurity practitioners from leading financial, legal, and technological industries, as well as experts working in law enforcement, whose work and advice inspired this book but who wished to remain anonymous. Original artwork for this book was produced by **Alexander Kharlamov**, an award-winning artist and photographer, in collaboration with the authors.

Disclaimer

All company names, trade names, trademarks, trade dress designs/logos, copyright images, and products referenced in this book are the property of their respective owners. No company references in this book sponsored this book or the content thereof.

Contents

About the Authors

Ganna Pogrebna is Professor of Behavioral Economics and Data Science at the University of Birmingham and Fellow at the Alan Turing Institute. Blending behavioral science, computer science, data analytics, engineering, and business model innovation, Ganna helps businesses, charities, cities, and individuals to better understand why they make the decisions they make and how they can optimize their behavior to achieve higher profit, better (cyber)security, more desirable social outcomes, as well as flourish and bolster their well-being. She is interested in analyzing individual and group decision–making under risk and uncertainty (ambiguity) using laboratory experiments, field experiments and non-experimental data (specifically, large non-experimental datasets). She studies how decision-makers reveal their preferences, learn, co-ordinate, and make trade-offs in static and dynamic environments. Her work aims to develop quantitative models capable of describing and predicting individual and group behavior under risk and uncertainty. Using an algorithmic approach, Ganna works on hybrid models at the intersection between decision theory and machine learning (particularly, Anthropomorphic Learning). Her recent projects focus on smart technological and social systems, cybersecurity, AI, human–computer interaction (HCI), human–data interaction (HDI), and business models. Ganna is one of the authors of the Cyber Domain-Specific Risk Taking scale (CyberDoSpeRT), a tool which allows practitioners to construct behavioral segmentation in order to design cybersecurity solutions, and which received the Organizational Psychology Award from the British Academy of Management in 2018. Her work on risk modeling and understanding human behavior under risk and uncertainty was published in highly reputable peer-refereed academic journals and recognized by numerous awards, including the Leverhulme Fellowship Award as well as the Economic and Social Research Council/the Alan Turing Institute Fellowship Award. Since 2002, Ganna has used her expertise to develop practical solutions for businesses as a consultant.

Mark Skilton is Professor of Practice in Information Systems and Management at Warwick Business School, the University of Warwick, UK. He has over 30 years' experience as a professional consultant with a track record in the top 1000 companies in over 20 countries and across multiple public, private, and start-up sectors. He is also currently a member of the senior executive team as Head of the Applied Research and Collaboration Labs (ARC) UK at Enzen, an international energy and utility consultancy based in the UK, India, the EU, Australia, and North America. He has direct industrial experience of commercial practice leadership, boardroom, and investor strategy to program team and transformation management at scale. Mark has previously published two international practitioner books on building the digital enterprise and digital ecosystem architectures. He is a recognized international thought leader in digital, IoT, automation and AI, cyber-physical systems, cybersecurity, company strategy, telecoms, digital markets and M&A strategies, CxO practices, and technology governance. His work and views have been published in the *Financial Times*, *New York Times*, *Wall Street Journal*, *Washington Post*, *New Scientist*, *Nature*, and *Scientific American*, by Bloomberg and the Associated Press, and on many TV and radio channels around the world, including the BBC, Sky, ITV, Al Jazeera, and many others. Mark has an MBA and postgraduate qualifications in Production Engineering, Design Management, and Material Sciences from the University of Warwick, the University of Cambridge, and the University of Sheffield, UK, respectively.

Notes on Advisors

Debi Ashenden is Professor of Cyber Security in the School of Computing at the University of Portsmouth. Debi was previously Head of the Centre for Cyber Security at Cranfield University at the Defence Academy of the UK. Before becoming an academic, she was a Managing Consultant at QinetiQ (formerly DERA) and has worked in cybersecurity since 1998. Debi holds a Ph.D. in Computer Science from UCL, an M.B.A., M.Sc. in Computer Science, M.A. in Victorian Literature and B.A. (Hons) in English Literature. She has worked extensively across the public and private sector for organizations such as the UK Ministry of Defence (MoD), UK Cabinet Office, UK Home Office, Euroclear, Prudential, Barclaycard, Reuters, and Close Bros. Debi has had a number of articles on cybersecurity published, presented at a range of conferences and co-authored a book for Butterworth-Heinemann, *Risk Management for Computer Security: Protecting Your Network and Information Assets*.

Jon Crowcroft is the Marconi Professor of Communications Systems, Computer Laboratory, University of Cambridge, UK. He is also Associate Fellow of the Centre for Science and Policy and Fellow at the Alan Turing Institute, UK. Jon Crowcroft joined the University of Cambridge in 2001, prior to which he was Professor of Networked Systems at UCL in the Computer Science Department. He is a Fellow of the Royal Society, Fellow of the Association for Computing Machinery, a Chartered Fellow of the British Computer Society, a Fellow of the Institution of Electrical Engineers and a Fellow of the Royal Academy of Engineering, as well as a Fellow of the Institute of Electrical and Electronics Engineers. He was a member of the Interactive Advertising Bureau (1996–2002) and went to the first 50 meetings of the Internet Engineering Task Force; was General Chair for the ACM SIGCOMM (1995–1999) and was a recipient of the SIGCOMM Award in 2009. He is the Principal Investigator in the Computer Lab for the EU Social Networks project, the Horizon Digital Economy project, funded by the Engineering and Physical Sciences Research Council and hubbed at Nottingham, and the EPSRC–funded federated sensor networks (i.e., sensor nets) project FRESNEL, in collaboration with Oxford, along with a new five-year project towards a Carbon Neutral Internet with Leeds. Jon has made major contributions to a number of successful start-up projects, such as the Raspberry Pi and Xen. He has been a member of the Scientific Council of IMDEA Networks since 2007. He is also on the advisory board of the Max Planck Institute for Software Systems. Jon has written, edited, and co-authored a number of books and publications which have been adopted internationally in academic courses, including *TCP/IP and Linux Protocol Implementation: Systems Code for the Linux Internet, Internetworking Multimedia* (2001) and *Open Distributed Systems* (1995). Jon's research interests include communications, multimedia, and social systems, especially Internet related.

Anthony Phipps is a Senior Manager leading the Digital Cyber Research team at one of the largest financial institutions in Europe. Tony started his career as an engineer and has worked in a variety of fields including electrical and electronic engineering, and, more recently, information technology. For the last 20 years he has specialized in information, cyber and physical security. He obtained his first degree in Electrical and Electronic Engineering from the University of Greenwich in 1997 and a Master's degree from the University of Westminster in Information Technology Security in 2002. He is currently working towards obtaining a Ph.D. in cybersecurity.

Haydn Povey is a CEO and Founder of Secure Thingz Inc. He is also a board member of the IoT Security Foundation. He is a recognized international expert in IoT security development. Prior to establishing Secure Thingz, he spent ten years at ARM as Director of Marketing of Security across industry sectors and in the Processor Division and product management. Secure Thingz is a provider of advanced security solutions for embedded systems in the Internet of Things. It was founded by Haydn in 2016 and recently sold to IAR Systems AB, a Swedish developer of embedded systems tools, for £20 million. The company's Secure Deploy™ architecture has been developed to solve the major security issues challenging the IoT. It claims that its solutions ensure a cost-efficient root of trust in low-cost microcontrollers to deliver a core set of critical services through the product lifecycle, alongside a secure deployment, production, and update infrastructure in the field of embedded trust.

Karen Renaud is Professor of Cybersecurity, Division of Cybersecurity, at the Abertay University, Professor Extraordinarius at the University of South Africa, Fulbright Cyber Security Scholar 2016/2017, as well as Honorary Research Fellow (Computing Science) at the University of Glasgow, UK. Karen is a graduate of the universities in Pretoria, South Africa, and Glasgow, UK. Her main research interest is Usable Security. She publishes widely in this area and collaborates with academics in the UK, South Africa, and Canada. She also has interests in email usage in organizations, electronic voting, and technology acceptance, specifically with respect to learning support systems. Karen's research interests include the usability of security systems, graphical authentication mechanisms, security and email acceptable-use policies, the use of technology in organizations, electronic voting, and privacy. She has written many academic publications in the field of security, along with numerous book contributions, and is a frequent speaker at cybersecurity conferences.

Boris Taratine is a passionate visionary and an influential ambassador of cybersecurity and cyberdefense. He has worked for world-renowned companies across the globe, holding different senior cyber and information security technical and leadership roles, was engaged in consulting with numerous organizations and is an active participant in various industry and law enforcement forums influencing global cybersecurity development. He is a frequent speaker at various industry events. He serves as a Strategic Executive Advisor to CEOs and a member of advisory boards to new cybersecurity start-ups. Boris has nearly 30 years' experience in the cybersecurity, information security, and information technology fields, spanning different industries. He possesses extremely strong analytical and problem-solving skills and is able to find and integrate complex solutions consistent with the customer and regulatory requirements. Boris is the author of six scientific publications and nine patents (including four granted under the NATO HiTech project), and has dozens of patents pending. He is a Ph.D. candidate and graduated from the Saint-Petersburg State University with the highest honor.

Maria Vello is a CEO of the Cyber Defence Alliance (CDA). She joined the CDA in April 2016. Prior to this, she was the CEO and President of the NCFTA (National Cyber-Forensics and Training Alliance) for three years.

Before her appointment as CEO and President, Maria served on the Board of Directors of the NCFTA from its inception in 2002 to 2012, and as the Board Secretary at the NCFTA for four years. Under Maria's leadership, the NCFTA weathered several significant cyber storms (e.g., those instigated by Gameover ZeuS and Darkode), playing an instrumental role in major successes across cybersecurity industry and in law enforcement. During her leadership, in 2014, the NCFTA was named in the President Obama's Executive Order. Maria was the constant driving force for the NCFTA's growth in revenues and reach. She also helped ensure the increase in the number of cybercriminal arrests as well as cases taken on by the law enforcement partners. Maria brings a wealth of experience in trust-based collaboration and information sharing across businessed in different industries. She often acts as an ambassador linking businesses with law enforcement, government and academia to proactively detect, protect, deter, dismantle, and stop cybercrime and cyberthreats. She has effectively led multinational teams to leverage cross-sector resources and threat intelligence in order to more efficiently analyze, correlate, and attribute critical real-time intelligence against emerging cyberthreats as well as to deliver actionable intelligence to both industry and law enforcement.

With more than 25 years' experience in the security, design, integration, risk, architectural design, and implementation of global corporate systems, security architectures, and networks, Maria has been responsible for integrating security best practices, risk, and compliance, as well as raising awareness at every level in every organization for which she has worked. Maria managed a Fortune Global 100 network infrastructure and systems from security, LAN, WAN, Voice, Video, Voicemail, gateways to network architecture. She was the owner of network security and vulnerability assessment company and worked for Cisco Systems in security for 7 years. Maria has been recognized as a leading expert in security throughout her career. She received the AT&T Leaders Council Award, finishing in the top 2% of the AT&T expert rankings and was the number one Regional Manager in Security while she worked for Cisco Systems. She was also honored by the FBI Executive team within the FBI Cyber Unit, Department of Justice, and the FBI Cyber Initiative Resource and Fusion Unit (CIRFU) for her exemplary service, partnership, and contributions with the Cyber Division. In 2014, she was named one of the top ten Women in Cloud. Maria received her Bachelor's degree from Duquesne University, Pittsburgh, Pennsylvania, and studied further at the Massachusetts Institute of Technology and the University of Pennsylvania's Wharton School of Business. She has also attended numerous executive leadership and management training courses, including the Carnegie Mellon University Software Engineering Institute's certification program in the delivery, facilitation, consulting, and training of the Institute's OCTAVE methodology. In addition to being a Certified Information Systems Security Professional (CISSP), Maria also has the RAM-W physical security certification for the water industry.

Tim Watson is the Director of the Cyber Security Centre at Warwick Manufacturing Group (WMG) within the University of Warwick. With more than 25 years' experience in the computing industry and in academia, he has been involved with a wide range of computer systems on several high-profile projects and has acted as a consultant for some of the largest telecoms, power, and oil companies. He is an advisor to various parts of the UK government and to several professional and standards bodies. Tim's current research includes EU-funded projects on combating cybercrime and research into the protection of infrastructure against cyberattack. He is the Vice President (Academia) of the Trustworthy Software Initiative, a UK government–sponsored project to make software better, and a key deliverable of the UK National Cyber Security Programme. Tim is also a regular media commentator on digital forensics and cybersecurity.

Sir Alan Wilson is a current Executive Chair of the Ada Lovelace Institute, a former CEO of the Alan Turing Institute and Professor of Urban and Regional Systems in the Centre for Advanced Spatial Analysis at UCL. He is Chair of the Home Office Science Advisory Council. Alan is a Cambridge Mathematics graduate and began his research career in elementary particle physics at the Rutherford Laboratory. He turned to the social sciences, working on cities, with posts in Oxford and London before becoming Professor of Urban and Regional Geography in Leeds in 1970. He was a member of Oxford City Council from 1964 to 1967. In the late 1980s, he was the co-founder of GMAP Ltd, a university spin-out company. He was Vice Chancellor of the University of Leeds from 1991 to 2004, when he became Director–General for Higher Education in the then DfES. After a brief spell in Cambridge, he joined UCL in 2007. From 2007 to 2013, he was Chair of the Arts and Humanities Research Council; and from 2013 to 2015, he was Chair of the Lead Expert Group for the Government Office for Science Foresight on The Future of Cities project. His research field covers many aspects of the mathematical modeling of cities and the use of these models in planning. These techniques are now in common use internationally—including the concept of entropy in building spatial interaction models, summarized in *Entropy in Urban and Regional Modelling* (reissued in 2011 by Routledge). These models have been widely used in areas such as transport planning, demography, and economic modeling. Alan's recent research focused on the applications of dynamical systems theory in relation to modeling the evolution of urban structure in both historical and contemporary settings. This led to the laying of the foundations of a comprehensive theory of urban dynamics described in *Complex Spatial Systems* (2000). He has published over 200 papers and his recent books include *The Science of Cities and Regions* (2012), his five-volume *Urban Modelling* (2012, edited), *Explorations in Urban and Regional Dynamics* (2015, with Joel Dearden), *Global Dynamics* (2016, edited), and *Geo-mathematical Modelling* (2016, edited). Alan has a particular interest in interdisciplinarity and published *Knowledge Power* in 2010; he also writes the quaestio blog (www.quaestio. blogweb.casa.ucl.ac.uk).

Karen Yeung is the University of Birmingham's first Interdisciplinary Chair, taking up the post of Interdisciplinary Professorial Fellow in Law, Ethics, and Informatics in the School of Law and the School of Computer Science in January 2018. She has been a Distinguished Visiting Fellow at Melbourne Law School since 2016. Together with Andrew Howes and Ganna Pogrebna, she informally leads a group of over 90 researchers at the University of Birmingham from a wide range of disciplines under the theme of *Responsible Artificial Intelligence*. Karen is actively involved in several technology policy and related initiatives in the UK and worldwide, including initiatives concerned with the governance of AI, which is one of her key research interests. In particular, she is a member of the EU's High Level Expert Group on Artificial Intelligence (since June 2018), as well as a member and rapporteur for the Council of Europe's Expert Committee on human rights dimensions of automated data processing and different forms of artificial intelligence (MSI-AUT). Since March 2018, she has been the ethics advisor and member of the Expert Advisory Panel on Digital Medicine for the Topol Independent Technology Review for the NHS. Between 2016 and 2018, she was Chair of the Nuffield Council on Bioethics Working Party on Genome Editing and Human Reproduction. During this period, she was also a member of the World Economic Forum Global Future Council on Biotechnology. Her recent publications include *The Oxford Handbook of Law, Regulation and Technology* (2017, co-edited with Roger Brownsword and Eloise Scotford), and the Royal Society/British Academy report *Data Management and Use: Governance in the 21st Century* (2017). She is qualified to practice as a barrister and solicitor at the Supreme Court of Victoria (Australia), having completed a brief stint in professional legal practice. Karen is on the editorial boards of *Big Data & Society* and *Public Law*. As an Interdisciplinary Chair, she is keen to foster collaboration between academics from across a range of disciplines, and to initiate dialogue between academics and policy–makers across various disciplines concerned with examining the social, legal, democratic, and ethical implications of technological development, as well as seeking to promote informed, inclusive, and human-centered technology policy-making and implementation.

Abbreviations, Acronyms and Glossary

AG	Attack graph. A model of vulnerabilities and possible attack paths.
AI	Artificial intelligence—sometimes called machine intelligence—is intelligence demonstrated by machines, in contrast to the natural intelligence displayed by humans and other animals. In computer science, AI research is defined as the study of "intelligent agents": any device that perceives its environment and takes actions that maximize its chance of successfully achieving its goals (Poole and Goebel 1998). Colloquially, the term "artificial intelligence" is applied when a machine mimics "cognitive" functions that humans associate with other human minds, such as "learning" and "problem-solving" (Russel and Norvig 2009).
Anonymous	A decentralized international hacktivist group that is widely known for its various distributed denial-of-service (DDoS) cyberattacks against several governments, government institutions and agencies, corporations, and the Church of Scientology.
API	Application Programming Interface.
APT	Advanced Persistent Threat.
ATM	Automated Teller Machine.
AG	Attack Graph—the graphical mapping of a cyberattack.
Attack Policy	A model of methods and rules to respond to an attack graph model of vulnerabilities and possible attack paths. A contingent attack policy defines an action for each situation that may arise during an attack. This allows

	identification of not only the actions likely to be executed by a rational attacker, but also the order of their execution.
Attack Strategy	The attack strategies are all contingent plans consistent with the attack graph.
Attack Surface	Also known as threat surface. The attack surface of a software environment is the sum of the different points (the "attack vectors") where an unauthorized user (the "Attacker") can try to enter data to or extract data from an environment. Keeping the attack surface as small as possible is a basic security measure (Manadhata and Wing 2008).
BAT	Baidu, Alibaba, and Tencent, China's leading Internet companies.
BCT	Blockchain Technology.
BCW	Behavior-Change Wheel.
BlackSec	A hacking group involved with LulzSec and Anonymous in Operation AntiSec.
Botnet	Several Internet-connected devices, each of which is running one or more bots. Botnets can be used to perform a distributed denial-of-service (DDoS) attack, infect (Trojan) and steal data, send spam, and allow the attacker to access the device and its connection.
BYOD	Bring-You-Own-Device.
CareCERT	The NHS Digital cybersecurity CERT team.
CARTA	Continuous Adaptive Risk and Trust Assessment, a commercial framework by Gartner.
CBT	Cognitive Behavioral Therapy.
CEH	Certified Ethical Hacker from the EC-Council. Also known as a white-hat hacker.
CERT	A team of cybersecurity specialists who investigate cybersecurity attacks and can investigate and plan fixes. They provide alerts on attacks and can be notified of attacks to investigate. Examples include US-CERT, CareCERT.
CIIA	Critical Infrastructure Information Act (2002).
CISSP	Certified Information Systems Security Professional is an independent information security certification granted by the International Information System Security Certification Consortium, also known as (ISC). CISSP designation was accredited under the ANSI ISO/IEC Standard 17024:2003. It is also formally approved by the US Department of Defense (DoD) in both their

Information Assurance Technical (IAT) and Managerial (IAM) categories for their DoDD 8570 certification requirement. CISSP has been adopted as a baseline for the US National Security Agency's ISSEP program. CISSP is a globally recognized certification in the field of IT security.

Cloud-IAP   Cloud Identity-Aware Proxy.

CNI   Critical national infrastructure attack.

Cookies   A HTTP cookie (also called web cookie, Internet cookie, browsercookie, or simply cookie) is a small piece of data sent from a website and stored on the user's computer by the user's web browser while the user is browsing. Cookies were designed to be a reliable mechanism for websites to remember stateful information (such as items added in the shopping cart in an online store) or to record the user's browsing activity (including clicking buttons, logging in, or recording which pages were visited in the past). They can also be used to remember arbitrary pieces of information that the user previously entered in form fields, such as names, addresses, passwords, and credit card numbers.

Other kinds of cookies perform essential functions in the modern web. Perhaps most importantly, authentication cookies are the most common method used by web servers to establish whether the user is logged in or not, and which account they are logged in with.

Security vulnerabilities may allow a cookie's data to be read by a hacker, used to gain access to user data, or used to gain access (with the user's credentials) to the website to which the cookie belongs (see Cross-site Scripting [XSS]) and Cross-site Request Forgery [CSRF, XSRF]) (Vamosi 2008).

CPMI   Committee on Payments and Market Infrastructures.

CRISC   Certified in Risk and Information Systems Control certified by Information Systems Audit and Control Association (ISACA).

Cross-site Scripting   Cross-site scripting (XSS) is a type of computer security vulnerability typically found in web applications. XSS enables attackers to inject client-side scripts into web pages viewed by other users. A cross-site scripting vulnerability may be used by attackers to bypass access controls such as the same-origin policy.

CSEA	Cyber Security Enhancement Act (2002).
CSIS	Center for Strategic and International Studies.
CSL	China's Cyber Security Law, which took effect in June 2017. Contains the MLPS framework.
CSRF	Cross-site request forgery, or XSRF or Sea Surf, refers to an attack against authenticated web applications using cookies.
CTI	Cyberthreat intelligence.
Cyber Assurance	Grounds for confidence that the other four security goals (integrity, availability, confidentiality, and accountability) have been adequately met by a specific implementation (NIST Glossary 2013).
DARPA	Defense Advanced Research Projects Agency.
DCMS	Department for Digital, Culture, Media and Sport, UK.
DDoS	Distributed denial of service. A type of DoS attack where multiple compromised systems, which are often infected with a Trojan, are used to target a single system, causing a denial-of-service (DoS) attack (see DoSing).
DDoSing	Distributed denial of service. An attack becomes a distributed denial of service (DDoS), when it comes from multiple computers (or vectors) instead of just one. This is the most common form of DoS attack on websites.
DHS	Department of Homeland Security, US government.
Diagnostic	A distinctive symptom or characteristic. Concerned with the diagnosis of, for example, an illness or state of an asset or other problems.
Digital Forensics	A branch of forensic science encompassing the recovery and investigation of material found in digital devices, often in relation to computer crime.
DMZ	Demilitarized zone on a computer network.
DNS	Domain name servers are the Internet's equivalent of a phone book. They maintain a directory of domain names and translate them to Internet protocol (IP) addresses.
DoD	US Department of Defense.
DoSing	Denial of service. The perpetrator seeks to make a machine or network resource unavailable to its intended users by temporarily or indefinitely disrupting the services of a host connected to the Internet. DoS attacks can range in duration and may target more than one site or system at a time. DoS events often occur when a service's underlying systems are overloaded with high volume of request calls.

DPA	Differential Power Analysis.
ECHR	European Convention on Human Rights.
ECJ	European Court of Justice.
EEA	The European Economic Area allows for the free movement of persons, goods, services, and capital within the European Single Market, including the freedom to choose residence in any country within this area. The EEA includes EU countries and Iceland, Liechtenstein, and Norway. Switzerland is neither an EU nor EEA member but is part of the single market.
Email Spoofing	Creation of email messages with a forged sender address.
ENISA	European Union Agency for Network and Information Security.
Ethical Hacker	A computer and networking expert who systematically attempts to penetrate a computer system or network on behalf of its owners to find security vulnerabilities that a malicious hacker could potentially exploit. Also known as a white-hat hacker.
Exploit	"To use something to one's own advantage" is a piece of software, a chunk of data, or a sequence of commands that takes advantage of a bug or vulnerability to cause unintended or unanticipated behavior to occur in computer software, hardware, or other electronic equipment (usually computerized). Such behavior frequently includes, for example, gaining control of a computer system, allowing privilege escalation, or a denial-of-service (DoS or related DDoS) attack.
FAANG	Facebook, Apple, Amazon, Netflix, Alphabet's Google, the USA's leading Internet companies.
FISMA	Federal Information Security Management Act (2002).
Fix	A patch or other type of solution to a known or discovered vulnerability or exploit.
FSB	Russian Federal Security Service (formerly the KGB).
FTC	Federal Trade Commission.
Gamification	A mechanism to reinforce communication and behavior by using incentivized games.
GDPR	EU General Data Protection Regulation Law for the European Union and European Economic Area (EEA).
GLBA	Gramm–Leach–Bliley Act (1999).
Hacker	Anyone with technical skills, but it often refers to a person who uses his or her abilities to gain unauthorized access to systems, networks, or data to commit crimes.

HIPAA	Health Insurance Portability and Accountability Act (1996).
HIPS	A host-based intrusion prevention system is a system or a program employed to protect critical computer systems containing crucial data against viruses and other Internet malware. Starting from the network layer all the way up to the application layer, HIPS protects from known and unknown malicious attacks [1].
Honeypot	A computer security mechanism set to detect, deflect, or, in some manner, counteract attempts at unauthorized use of information systems. Generally, a honeypot consists of data (for example, in a network site) that appears to be a legitimate part of the site (but is actually isolated and monitored) and seems to contain information or a resource of value to attackers, who are then blocked. Colloquially known as "baiting" a suspect, it resembles a police sting operation (Cole and Northcutt 2018).
HP	Honeypot.
HSA	Homeland Security Act (2002).
IDS	Intrusion Detection System.
IHRL	International Human Rights Law.
Interpol	The International Criminal Police Organization, more commonly known as Interpol, is the international organization that facilitates international police co–operation.
IoC	Indicators of compromise threat intelligence.
IOSCO	International Organization of Securities Commission.
IoT Botnet	(Internet of Things botnet) is a group of hacked computers, smart appliances, and Internet-connected devices that have been co-opted for illicit purposes.
IP	Intellectual property. A category of property that includes intangible creations of the human intellect, and primarily encompasses copyrights, patents, and trademarks (Sullivan 2016).
IP	Internet protocol. The principal communications protocol in the Internet protocol suite for relaying datagrams across network boundaries. Its routing function enables Internetworking, and essentially establishes the Internet. The first main version was IP v4, a 32-bit numeric decimal address system. This was replaced by the latest version, IP v6, a 128-bit hexadecimal address system with many new features.

IPS	Intrusion Prevention System.
ISACA	Information Systems Audit and Control Association.
(ISC)²	International Information System Security Certification.
ISP	Internet Service Provider.
ISSEP	Information Systems Security Engineering Professional.
IT	Information Technology.
Kill Chain	A concept developed by Lockheed Martin in 2011 to categorize different phases of a cyberattack they describe as adversary campaigns and intrusion kill chains.
LulzSec	A black-hat computer hacking group that claimed responsibility for several high-profile attacks, including the compromise of user accounts from Sony Pictures in 2011.
M2M	Machine-to-Machine.
Malware	A malicious software is any program or file that is harmful to a computer user. Malware includes computer viruses, worms, Trojan Horses, and spyware.
Masquerade	The attacker pretends to be an authorized user of a system to gain access to it or to obtain greater privileges than they are authorized for.
MFA	Multifactor Authentication.
MIT	Massachusetts Institute of Technology.
MLPS	Chinese government's Multilevel Protection Scheme contained in the CSL. MLPS classifies information systems physically located in China according to their relative impact on national security, social order, and economic interests should the system be damaged or attacked.
MPS	China's Ministry of Public Security.
MulVAL	An end-to-end framework and reasoning system that conducts multihost, multistage vulnerability analysis on a network.
NAC	Network Access Control.
NAO	UK government's National Audit Office.
NCSC	National Cyber Security Centre, UK.
NECSI	New England Complex Systems Institute.
NIST	National Institute of Standards and Technology, USA.
NSA	National Security Agency, US government.
OEM	Original Equipment Manufacturer.
Operation Anti-Security	Also referred to as Operation AntiSec or #AntiSec. A series of hacking attacks performed by members of the hacking groups LulzSec and BlackSec, Anonymous, and others.

OVAL	Open Vulnerability and Assessment Language is an international information security community standard to promote open and publicly available security content, and to standardize the transfer of this information across the entire spectrum of security tools and services. OVAL includes a language used to encode system details, and an assortment of content repositories held throughout the community.
OWASP	Open Web Application Security Project—a not-for-profit charitable foundation established in the USA in 2004.
Patch	A set of changes to a computer program or its supporting data designed to update, fix, or improve it. This includes fixing security vulnerabilities and other bugs. Usually referred to as bugfixes or bug fixes, they improve usability or performance.
Pen Test	A penetration test of a company typically carried out by security professional or by hackers seeking to find vulnerabilities.
Phishing	An attempt to obtain sensitive information such as usernames, passwords, and credit card details (and money), often for malicious reasons, by disguising as a trustworthy entity in an electronic communication.
PIR	Passive Infrared Sensor.
PKI	Public-Key Infrastructure.
Polymorphic Code	A computer virus is a type of malicious software that, when executed, replicates itself by modifying other computer programs and inserting its own code. When this replication succeeds, the affected areas are then said to be "infected" with a computer virus.
POTS	Also known as Honeypot.
PoUW	Proof of Useful Work.
PP	Privacy Policies.
Prognostic	Relating to or serving to predict the likely course of, for example, a medical condition.
PUA	A program that contains adware, installs toolbars, or has other unclear objectives that a user may perceive as potentially unwanted.
Reachability	The ability of an attacker to reach a location in an attack graph, a point in a network.
REBT	Rational-Emotive Behavior Therapy.
Risk Perception	Risk perception is the subjective judgment people make about the severity and probability of a risk and may

	vary from person to person. Any human endeavor carries some risk, but some are much riskier than others (Hansson and Zalta 2014).
Risk	The potential to gain or lose something of value. Values (such as physical health, social status, emotional well-being, or financial wealth) can be gained or lost when taking a risk resulting from a given action or inaction, foreseen or unforeseen (planned or not planned). Risk can also be defined as the intentional interaction with uncertainty (Preston 2015). Uncertainty is a potential, unpredictable, and uncontrollable outcome; it is a consequence of action taken despite uncertainty.
SEC	Securities and Exchange Commission.
SEM	Security Event Management.
SETI	Search for Extraterrestrial Intelligence.
SIEM	Security information and event management is an approach to security management that combines SIM (security information management) and SEM (security event management) functions into one security management system.
SIM	Security Information Management.
Social Engineering	Refers to the psychological manipulation of people into performing actions or divulging confidential information. A type of confidence trick for information gathering, fraud, or system access, it differs from a traditional "con" in that it is often one of many steps in a more complex fraud scheme. It is also broadly described as an act of psychological manipulation of another human being (Anderson 2008).
Software Bug	A software bug is an error, flaw, failure or fault in a computer program or system that causes it to produce an incorrect or unexpected result, or to behave in unintended ways.
Spyware	Software that aims to gather information about a person or organization sometimes without their knowledge. It may send such information to another entity without the consumer's consent, assert control over a device without the consumer's knowledge, or send such information to another entity with the consumer's consent, through cookies.

SQLi	SQL injection is one of the many web attack mechanisms used by hackers to steal data. It is perhaps one of the most common application layer attacks.
SSO	Single sign-on is a property of access control of multiple related, yet independent, software systems. With this property, a user logs in with a single ID and password to gain access to a connected system and/or accomplishes this using the Lightweight Directory Access Protocol (LDAP) as well as stored LDAP databases on (directory) servers. A simple version of single sign-on can be achieved over IP networks using cookies but only if the sites share a common DNS parent domain.
STIX™	Structured Threat Information eXpression. STIX is a language developed for cyberthreat intelligence sharing.
TAXII™	A transport mechanism for sharing cyberthreat intelligence.
Threat Actor	"The Attacker"—a person, group, organization, or government that carries out cyberattacks.
Threat Surface	Also known as Attack Surface. The attack surface of a software environment is the sum of the different points (the "attack vectors") where an unauthorizeduser (the "Attacker") can try to enter data to or extract data from an environment. Keeping the attack surface as small as possible is a basic security measure (Manadhata and Wing 2008).
Threat Target	A threat target is anything of value to the Threat Actor. It could be a PC, mobile, vehicle, your online bank account … or you (stealing your identity), intellectual property (IP) influence, ideology (adapted from Withers 2011).
Threat Vector	Also known as attack vector or information security threat vector. A threat vector describes a method of cyberattack that is a path or tool used by a threat actor to attack the target (Withers 2011). They are the routes that malicious attacks may take to pass your defenses and infect and carry out the attack on your network, person, organization, or sovereignty.
ToS	Terms of Service.
Tracking Cookies	Tracking cookies, and especially third-party tracking cookies, are commonly used as ways to compile long–term records of individuals' browsing histories, a potential privacy concern that prompted European (EU cookies 2013) and US lawmakers to act in 2011. European law

	requires that all websites targeting European Union member states gain "informed consent" from users before storing non-essential cookies on their device. Google Project Zero researcher Jann Horn describes the ways cookies can be read by intermediaries, such as Wi–Fi hotspot providers. He recommends using the browser in incognito mode in such circumstances (Horn, accessed 2018).
Trojan	A virus. Trojans are also known to create a backdoor on a computer that gives malicious users access to your system, possibly allowing confidential or personal information to be compromised. Unlike other viruses and worms, Trojans do not reproduce by infecting other files, nor do they self-replicate.
UAI	Uncertainty Avoidance Index.
UDHR	Universal Declaration of Human Rights, United Nations General Assembly, Resolution 217.
UEBA	User and Entity Behavior Analytics.
US-CERT	United States Computer Emergency Readiness Team. A cybersecurity attack alerts service.
Virus	A piece of software code which can copy itself and typically has a detrimental effect, such as corrupting the system or destroying data.
VM	A virtual machine is a computer file, typically called an image, that behaves like an actual computer. Multiple virtual machines can run simultaneously on the same physical computer. For servers, the multiple operating systems run side by side, managed by a piece of software called a hypervisor, while desktop computers typically employ one operating system to run the other operating systems within its programwindows. Each virtual machine provides its own virtual hardware, including CPUs, memory, hard drives, network interfaces, and other devices. The virtual hardware is then mapped to the real hardware on the physical machine, which minimizes costs by reducing the need for physical hardware systems (and their associated maintenance costs), as well as reducing power and cooling demand.
VPN	Virtual Private Network.
Vulnerability	A flaw in a system that can leave it open to attack. A vulnerability may also refer to any type of weakness in a computer system itself, in a set of procedures, or in anything that leaves information security exposed to a threat.

WEF	World Economic Forum.
Worm	A standalone malware computer program that replicates itself and spreads to other computers.
XSRF	Cross-site scripting forgery (see also CSRF).
Zero-day Attack	A zero-dayexploit is a cyberattack that occurs on the same day a weakness is discovered in software. At that point, it is exploited before a fix becomes available from its creator.
Zero-day	A zero-day vulnerability is a vulnerability, unknown to or undiscovered by those who would be interested in mitigating the vulnerability (including the vendor of the target software). Until the vulnerability is mitigated, hackers can exploit it to tamper with computer programs, data, systems and networks.
Zero-trust	Zero-trust is a security model based on the principle of maintaining strict access controls and not trusting anyone by default ("never trust, always verify" principle).
ZKP	Zero-Knowledge Proof.

References

1. Host-Based Intrusion Prevention System (HIPS), Technopedia https://www.techopedia.com/definition/…/host-based-intrusion-prevention-system-hips.
2. What is a Zero-Day Vulnerability?, pctools by Symantec https://web.archive.org/web/20170704035927/, http://www.pctools.com/security-news/zero-day-vulnerability/.

List of Figures

List of Tables

1

Introduction

This is a story about trust.

We live in an era that might be described as a "post-Snowden" world where the assumptions about trust and anonymity from issues such as *what is your privacy and personal rights* to *what is classified information* and *how information is communicated as fact or opinion* are being challenged by the convergence of new information technology.

Edward Snowden first exposed the bombshell story to the journalist Glenn Greenwald and the *Guardian* newspaper in 2013 about how the National Security Agency (NSA) had collected millions of domestic phone records of unsuspecting citizens under a top-secret court order issued in April of that year [1, 2]. Facts which surfaced as a result of this story formed what was later described as a "treasure trove" of information, that at the time resulted in a trickle feed of revelations from government wiretapping, spying on friend and foe politicians, tracking Google, Facebook, Microsoft, Apple, and many others, to exposing expert hacking techniques and attempts to crack the encryption and undermine the entire Internet security [3] Much of this was later contested and counter-argued, but the genie was out and Pandora's box was open. Another innocence had been torn down. After surviving the 9/11 attacks, international terrorism catalyzation, as well as the 2008 financial crisis, the humanity had been hit with a new challenge of how to uncover and understand the underlying truths of what was real and what was hiding behind the façade of everyday living. Snowden, who was a contractor at the time of obtaining the controversial materials from the NSA, disclosed his identity in the media [4]. From his point of view, as a self-appointed "whistle-blower", he had to raise a moral objection to

© The Author(s) 2019
G. Pogrebna and M. Skilton, *Navigating New Cyber Risks*,
https://doi.org/10.1007/978-3-030-13527-0_1

surveillance practices that hitherto were unknown to the public at large and he could not remain anonymous.

This in itself was not new: several years earlier, in 2010, Julian Assange had introduced a new term into the lexicon of several generations. This term was "WikiLeaks" and described an international non-profit organisation, committed to publishing secret information, news leaks, and classified media provided by anonymous sources [5]. Even though WikiLeaks was established in 2006, the disclosure of 750,000 classified and sensitive military and governmental documents by Chelsea Manning in 2010, including war logs about the Iraq and Afghanistan conflicts, private cables from the State Department as well as assessments of Guantánamo prisoners made the organization the most talk about in decades [6]. The WikiLeaks publications and their subsequent media footprints [7] revealed that information as well as the digital access to information were and continue to be weapons as well as targets or valuable commodities for a large number of interested parties. In its essence, information became the new valuable and monetizable asset obtained through and exchanged by a variety of agents who can be individuals, groups, and organizations, and even nation states, activists.

It would seem that we live in the age of the liar's paradox. The classical definition of the paradox refers to a situation when a liar makes a declaration that he or she is lying. By making such a declaration the liar is telling the truth about his or her lying. Yet, his or her declaration does not change the fact that the liar is in fact lying.

Therefore, when we say that in the modern digitized world "all people lie", what does this mean? If a particular person is a liar, is this a classic tautological contraction or is this a false statement that becomes invalid if we can identify at least one person who is not a liar? How do you verify what is *true* and what is *false*? Who do you trust?

It is clear now that with the development of digital technology understanding what a "safe place" is and learning how to verify and validate what is "true" and "safe", have become a whole lot more complicated. Considering that we are struggling to define *disclosure* and *protection* in the context of the new digital communication, it is hardly surprising that the terms *privacy* and *safely* become more and more obscure and context-dependent.

In 2013, 3 billion Yahoo! user account details were compromised as a result of one of the largest data breaches in human history. Stolen information included names, email addresses, telephone numbers, birth dates, encrypted passwords and, in some cases, security questions. It is believed that a "state-sponsored actor" was behind this act [8]. Yahoo! allegedly remained unaware of this for three years and only disclosed the information about the breach to the general public in 2016 [9]. The company breaches like the one which affected Yahoo! are, *as such*, not new as innovative forms of insidious and panoptical attacks emerge on a daily if not hourly basis worldwide. Consider, for example, the 2015 attack with malware which lurked in the background of the computer systems at the world's most successful banks and allowed a team of Russian-based hackers to steal €1 billion globally [10]. Note that this is just the amount which was publicly disclosed. In reality, the amount could have been significantly higher due to the fact that the malware might have been in place at these banks for months or even years. We may also recall another global cyberattack in 2017 when the WannaCry malware was deployed in 110 countries worldwide. Its targets included large corporations as well as public entities such as Telefónica, one of Spain's largest telecommunications operators; Renault, the French automotive manufacturer; the German railway system Deutsche Bahn; many ministries of the Russian government; FedEx; and the British National Health Service [11]. These examples lead to one simple conjecture: the scope and scale of modern cyberattacks as well as the fact that even the most resourceful and carefully designed cybersecurity systems can be bypassed by highly motivated adversaries show that any individual, group, organization or even a state as a whole can become a target.

But the targets in our living and working spaces are not just people and organizations, but also the objects, buildings, vehicles, malls, highways, and infrastructure networks, enabled with the Internet of Things (IoT), machine learning (ML) and artificial intelligence (AI) algorithms, along with blockchain technologies (BCT), 3D printing, as well as immersive new experiences, which use virtual reality, augmented reality, mixed reality, and extended reality (VR, AR, MR, X-R). Many of these new technologies are fusing into our products and services and living spaces. Yet, despite all the advantages which these technologies may possess, they also make our lives more vulnerable to new cyberattacks and risks.

Exploiting security flaws in IoT and its detrimental consequences for urban infrastructure were demonstrated in a case study of road traffic lights conducted by researchers at Michigan State University in 2014. They showed that unencrypted wireless connections, widely used in traffic control systems, as well as default usernames and passwords, which could be found online, were also easy attack targets [12]. It soon became apparent that automotive vehicles and even aircrafts could be compromised in a similar fashion. Moreover, the widespread nature of such cyberattacks delivered a simple message to individuals, businesses and cities. The cyberthreats are real as attacks are happening here and now: be it the switching of all the traffic lights simultaneously to green at a particular city junction; taking control and disabling the engine of a Jeep Cherokee on a highway [13]; or claiming to have bypassed the onboard flight engine control systems of an aircraft [14]. In the aviation sector alone, over 1000 attacks were reported monthly in 2016 by Strategy and Safety Management at the European Aviation Safety Agency (EASA) [15]. It is also clear that cybercriminals polish their sophistication not only by penetrating multiple sectors and systems. They also enhance their tools by carefully studying cybersecurity safeguard mechanisms and algorithms used by various organizations. For example, a recent study into cybersecurity tools stolen from the CIA and the NSA showed that they were subsequently used by hackers in over half of all cyberattacks in the healthcare sector in 2017 [16, 17]. That same year, the American Food and Drug Administration (FDA) requested 500,000 heart pacemakers to be recalled due to a hacking risk stemming from the fact that their firmware update designed to fix security vulnerabilities actually created new vulnerabilities [18]. Apart from major attacks on personal devices as well as organizational and urban infrastructure, cybercriminals are also targeting critical national infrastructure. For example, in 2018, the US Homeland Security reported that Russian hackers had allegedly breached the US utility network control rooms via trusted vendors, which resulted in access to confidential information about equipment as well as data on how utility networks are configured to be compromized. This created a real risk of adversarially-controlled blackouts [19].

Whether the target of a particular cybercriminal is a heart pacemaker or a power station, the risk of a cyberattack threatens human lives rather than just human data. As a result, cybersecurity progressively becomes a matter of national safety and security.

The knowledge and intelligence to carry out cyberattacks as well as to design effective cyber defense mechanisms are also no longer just the domain of human intelligence, human skills, and human experience. The rise of ML and AI is moving cyberattack vectors to a new level. In early 2017, it was reported that a commercial cybersecurity firm Darktrace Inc had spotted a new type of attack on a client company in India. The cyberattack software used a sophisticated ML algorithm to observe and learn patterns of normal user behavior inside the victim company's computer network. This software then began to mimic user behavior. As a result, the malicious algorithm was almost undetectable for the company's security architecture. [20] In 2018, MIT researchers reported the rise of the weaponization of AI as a new AI-driven arms race [21] deployed in a broad set of manifestations, including cyber-physical attacks on Ukraine's national electricity infrastructure that plunged large parts of the country into darkness in December 2015 and 2016 [22]. The use of AI is also rapidly growing in both detecting and committing financial fraud [23, 24]. We also observe the rise of automated social media "bot-farms", which plant fake news, fake "likes", and generally imitate user traffic [25].

So, what is the future of cyberdefense systems?

The technology of cybersecurity attack and defense is constantly evolving. The keynote discussion at the annual Arm TechCon in 2017 facilitated a debate about contemporary trends in security, especially about the way in which cybersecurity system should be built in order to safeguard and manage all areas of computing, from microchips to clouds [26]. The ubiquity of the IoT era means that building security principles into the ecosystem of computing systems both in its end use and down to the chip level architecture is extremely important. Today, manufacturers, service providers and even individual users need to move to a new culture of "security-by-design" and "security-in-use" [27], treating everything as potentially untrustworthy and requiring constant verification and validation. One manifestation of this new approach to cybersecurity are the so-called "zero-trust" systems and principles [28]. This culture is necessary to protect users and enterprises, as well as the wider society. Yet, it is also recognized that technology (including technology which is based on "zero-trust") is not the silver bullet [29]. Equally, AI-enabled technology cannot fully protect individuals and organizations: while we can use AI to monitor and detect patterns in human and machine behavior and activity much faster, 24 hours a day, 7 days a week, new threats may evolve that AI may not have encountered. AI-enabled security suffers from a number of other problems. For example, an AI algorithm may accrue generated bias (due to imperfections in the training sets which informs it) that could affect its performance. This might make it vulnerable to manipulation or prone to errors. Equally, legal basis as well as government policy and regulatory landscape may need to catch up with the rapidly evolving technological advances. For example, if AI could increasingly mimic humans, or, moreover, operate at speeds and multiply across vast attack surfaces, then technical analysis alone would not be enough. The response needs to incorporate technical, cultural, psychological, legal, and sociological as well as policy aspects. Let us not forget that while individuals, organizations and state have access to the AI technology, so do cybercriminals, who can also make use of the smart algorithmic solutions.

It is now clear that response to the cybersecurity risks of the future should be based on effective communication, information, knowledge, and intelligence shared among individuals and organizations which collect and store valuable data. By exchanging information about cyberattacks, their features and patterns these individuals and organizations will ensure that existing and future cybersecurity threats will be easier to detect and alleviate. After all, individuals, businesses, and governments are facing cybercriminals who excel in communication and information sharing, and we now need to develop an equivalent, if not more advanced, communication mechanisms and channels.

Business strategies must evolve not only to handle new kinds of cyberattacks, but also the rising expectations about compliance and personal data protection as seen in the recent new laws which emerged in many countries worldwide such as the 2018 European Union's (EU) General Data Protection Regulation (GDPR), the 2002 US Homeland Security Act; telecommunications, financial services, and healthcare industrial data regulations, as well as the development of the novel social media regulations.

Threats evolve, and governments and regulators formulate new laws to control digital expansion, privacy, as well as human digital rights. In 2016 the US government issued a cyberdefense readiness condition (DEFCON) scale, which represented a cyber incidence severity measure ranging from one (high risk of harm) to five (low risk of harm) and allowed individuals and organizations to capture the imminent cyberthreat propensity in different contexts [30].

Being ready, understanding threats and vulnerabilities, and managing consequences—all these components are necessary to respond adequately and appropriately to threats and exploits. While the DEFCON scale attempts to provide a useful and simple risk management tool, it is not clear whether and to what extent it is applicable in practice when addressing a live attack in the real time.

It is also clear that cybersecurity is a complex and constantly evolving issue. In fact, cybersecurity space is developing and changing so rapidly that by the time this book is in print, many of our examples may seem dated, as in a matter of weeks, days or even hours new attacks may occur which will dwarf events described above. In this regard, two very recent examples come to mind. In September 2018, Facebook reported a data breach, with up to 50 million account credentials stolen, highlighting the importance and evolving nature of cybersecurity threats [31]. The worrying fact was not only the scale of the harmful impact, even though the incident was reported quickly to the Irish data regulator, but also the fact that Facebook significantly underestimated the potential risk of this attack when in July 2017, 14 months prior the attack, they introduced a new "update feature" into a product through which cybercriminals were able to infiltrate the system and gain access to user data [32]. In a similar fashion, another digital giant, Google, revealed its decision in 2018 to shut down its social media product, Google+. Initial suspicions that this was due to low user uptake were overshadowed by the company's admission that the network was being shut down over cybersecurity concerns. Google revealed that a vulnerability in the system had been discovered which put over 500,000 user profiles at risk.[1] Even though Google made statements that they did not have any reason to believe that the discovered vulnerability was ever exploited by cybercriminals, time will tell whether Google+ data will surface somewhere on the Dark Web in the future.

These examples clearly show that even the largest digital companies who earn their living through handling, analyzing, and packaging data into a variety of products do not have enough capacity to ensure safety against the enormous attack surface of the current, ever-expanding digital environment.

Considering all this, the main question which this book is trying to answer is the following: what are the new cyber risks and how do we plan, build, and manage safe spaces in the digital age?

Structure of the Book

The book is intended for executives, risk assessment analysts, and practitioners interested in receiving practical guidance about how to diagnose, anticipate, and address new risks and vulnerabilities while building secure digital environments inside and around their businesses. It will be of interest to start-ups who have just begun to navigate their journey in the dynamic environment of the digital business and want to be more aware of the potential risks they are likely to encounter in cyber spaces. This book will also help policy-makers to better understand the complexity of strategic and tactical business decision-making in the digital economy, which, in turn, can help inform new policies in the domain of cybersecurity and beyond.

Additionally, the book may be useful for anyone who communicates about complex risky environments in the cyber space, from business speakers, bloggers, scientists, journalists, educators, and political aides to concerned citizens. It can assist communicators in reaching two key audiences—the general public and decision-makers from government and business—more effectively in order to help built safe and secure human-cyber

---

[1]See https://www.searchenginejournal.com/google-is-shutting-down-google-admits-low-consumer-adoption/273113/ for more detail.

spaces. The principles found in this book should help to explain how to anticipate new risks more effectively and how to communicate information about these risks in business-to-consumer, within business, as well as business-to-business environments.

The book offers an innovative approach of combining technical and behavioral fields in seeking to understand the intersection of vulnerabilities, risks, and responses. We build on the body of knowledge in cybersecurity, risk management, ML, behavioral science, and business model innovation to suggest practical mechanisms of detecting new risks in cyber spaces. The book provides insights from academics and practitioners, and presents new evidence from field studies and experiments which illustrate how new risks in the digital economy can be identified, quantified, and alleviated.

The book is organized in four parts:

PART I New Cyberthreats and Why We Should Worry About Them
PART II Existing Solutions and Cybersecurity for Business
PART III Future Threats and Solutions
PART IV Cybersecurity: The New Frontier

References

1. *Edward Snowden Biography*. Accessed September 2018. https://www.biography.com/people/edward-snowden-21262897.
2. Greenwald, G. (2013, June 6). NSA collecting phone records of millions of Verizon customers daily. *The Guardian*. https://www.theguardian.com/world/2013/jun/06/nsa-phone-records-verizon-court-order.
3. Greenwald, G., MacAskill, E., & Poitras, L. (2013, June 11). Edward Snowden: The whistleblower behind the NSA surveillance revelations. *The Guardian*. https://www.theguardian.com/world/2013/jun/09/edward-snowden-nsa-whistleblower-surveillance.
4. Franceschi-Bicchierai, L. (2014, June 5). The 10 biggest revelations from Edward Snowden's leaks. MashablesUK. https://mashable.com/2014/06/05/edward-snowden-revelations/?europe=true#E9W_W2HdFPqV.
5. Assange, J.,& Rusbridger, A. (2011, January). WikiLeaks: The Guardian's role in the biggest leak in the history of the world. *The Guardian*. https://www.the-guardian.com/media/2011/jan/28/wikileaks-julian-assange-alan-rusbridger.
6. *Chelsea Manning Biography*. Accessed September 2018. https://www.biography.com/people/chelsea-manning-21299995.

7. Ellison, S. (2011, February). The Man who spilled the secrets. *Vanity Fair.* https://www.vanityfair.com/news/2011/02/the-guardian-201102.

8. Stempel, J., & Finkle, J. (2017, October). Yahoo says all three billion accounts hacked in 2013 data theft. *Reuters.* https://www.reuters.com/article/us-yahoo-cyber/yahoo-says-all-three-billion-accounts-hacked-in-2013-data-theft-idUSKCN1C82O1.

9. Perlroth, N. (2016, September). Yahoo says hackers stole data on 500 million users in 2014. *New York Times.* https://www.nytimes.com/2016/09/23/technology/yahoo-hackers.html.

10. Evens, M. (2015, February). Hackers steal £650 million in world's biggest bank raid. *The Telegraph.* https://www.telegraph.co.uk/news/uknews/crime/11414191/Hackers-steal-650-million-in-worlds-biggest-bank-raid.html.

11. Palmer, D. (2018, May). WannaCry ransomware crisis, one year on: Are we ready for the next global cyber attack? zdnet. https://www.zdnet.com/article/wannacry-ransomware-crisis-one-year-on-are-we-ready-for-the-next-global-cyber-attack/.

12. Ghena, B., Beyer, W., Hillaker, A., Pevarnek, J., & Halderman, J. A. (2014, August) Green lights forever: Analyzing the security of traffic infrastructure. In *Proceedings of the 8th USENIX Workshop on Offensive Technologies (WOOT'14).*

13. Greenberg, A. (2015, July). Hackers remotely kill a jeep on the highway—With me in it. *Wired.* https://www.wired.com/2015/07/hackers-remotely-kill-jeep-highway/.

14. Perez, E. (2015, May 19). FBI: Hacker claimed to have taken over flight's engine controls. CNN. https://edition.cnn.com/2015/05/17/us/fbi-hacker-flight-computer-systems/index.html.

15. Valero, J. (2016, July). Hackers bombard aviation sector with over 1000 attacks per month. EuroActiv. https://www.euractiv.com/section/justice-home-affairs/news/hackers-bombard-aviation-sector-with-more-than-1000-attacks-per-month/.

16. Jay J. (2018, May). Healthcare sector suffered more than half of all cyber-attacks in 2017. SC Media. https://www.scmagazineuk.com/healthcare-sector-suffered-half-cyber-attacks-2017/article/1472744.

17. 2017 Cylance Threat Report. Accessed September 2018. https://pages.cylance.com/2018-03CylanceThreatReport2017.html.

18. Hern, A. (2017, August 31). Hacking risk leads to recall of 500,000 pacemakers due to patient death fears. *The Guardian.* https://www.theguardian.com/technology/2017/aug/31/hacking-risk-recall-pacemakers-patient-death-fears-fda-firmware-update.

19. Smith, R. (2018, July 23). Russian hackers reach U.S. utility control rooms, Homeland security officials say. *Wall Street Journal.* https://www.wsj.com/articles/russian-hackers-reach-u-s-utility-control-rooms-homeland-security-officials-say-1532388110.

20. Rosenbush, S. (2017, November 16). The morning download: First AI-powered cyberattacks are detected. *CIO Journal, Wall Street Journal.* https://blogs.wsj.com/cio/2017/11/16/the-morning-download-first-ai-powered-cyberattacks-are-detected/.

21. Giles, M. (2018, January). Six cyberthreats to really worry about in 2018. *MIT Technology Review.* https://www.technologyreview.com/s/609641/six-cyber-threats-to-really-worry-about-in-2018/.

22. Ukraine power cut "was cyber-attack". (2017, January 11). BBC. https://www.bbc.co.uk/news/technology-38573074.

23. Dickinson, B. (2017, May 3). This is what fraud looks like in the age of Artificial Intelligence. The NextWeb. https://thenextweb.com/contributors/2017/05/03/what-fraud-looks-like-in-the-age-of-artificial-intelligence/.

24. AI and ML curbing financial fraud. (2018, March 6). Fintech Futures. https://www.bankingtech.com/2018/03/ai-and-ml-curbing-financial-fraud/.

25. Williams, S. (2017, May 12). Inside China's phoney "click farm": Tiny office uses 10,000 handsets to send fake ratings and "likes" for boosting clients' online popularity. *The DailyMail.* https://www.dailymail.co.uk/news/article-4499730/click-farm-10-000-phones-boost-product-ratings.html.

26. Tackling the challenges of securing a trillion connected devices at Arm TechCon 2017. (2017, September 6). ARM TechCon2017. https://www.arm.com/company/news/2017/09/tackling-the-challenges-of-securing-a-trillion-connected-devices-at-arm-techcon-2017.

27. *Secure-by-design.* UK Government. Published 7 March 2018. https://www.gov.uk/government/publications/secure-by-design.

28. Pratt, M. K. (2018, January 16). What is Zero Trust? A model for more effective security. CSO. https://www.csoonline.com/article/3247848/network-security/what-is-zero-trust-a-model-for-more-effective-security.html.

29. Bird, J. (2018, September 26). AI is not a "silver bullet" against cyber attacks. *Financial Times.* https://www.ft.com/content/14cd2608-869d-11e8-9199-c2a4754b5a0e.

30. The White House just issued a Defcon scale for cyber attacks. (2016, August 3). The Fanatical Futurist. https://www.fanaticalfuturist.com/2016/08/the-white-house-issued-a-defcon-scale-for-cyber-attacks/.

31. Lee, D. (2018, September). Facebook security breach: Up to 50 m accounts attacked. BBC News. https://www.bbc.co.uk/news/technology-45686890.

32. Kuckler, H. (2018, September 28). Facebook reveals cyber attack affecting up to 50 m users. *Financial Times.* https://www.ft.com/content/c5f13f30-c33f-11e8-8d55-54197280d3f7.

Part I

New Cyberthreats
and Why We Should Worry about Them

2

Cybersecurity Threats: Past and Present

In the contemporary business environment, we are surrounded by labels and keywords which refer to various cyberthreats. It is hard to find a business owner, CEO, board member, or an employee who has never heard of a hacking attack, identity theft, or a computer virus. But what are cybersecurity threats? Are they different from cybercrimes? And if so, how?

A "threat" in general terms is always related to two important constructs—"chance" or "probability" and "harm". A threat in a general business sense implies a chance of an event which leads to harm, loss, or damage. This "negative" or "adverse" event may be due to action or inactivity.[1] In non-cyber environments, a threat may be man-made (inflicted by human or a group of humans) or be a consequence of non-human factors (e.g., natural phenomena such as earthquake, tornado, flood, etc.).

How do cyberthreats differ from threats a business is facing in non-cyber environments? There is no consensus among experts on the definition of cyberthreat. The *Oxford English Dictionary* provides a very general explanation of the meaning of the term as "the possibility of a malicious attempt to damage or disrupt a computer network or system".[2] This definition is rather dated and quite incomplete, and yet it is helpful for understanding the cyberthreat phenomena. The useful part of the definition highlights that threat is related to risk ("possibility") and harm ("damage"). However, the second part which says that harm relates to a "computer network or system"

---

[1]See http://www.businessdictionary.com/definition/threat.html.

[2]See https://en.oxforddictionaries.com/definition/cyberthreat for more detail.

© The Author(s) 2019
G. Pogrebna and M. Skilton, *Navigating New Cyber Risks*,
https://doi.org/10.1007/978-3-030-13527-0_2

13

does not reflect reality. The contemporary adverse effects of malicious cyber activities may influence an individual's well-being (*harm to individual*), business profitability and survival (*harm to property*), national and international security (*harm to government*), and even break ethical and moral code (*harm to morality*), not only in cyberspace, but also in the "physical world" [1, 2]. Therefore, when we talk about cyberthreats, we need to consider a range of very complex phenomena which imply the use of unconnected computing devices, data, Internet-connected technology (ICT), and computer networks to cause damage in cyber and/or physical dimensions.

Even though scholars have grappled with the topology of cyberthreats for many years, there is no unified classification of threats. Below, we attempt to provide a topology of cyberthreats most relevant for the business environment, yet it is important to keep in mind that with the rapid development of technology and, as a result, the emergence of new threats on a daily basis, this topology does not pretend to be exhaustive or complete.

In relation to any business activity, cybersecurity threats can be broadly divided into two categories. First, there are threats due to simple technical faults such as system failures, where unexpected, unintended, non-malicious things can happen to computer systems and, as a result, affect business operations causing damage. These faults may happen due to the failure of technology, human error, human negligence, or failure of organizational procedures. While these threats are, of course, very important, in this book we concentrate on threats related to the malicious attempts by other people or organizations (which we call "*adversaries*") to infiltrate organizational computer systems and cause financial or non-monetary (e.g., reputational) damage. In the cybersecurity literature, such threats are often related to criminal activities in cyberspace, or *cybercrimes*.

But what are cybercrimes? Are they "traditional" crimes committed in cyber space or are they something special, "*an animal of its own kind*"? Susan Brenner, an expert on cybercrime history who has written extensively on this topic, asserts that "*Cybercrime, like crime, consists of engaging in conduct that has been outlawed by a society. Cybercrime differs from crime primarily in the way it is committed: where real-world criminals use guns to commit crimes, cybercriminals use computer technology to engage in socially outlawed conduct*" [1, p. 706]. Professor Brenner argues that much of the criminal activity in cyberspace is a reincarnation of traditional crime (such as fraud, theft, extorsion, acts of terrorism, etc.) in digital environments. Yet, she also accepts that cybercrimes go beyond "*computer-facilitated commission of traditional crime*" [1, p. 706].

In popular culture, the term "cybercrime" is incredibly controversial and even paradoxical. On the one hand, for many, "cybercriminal" is synonymous with "hacker". Yet, while the term "cybercriminal" has a definite negative flavor, "hacker" is rather a positive term. We may blame Hollywood for this as hacker figures were popularized by many movie productions such as *The Matrix* trilogy (1999, 2003), *Swordfish* (2001), *BlackHat* (2015), etc., where a hacker is usually someone smart and incredibly cool. There was even a film those of us under 40 would probably never have heard of—*War Games*—which is believed to have inspired many hackers of the past when it came out in 1983. In fact, the roots of the positive connotation associated with "hackers" go a lot deeper, as the term dates back to 1950s when Massachusetts Institute of Technology (MIT) students coined the term to denote inventive college prankers [1]. By the late 1950s, through the MIT Intelligence Laboratory the term "hacking" spread into the information technology and computing community and generally referred to creative and innovative computer programming [1, 2].

But how far does the public view of cyberthreats and cybercrime differ from what they actually are? Of course, modern cyberthreats are a lot more diverse than hacking. They include a long list of things which vary significantly in their severity, volume, impact, and wider consequences.

Cyberthreats and Their Varieties

If you ask people who are not engaged in cybersecurity professionally to describe which threats they are facing, they will admit that they often have a hard time when they are trying to gain correct understanding of cyberthreats. One survey participant once told us: "*When you go online, there is just so much information about cyberthreats "staring" at you. And you don't even know whether it is relevant and how it is relevant.*" This is certainly true—it is really hard to navigate this space as there is no easy way in which cyberthreats can be classified and analyzed. Table 2.1 outlines our attempt to systematize the major cybersecurity threats, which individuals and organizations are facing today.[3] The resulting picture somewhat resembles the

---

[3]Derived from multiple sources including NCSC glossary, Cisco comprehensive list of malware. See Cisco Customer Assurance Security Programs (CASP). Specifically, https://www.cisco.com/c/en/us/about/security-center/virus-differences.html. See also Cisco 2018 Annual Cybersecurity Report, http://www.sans.org/resources/glossary.php; https://nvlpubs.nist.gov/nistpubs/SpecialPublications/NIST.SP.800-83r1.pdf; https://attack.mitre.org/wiki/Technique/T1067; and https://attack.mitre.org/wiki/Initial_Access.

Table 2.1   Periodic table of cybersecurity threats

Executable File file running an automatic task when a user clicks the file icon or when launched via a command				
Macro automated input sequence imitating keystrokes or mouse actions				
Exploit piece of software, a command, or a methodology that attacks a security vulnerability				
Web Crawler program systematically browsing the Internet indexing data				
Adware software automatically generating online ads				
Backdoor undocumented way of accessing a system, bypassing the normal authentication	Virus user-activated malware that propagates by inserting a copy of itself into and becoming part of another program	Worm self-propagating malware autonomously replicating itself without action by a user	Trojan harmful piece of software that looks legitimate	Wiper malware containing a disk/data wiping mechanism
Rootkit programs hiding the existence of malware by intercepting and modifying operating system API calls that supply system information	Bootkit malware modifying the boot sectors of a hard drive	Malicious Mobile Code malware transmitted from remote to local host and executed on the local host without user instruction	Malicious Crypto Miners software using system resources for large calculations with cryptocurrency awarded to the solvers	Malicious bot self-propagating malware used to infect a host and connect it to a central server acting as command and control
Logger action of recording the keys struck on a keyboard or generally recording user actions without user knowledge	Browser Hijacker software modifying web browser settings without user's permission to inject unwanted advertising into the user's browser	Spyware software aiming to gather, share, and assert control over information about a person/organization without their knowledge	Point of Sale (POS) malware used to target point of sale (POS) terminals to obtain credit/debit card information	Ransomware malware threatening to publish the victim's data or block access to it unless a ransom is paid
Social Engineering malicious use of human psychology to gain victim's trust and/or attain cooperation	Crimeware malware for automating cybercrime by perpetrating identity theft through social engineering or technical stealth in order to access user information	Phishing untargeted mass emails purporting to be from reputable source to induce individuals to reveal valuable information or directing them to malicious websites	Spear-phishing targeted phishing attack when an email is purporting to be from the source the targeted individual knows or trusts	Whaling highly targeted phishing attacks purporting to be from reputable sources aimed at senior executives
	Cyber Squatting registering, trafficking in, or using an Internet domain name with bad faith intent to profit from the goodwill of a trademark belonging to someone else	Stolen Devices loss of control over valuable information or data due to theft of devices (computers, smartphones, etc.)	Software Piracy illegal copying, distribution, or use of software	Malicious Insider threat which comes from people who have inside information about the organization's security, data and computer systems (e.g., employees)

periodic table of elements which many of us remember from studying chemistry and includes three broad categories of potential threats: *monomers*, *polymers*, and *composites*.

Monomers are "basic" threats which can cause damage on their own or, more often, can be combined into polymers and act as part of a more

Table 2.1 (continued)

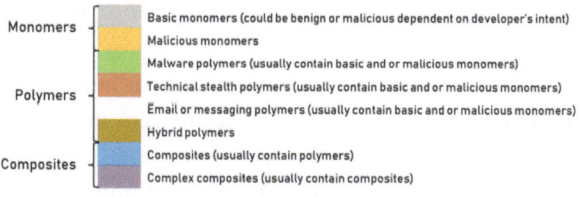

					(Cyber) Harassment using cyber means to harass, control, or manipulate individuals or organizations
Brute Force	CAPTCHA Bypass	Payload	Hacking	Advanced Persistent Threats (APT)	(Cyber) Theft
a trial and error method used to decode encrypted data such as passwords	faking response test used to determine whether or not the user is human	part of data transmission containing malware such as worms or viruses	gaining unauthorized access to systems	set of stealthy and continuous hacking processes targeting a specific entity	using cyber means to steal data or property (including identity theft, theft of data, property, etc.)
Denial of Service (DOS) attack	Man-in-the-Middle	Botnet	Network attack	Hijacking	(Cyber) Fraud
malicious attempts to cause the victim, site, or node to deny service to its customers	digital eavesdropping where communication among users is monitored and modified by an unauthorized party	network of compromised devices for launching broad-based, "remote-control", flood-type attacks	any method, process, or means used to compromise network security	network security attack in which the attacker takes control of network communication	use of cyber means for wrongful or criminal deception intended to result in financial or personal gain
Voice Fabrication	Data Diddling	Unwanted Programs/Apps	Drive-by-download	(Cyber) Extorsion	Cyber Terrorism
using technology to imitate user's voice	changing of data before or during entry into the computer system	software which users may perceive as unwanted including adware, spyware, browser hijackers, etc.	malware download happening without user knowledge	demanding payment through the use of or threat of malicious activity against a victim, such as data compromise or DOS attack	politically, ideologically, or religiously motivated use of computers or information technology to cause severe disruption or widespread fear
Spam	Water-holing	Malicious Research	E-mail crime	(Cyber) Espionage	Cyber Warfare
irrelevant or unsolicited messages sent to users for advertising, phishing, spreading malware, etc.	setting up a fake website (or compromising a real one) aiming to exploit visiting users	collecting information about individuals or organizations using malware, phishing or other malicious tools	intentional activity committed for personal gain or aimed at causing harm to individual or organization using email	use of cyber means to gain illicit access to confidential information usually held by private or public entity	use of computer technology or data to disrupt the activities of entire state and/or major sectors of state economy or infrastructure
Deceptive Callers	Phone Phreaking	Blockchain Majority (51%) Attack	Blockchain Price Infliction		
using telephone calls to lead users to believe something other than the truth with aim to cause harm	manipulation of telephone system	network attack by a group of miners controlling more than 50% of the network's mining hashrate, or computing power	using malicious informational tools (e.g. fake news) to affect price expectations on blockchain market		

complex threat structure. Monomers can be of two varieties: basic and malicious. The difference between the two is that basic monomers can be either benign or malicious dependent on how they are applied, while malicious are designed to cause harm. Basic monomers include, for example, *executable files* and *exploits* which, in principle, may be perfectly harmless or may be designed to cause serious damage. Malicious monomers, however, exercise "damage by design". For example, *backdoor* implies gaining access to systems through bypassing the usual authentication; *social engineering* refers to using psychological tools in malicious way to trick users into doing something they otherwise would not, etc.

Polymer threats are more complex threats which usually include several monomers. Dependent on the way in which polymers infiltrate and compromise systems, they can be partitioned into four varieties: malware polymers; technical stealth polymers; email or messaging polymers; and hybrid polymers. Malware polymers refer to various type of malicious software (or *malware*) and include *viruses* (user-activated malware), *worms* (self-propagating malware), etc. Technical stealth polymers represent threats which utilize various technical (e.g., programming) means and include *(distributed) denial-of-service (DoS) attacks* (malicious attempts to cause the victim, site, or node to deny service to its customers), *password brute force* (a trial and error method used to decode encrypted data), etc. Email and messaging polymers such as *phishing* (untargeted messages aimed at tricking users into revealing valuable information or taking actions advantageous to the cyberthreat instigator) spread through electronic communication. Finally, hybrid polymers usually involve a mixture of infiltration mechanisms from purely psychological to highly technical.

Polymers usually combine into composites, and composites, in turn, may be integral parts of complex composites. To illustrate the relationship between monomers, polymers, and composites, consider the following example. Monomers *backdoor* and *exploit* may be integral parts of such polymers as a *virus* or *worm*, and *payload* is a composite which may include viruses and worms. In turn, payload may be a part of a complex composite such as *(cyber) theft*.

From the security standpoint, it is easier to deal with monomers than polymers, and it is easier to deal with polymers rather than composites. Since the complexity of the threat elements increases from monomers to polymers and from polymers to composites, the complexity of solutions should also increase between these three categories.

Brief History of Cyberthreats

Looking at the variety and complexity of threats, it is not hard to understand why cybersecurity is such a "dry" topic. With such a broad variety of terminology and so many things which could potentially go wrong, one can encounter many difficulties in navigating not only potential threats but also the literature that describes those threats. Looking at the history

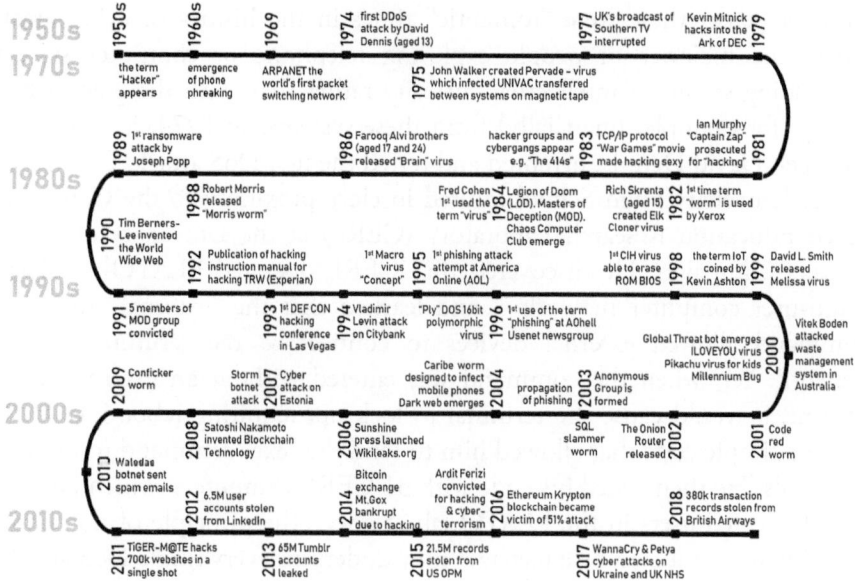

Fig. 2.1 Brief chronology of cyberthreats

of cyberthreats helps us to understand them better. The first cybersecurity threats started to appear in the period between the 1950s and 1970s and have diversified and intensified ever since. Figure 2.1 shows a brief chronology of cyberthreats covering the time period from the 1950s to 2018.

It is not our goal to provide a comprehensive and detailed history of Internet and cybersecurity.[4] Yet, a very brief account of events is useful to understand how various threats emerged, developed, and how this development led us to today's situation.

The Emergence of Cyberthreats (1950s–1979): Cyberthreats in general, and computer crime in particular, have grown out of their historic predecessor—"phone phreaking"—where telephone systems were studied and "attacked". These "attacks" were nothing of the kind you might imagine— essentially, phone phreaks carefully researched telephone networks and then made those systems do something they are not designed to do. For example, phone phreaks would be able to exploit the system to make free phone calls in the era when all calls had to be paid for.

---

[4]For those who want to know more, articles and monographs by Susan W. Brenner, as well as many other authors, provide a more detailed and comprehensive picture.

In some sense, these were "romantic" times in the history of cyberthreats, where the majority of people exploring telephone or computer systems were doing so out of intellectual curiosity rather than with the goal of benefiting (for example, financially) from these systems. In 1974, a 13-year-old teenager, David Dennis, invented and tested the first DoS attack. David went to the University High School located in close proximity to the Computer-based Education Research Laboratory (CERL) at the University of Illinois Urbana-Campaign. He discovered that CERL operated PLATO—a shared multi-user computer network— and learned that the "external" (or "ext") command allowed external devices to connect to the terminals on the network. Yet, when the command was entered without an external device present, it would cause the terminal to lock up, requiring rebooting. David wrote a simple code that allowed him to send the "ext" command to multiple terminals. He then tested his code with 31 CERL computers, which powered off all affected users in the PLATO lab at once. The principle of this simple experiment conducted by a teenager now underpins every single DoS attack.

Around the same time, the first attempts to develop viruses and instigate powerful attacks emerged. For example, in 1975 John Walker wrote the Pervade virus, which infected UNIVAC systems and was transferred between terminals using magnetic tape. In 1979, Kevin Mitnick designed and implemented the first large-scale hacking attack on The Ark, the computer system of the Digital Equipment Corporation (DEC). Mitnick used a combination of his technical skills and social engineering to infiltrate the system. Specifically, impersonating one of the DEC's top developers, he called the system administrator and pretended that he was unable to "log in". The system administrator simply gave away the precious password to Mitnick over the phone, which allowed the hacker to access The Ark.

The Development of Cyberthreats (1980–1989): In the 1980s, cyberthreats underwent a rapid development. There were many "firsts" during this time: first virus which affected personal (rather than industrial or institutional) computers; first worm; first hacker groups; first hacker wars; and even first convictions related to hacking activity. In this period, the global community came to the realization that cyberthreats were real and may potentially cause much harm. In 1982, Richard Skrenta, a 15-year-old ninth-grader from Pittsburg, created the first personal computer virus, which targeted Apple II computers. The Elk Cloner virus spread via infected disks. Interestingly, the term "virus" appeared only in 1984 when Fred Cohen used the term to describe "self–propagating code".[5] This definition was, of course, in many ways confusing because a virus required user activation—i.e., in order to set the malicious code in motion, the user needs to do something (e.g., open a file containing malicious software).

In 1986, the first "vengeful" virus was created by the Farooq Alvi brothers.[6] Basit Farooq Alvi and Amjad Farooq Alvi, who were, respectively, 17 and 24 years of age at the time, were running a computer shop in Lahore, Pakistan. They spotted that software for an MS-DOS operating system they had written and sold to their customers was being pirated and circulated for free. To prevent the piracy, the brothers developed the Brain virus, which only targeted machines with pirated software. The logic behind the virus was simple: it affected IBM computers by replacing the boot sector of the floppy disk with the pirated software which contained a copy of the virus. The brothers had developed a built-in counter in the software which allowed it to quickly and reliably diagnose whether the copy was genuine. Even though the initial motivation behind the development of the Brain virus was benign—i.e., stopping piracy—the consequences were not as positive as the Farooq Alvi brothers had hoped. When the virus information got out into the public domain, Brain "mutated" as malicious versions of the virus were developed based on the initial code.

In the 1980s, many young people became influenced by the movie *War Games* (1983). As a result, several hacker groups and cybergangs appeared during this time, including the 414s, Legion of Doom (LOD), Masters of Deception (MOD), Chaos Computer Club, and others [1]. Unlike the "noble hackers of the past", these groups often had mixed motives. They engaged in both intellectual and gainful activities, most probably due to the growing rivalry between the groups. One of the most notorious hacker wars was between LOD and MOD, which became progressively more dangerous as they tried to outperform and outsmart each other [1].[7]

---

[5]See https://www.edn.com/electronics-blogs/edn-moments/4406021/1st-computer-virus-is-written--January-30--1982 for more detail.

[6]See https://www.youtube.com/watch?v=dVwLAbMwqQ0 for a brief account of this story.

[7]Much later, in 1991, five members of MOD were convicted on conspiracy, wire fraud, computer fraud, computer tempering, and wiretapping charges [1].

This period also saw the first global ransomware attack, which was labelled the AIDS Trojan or the PC Cyborg attack.[8] In 1989, a postdoctoral AIDS researcher, Joseph Popp, sent out 20,000 floppy disks to AIDS researchers in more than 90 countries around the globe. Each disk was said to contain a risk-assessment questionnaire and a program which would estimate the risk of a particular individual contracting AIDS. The problem was that the disk contained ransomware with lagged activation (it activated after the computer terminal was powered on 90 times). After activation, the ransomware showed a message demanding a payment of $189 and $378 in exchange for the "software lease".

This period also saw the first convictions related to computer crime. Researchers [1, 2] often name Ian Murphy (aka "Captain Zap") as the first person ever to be convicted of "hacking"-related crime, in 1981. However, it is important to note that at the time, computer crime did not exist in the legal language and Murphy was prosecuted on theft charges. Therefore, Captain Zap's title of the first prosecuted hacker is often contested by the case of Gerald Wondra and two other members of the 414s hacker group, who, in 1983, were convicted for "harassing telephone calls" and received two years' probation. Strictly speaking, if we agree that phone phreaking was the predecessor of hacking, the 414s can probably claim to be the first convicted hackers as they were formally charged with phone phreaking rather than theft.

Yet, probably the most important event in the 1980s was the release of the "Morris Worm" by Robert Tappan Morris on November 2, 1988. This day was labelled in computer technology history as "Black Thursday" [2]. In contrast to the existing virus malware which required user activation, Morris released a self-propagating malware—a worm—which spread through the ARPANET (the predecessor of the Internet) and affected many[9] of the 60,000 computers which were connected to the network at the time, mostly belonging to NASA and the Pentagon, as well as to MIT, Stanford, Berkeley, and other universities. Morris was the first person convicted under the 1986 Computer Fraud and Abuse Act and sentenced to three years' probation, 400 hours of community service, and a fine of $10,050. In his defense,

---

[8]See   https://www.beckershospitalreview.com/healthcare-information-technology/first-known-ransomware-attack-in-1989-also-targeted-healthcare.html for more detail.

[9]According to some estimates, the damage was caused to 6000 computers (10% of connected computers), yet research shows that these estimates are most probably based on an approximation [2].

Morris argued that he was motivated by intellectual curiosity and did not benefit from his actions financially. Even though Morris was the first to conduct a "live test" of the worm malware, the term "worm" had been coined by Xerox in 1982—six years earlier [2]. Another interesting fact about the Morris worm is that the first official definition of the term "Internet" in its contemporary sense was documented in the case of "The United States of America v. Robert Tappan Morris" in 1991, which explained that: "Morris released the worm into INTERNET, which is a group of national networks that connect university, governmental, and military computers around the country" [2].

The Era of Charismatic "Despicable MEs" (1990–1999): The 1990s was one of the most interesting periods in the history of cyberthreats as it was a period dominated by individual hackers. The names of these individuals are known to the majority of those interested in cybersecurity. Let us remember several examples. In 1994, Kevin Poulsen (aka Dark Dante) was prosecuted and convicted for hacking into the Pacific Bell Telephone company system. He received a 51-month jail sentence and was ordered to pay $56,000 in restitution. In 1995, Kevin Mitnick (aka The Condor, The Darkside Hacker) was convicted on 5 of 21 counts of access to device fraud, wire fraud, computer damage, and wiretapping. In 1996, a 21-year-old, Julio Ardita, was charged with hacking into the Harvard University computer system. It turned out that Ardita had used the university system to instigate further attacks on other systems.

In March 1999, David L. Smith (aka Kwyjibo) released the Melissa virus, which affected Microsoft systems and spread via email attachment. This was the first mass–mailing computer virus. When the Melissa attachment was opened, the virus would be resent to the first 50 contacts in every affected user's Microsoft Outlook address book. Even though the virus did not cause any harm to the affected computers' data, it created serious disruptions to the global computer networks by sabotaging the email traffic, leading to over $80 million worth of damages. Smith was sentenced to ten years and ordered to pay $5000 in restitutions. He ended up serving 20 months.

The Proliferation of Cyberthreats (2000–2009): The early 2000s was the period when cyberthreats spread and became (i) more harmful and (ii) more impactful. With the development of the Internet and ICTs, the means to access information became available to large numbers of people. Equally, information about cyberthreats as well as malicious code became more accessible.

The year 2000 hit the global computerized community with several new challenges. In May 2000, the ILOVEYOU virus spread throughout the global computer network affecting Microsoft systems. The email subject of the spreading email was "ILOVEYOU" and it carried an attachment "LOVE-LETTER-FOR-YOU.txt.vbs". Even though the virus in its essence was very similar to Melissa and spread via an email attachment, it damaged files on the victims' machine and sent itself to all contacts in the Microsoft Outlook address book. The investigation led to the Philippines, where two programmers, Reonel Ramones and Onel de Guzman, became suspects. However, the Philippines did not have suitable laws to prosecute computer crime and eventually all charges against Ramones and de Guzman were dropped.

The year 2000 showed that malware was not only for grown-ups but also for kids. The Pikachu virus (named after the famous Pokémon series character) spread via email attachment and replicated itself in the same fashion as ILOVEYOU. In addition, it also attempted to delete several important Windows directories. However, the victims were given a deletion prompt, which is why the virus did not cause as much damage as ILOVEYOU.

The same year also saw the emergence of the Global malicious bot (self-propagating malware used to infect a host and connect it to a central server acting as command and control). It also brought about the Millennium bug problem: many programs used the last two digits to represent calendar years and there were wide concerns that the year 2000 would be indistinguishable from 1900, causing overwhelming computer failures due to the incorrect display of dates. Yet, the global community had prepared for the problem and addressed it with updates prior to 2000.

The emergence of large social media networks (such as Facebook in 2004) led to the increase in global communication. This, among other things, led to the further development of various hacker groups, including cybergangs. Better and faster access to information and the ability to quickly make a global impact also led to the emergence of hacktivist organizations such as The Anonymous in 2003.[10] Open web sources for hacktivists (such as Wikileaks.org in 2006) also appeared during this time.

The early 2000s also saw the emergence of the Dark Web, also known as the Dark Net—a portion of the World Wide Web where users remain anonymous. In the mid-1990s, the US navy created Tor—the "Onion Router" or

---

[10]See https://anonofficial.com/ for more detail.

"Onion Routing Browser". By 2002, the onion router technology became known to a limited number of users and in 2004 the Tor was open-sourced. Since Tor allowed for anonymous surfing of the Internet, it became the main Dark Web browser. On a daily basis, the Dark Web is surfed by a large number of users, who may range from curious teenagers to cybercriminals and cyberterrorists. The emergence of the Dark Web also allowed cybercriminal organizations to solicit services, communicate, and execute transactions at a global scale.

In 2007, the first global scale botnet attack, which became known as the Storm botnet or Storm worm botnet, affected millions of computer systems. The botnet spread via an email spam and allowed the instigators to remotely control a network of affected computers. To date, the adversaries behind the Storm botnet remain unidentified.

Another important event during this period was the invention of blockchain technology (a public ledger consisting of a growing number of blocks linked using cryptography) by Satoshi Nakamoto. The main idea behind blockchain is that it is a distributed and decentralized public ledger which is kept in the digital form. Since the ledger is used to record transactions live and across many computers simultaneously, the records on the ledger cannot be changed or tampered with retrospectively without attracting attention. To date, it is disputed whether Nakamoto is one person or a group of people. It is also unknown whether Nakamoto is actually from Japan or if it is an alias used by someone from another country. Between 2008 and 2009, Nakamoto published two papers [3, 4] explaining how a distributed ledger can be used to form a peer-to-peer electronic cash system, which gave rise to the bitcoin cryptocurrency. In 2009, Nakamoto publicized the first bitcoin software and launched the first bitcoin network. Even though blockchain technology generated a lot of positive outcomes and is currently employed by millions of individual users and organizations for a variety of purposes (e.g., tracing the diamond origins for blood diamond smuggling prevention; smart contracting, etc.), cryptocurrencies in general and bitcoins in particular remain the important means of payment and transaction for cybercriminals.

The Cyberthreat Renaissance (2010–Present): The period of the 2010s can be described as the rebirth or renaissance of cyberthreat activities. With much code being openly available and any teenager being able to access information about how to create a "nuclear cyberbomb" online in several clicks, it becomes very easy to access the means to infiltrate complex cyber systems.

In recent years, cybersecurity breaches became widespread and started to target a large number of businesses and individuals primarily with the aim of financial gain [5–7]. The further development of technology not only allowed systems to be infiltrated, but also to do this very rapidly. Examples of such activities include the massive data breaches which affected 6.5 million LinkedIn users in 2012 and 65 million Tumbler accounts in 2013; concerted attacks on blockchains and cryptocurrencies in 2014 and 2016; the WannaCry and Petya virus attacks in 2017 which paralyzed not only individual businesses but industries and entire countries. This period also saw the first ever conviction for both hacking and cyber terrorism.

Overall, the variety of tools and availability of information since 2010 has led to a situation in which the attacks have become more and more common, progressively powerful and less easy to cope with.

Distinguishing Between Vulnerability, Threat, and Risk in Cyberspace

As we can see from the previous subsections, cyberthreats are multifaceted and widespread. So far, we have looked at the various types of cyberthreats and tried to sketch how some of those threats came about. However, when we talk about businesses and their ability to build safe cyber spaces, we often consider not only cyberthreats, but also vulnerabilities and risks. And this is where the terms start getting confused. This confusion comes from the fact that all three terms (cyberthreat, cyber vulnerability, and cyber risk) relate to "harm" and "chance" or "probability", yet, they do not mean the same thing. The easiest way to understand the difference between the three terms is to imagine cyber risk as an overlap between cyberthreat and cyber vulnerability. Let us look at this issue more closely.

When we talk about threats, vulnerabilities, and risks in cyber space, we always refer to "probabilistic" or "chance" events. In other words, events which may or may not happen. Therefore, a *probability* is usually defined as an extent to which a particular event is likely to happen. Probability is usually represented as odds (e.g., 1 in 10 chances of something happening) or, more often, as a percentage chance of something happening (e.g., 10% chance of something happening).

As we explained earlier, cyberthreat is the *objective general* probability of a malicious cyber act which results in cyber or physical harm damaging individuals (private or public), organizations, the international community, or moral code. This probability is *objective* and *general* because the malicious cyber act can happen *in principle* (or *on average*) with some *positive* probability (probability greater than 0). Cybervulnerability is an *objective specific* probability with which a particular security system could be compromised. In other words, it is a probability with which a *specific* security system has a gap that, *in principle*, could be exploited. Cyber risk, therefore, is the *precise* probability with which a cyberthreat and a cyber vulnerability coincide at a specific place and time and result in harm.

To make these definitions less abstract, let us consider the following example. In October 2015, the telecommunication giant TalkTalk was hit by a major cyberattack, as a result of which thousands of customer online records that included identity information (names, email addresses, telephone numbers, as well as bank account numbers) were compromised.[11] The global cybersecurity data collected from businesses shows that 63% of all data breaches around the globe target identity data [5] —i.e., the data that can help cybercriminals masquerade as a particular individual. This means that there exists a cyberthreat of identity theft which may occur with an *objective general* probability (equal to 63%), irrespective of the type of business you own, the type of security system you run, etc. In other words, cyberthreat probability tells you to what extent, *on average*, any business (including TalkTalk or your business) can become a victim of identity theft.

Now, cyber vulnerability tells you how likely it is that a specific business (TalkTalk or your business) has a gap or gaps in its security system through which identity information can be stolen. In theory, you can have an impervious system which makes extracting identity information impossible (e.g., you do not store any identity data digitally[12]) or almost impossible (you only store partial data digitally), or you can have a highly fragile system offering many opportunities for an attack. Again, in theory, if you analyze all the possible ways in which someone can get to the identity data you store, you should be able to come up with an objective and specific probability estimate which would tell you how vulnerable your system is.

---

[11]See https://www.bbc.co.uk/news/business-34743185 for more detail.

[12]This is, however, highly unlikely as even if you do not store customer data, you almost certainly store employee data in the digital form.

You might ask—why can't we just assume that cyber vulnerability is the same as cyberthreat? It would be incorrect to do this because cybersecurity is costly. If you assume that you have a 63% vulnerability to cyberthreats when in fact it is 5%, you would be directing valuable labor and monetary resources to something not very relevant to your business.[13] Using our example, in theory, TalkTalk should be able to analyze various security gaps and come up with an objective and specific probability with which the identity data they store could be stolen.

Yet, because both cyberthreat and cyber vulnerability are "probabilistic" constructs—i.e., they depend on the realization of chance events—we need to introduce the concept of cyber risk, which shows the probability with which cyberthreat and cyber vulnerability are likely to coincide and result in harm. For example, you might have a cyber vulnerability but this vulnerability is highly unlikely to be exploited by a particular threat—then the actual cyber risk is low. At the same time, you can have a high likelihood of a cybersecurity threat but a very robust security system (low cyber vulnerability), in which case cyber risk will also be low. In other words, by analyzing threats versus existing vulnerabilities, in theory, one should be able to calculate precise value of cybersecurity risk. Going back to our example, in theory, TalkTalk should have been able to come up with a precise probability estimate of cyber risk related to identity theft given existing vulnerabilities in their cybersecurity system. In other words, they should have been able to estimate the probability with which the October 2015 attack could have occurred.

Notice that in our example we talk about the *theoretical* possibility of calculating *precise* probability estimates. We will see in the following chapters that what seems possible in theory is often not feasible in practice. This discrepancy between theoretical and practical cyber risk estimations is what makes the cybersecurity space so difficult to navigate, and this is why many businesses, much like TalkTalk in our example, fail to anticipate the oncoming attacks. But before we do this, let us consider who stands behind the various cyberattacks and why cyberattacks occur.

---

[13]We discuss actual and perceived probabilities with regard to cybersecurity threats, vulnerability, and risks later in this book.

References

1. Brenner, S. W. (2007). History of computer crime. In *The history of information security* (pp. 705–721). Amsterdam: Elsevier.
2. DeNardis, L. (2007). A history of internet security. In *The history of information security* (pp. 681–704). Amsterdam: Elsevier.
3. Nakamoto, S. (2009, May 24). *Bitcoin: A peer-to-peer electronic cash system* (PDF). Archived from the original on 20 March 2014. Retrieved 5 March 2014.
4. Nakamoto, S. (2008, 31 October). *Bitcoin P2P e-cash paper*. Archived from the original on 28 December 2012. Retrieved 5 March 2014.
5. Kharlamov, A., Parry, G., & Pogrebna, G. (2018). *Measuring vulnerability towards cybersecurity Risks* (Working Paper).
6. May, R. (2018). *The human firewall: Cybersecurity is not just an IT problem* (Kindle Edition).
7. Evans, K., & Reeder, F. (2010). *A human capital crisis in cybersecurity: Technical proficiency matters*. Washington, DC: CSIS.

3

A Sneak Peek into the Motivation of a Cybercriminal

There is a famous episode in Clint Eastwood's movie *One Million Dollar Baby* (2005) when Maggie, an aspiring professional fighter played by Hilary Swank meets her opponent in the first professional public fight. The opponent is tough and Maggie is struggling. When Maggie complains about her opponent to her coach Frankie (Clint Eastwood), he says: "*She is younger, she is stronger, and she is more experienced. Now, what are you going to do about that?*" In the next scene Maggie knocks the opponent out. In a way, this "*younger, stronger, and more experienced*" description is true about the majority of cybercriminals. Throughout the history of information technology development, young, educated, and very creative people became hackers. But what about their motivation? Why do they do the things they do?

Hackers of the past were mostly preoccupied with questions of intellectual curiosity. In his interview to hackstory.net, Ian Murphy (aka "Captain Zap"), regarded by many as the first person ever prosecuted for hacking-related activities on theft charges (see Fig. 2.1), said:

> *I have always been a hacker if you want to put it that way. I prefer to call it unorthodox or guerilla [sic] research protocols that test the limits of society, technological advances, overall impact upon our world and the never-ending thirst for finding out just what the hell is out there. I really think that the lack of our citizens to question technology, let alone understand how anything works keeps most people in a provincial view of technology and stifles their mind in general. Today, we have a huge society that does not understand the working of a simple light switch that is in their homes, and have to call an electrician to change it. And then complains that*

© The Author(s) 2019
G. Pogrebna and M. Skilton, *Navigating New Cyber Risks*,
https://doi.org/10.1007/978-3-030-13527-0_3

it cost 150 bucks for such a thing. Grow up and learn to hack your environment to understand what you are living in. Question everything that comes before you and don't take it for granted that it will be alright.[1]

Kevin Mitnick, the guy behind one of the first large-scale computer infiltration acts in 1979, as well as the first ever hacker to get onto the Federal Bureau of Investigation's (FBI) most-wanted list, also emphasized that his motivation was primarily intellectual curiosity. He wrote:

my crimes were simple crimes of computer trespass and making free telephone calls. I've acknowledged since my arrest that the actions I took were illegal, and that I committed invasions of privacy … My misdeeds were motivated by curiosity: I wanted to know as much as I could about how phone networks worked, and the ins and outs of computer security. I went from being a kid who loved to perform magic tricks to becoming the world's most notorious hacker, feared by corporations and the government … As I reflect back on my life for the last thirty years, I admit I made some extremely poor decisions, driven by my curiosity, the desire to learn about technology, and a good intellectual challenge.[2]

Yet, hacker motivation has progressively translated from primarily intrinsic to primarily financial. When did the switch from intrinsic to financial motives actually occur? Our dive into the history of cyberthreats (see Chapter 2) suggests that large-scale for-profit cyberattacks date back to the 1980s, with the first cyber-related convictions and the formation of the first organized hacker groups. However, it was only with the development of social networks and the Dark Web from the early 2000s that money became one of the main driving factors for the adversaries.

To explore the motives of cybercriminals, we collected and analyzed over 50 interviews with hackers who were either convicted felons or confirmed anonymous hackers who had expressed their thoughts to reputable journalists and websites.[3] By looking at the parts of interviews where they discussed their motivation, we were able to map their major incentives (see Fig. 3.1). Our analysis reveals that money is one of the major motivations for hackers. However, it would be incorrect to say that all hackers are after money. Figure 3.1 shows that they are also interested in information, privacy,

---

[1] See https://hackstory.net/Captain_Zap for more information.

[2] See https://www.theregister.co.uk/2003/01/13/chapter_one_kevin_mitnicks_story/ for more detail.

[3] Many studies rely on "self-reported" hacker data—i.e., on reports from people who would classify themselves as "hackers". We wanted to avoid any biases which such self-reported samples could bring and concentrated only on the direct speech of convicted or confirmed (verified) hackers.

Fig. 3.1 Adversary motivation from hacker direct speech

technology, research, and even in *"changing the world"*. Many mention their desire to fight against governmental surveillance and to obtain new knowledge. Some also say they do it for fun or the thrill.

Obviously, it is important to remember that our analysis is limited to individual hackers.

Yet, the current number and variety of *adversaries* involved in potentially damaging cyber activities has grown significantly and goes far beyond the hacker community.

Adversaries: Types and Varieties

To understand the scale of the problem, imagine for a moment that you open your laptop or switch on your PC and see the following message on your computer screen:

> *Your files have been encrypted! You can decrypt some of your files for free by clicking HERE. But if you want to decrypt all of your files, you need to pay. You only have three days to submit the payment. After that, the price will be doubled. If you don't pay in seven days, you won't be able to recover your files at all.*

The message is followed by detailed instructions about what amount in bitcoin you should pay and how you can do it. Obviously, if you get this message, you know that you have become a victim of a ransomware attack. Now, the question is who may be behind this attack? Is it an individual attacker, such as a teenager next door, a disgruntled employee you just fired, or even your ex? Is it a large ring of organized cybercriminals? Or is it an act of cyberwar instigated by an unfriendly state? The problem is—it can be any of these adversaries and it is highly likely that the source of the attack will not be found even after a detailed *ex post* analysis. It is true that ransomware attacks are mostly used by individual hackers and organized cybercriminals, but there is no reason why it cannot be an act of cyberwar. Consider, for example, the so-called Petya virus which spread across the global cyber network in June 2017, primarily affecting Ukrainian companies and public organizations.[4] While the Petya virus was first discovered in 2016, the 2017 attack is often called "NotPetya" due to its lack of similarity with the original Petya malware. While "NotPetya" masqueraded as a ransomware attack, it emerged in the process of *ex post* analysis that it was very likely an act of cyberwar against Ukraine. The malware spread primarily through the business tax-preparation software M.E.Doc. In 2018, several countries, including the USA, the UK, and Australia, issued statements in which they claimed that Russia was responsible for the attack.[5]

In current cyber spaces, we can distinguish between two major types of adversaries: individuals and organizations (see Fig. 3.2).

Individual adversaries can be split into five categories according to their motivation: Naïve, Ethical, Goal-oriented, Mercenaries, and Criminal Architects. Let us look at each category in more detail.

Naïve adversaries refer to creative individuals or copycats who tend to explore cyber vulnerabilities. They spend hours in front of the computer and by chance, or due to creative or deductive thinking, can penetrate complex systems. These adversaries tend to act alone or in a close group of like-minded individuals (e.g., high school friends) unconnected to hacker or terrorist groups, and/or organized criminals. A typical example of a naïve adversary attack was recently instigated on TalkTalk (an attack we used as an example in Chapter 2). In 2015, one such naïve actor (a 17-year-old teenager) discovered the so-called "zero-day" vulnerability (an unknown or unanticipated vulnerability) in the TalkTalk system. While he did not benefit from this discovery personally, he shared the details online. As a result, 156,959 consumer records were compromised, of which 15,656 had their bank account information stolen and 28,000 customers' credit and debit

---

[4]See https://www.wired.com/story/notpetya-cyberattack-ukraine-russia-code-crashed-the-world/ for more detail.

[5]See https://wccftech.com/australia-us-uk-russia-notpetya/ for more detail.

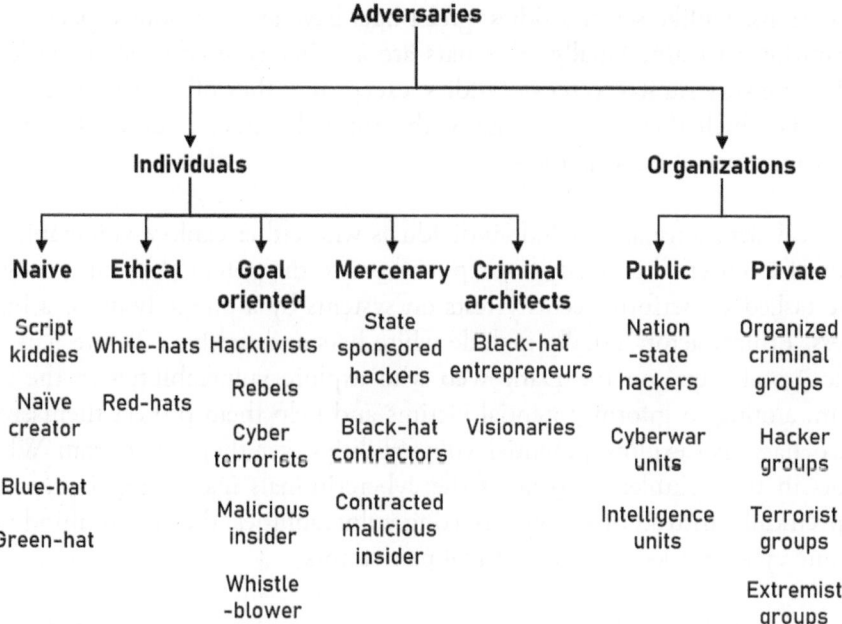

Fig. 3.2 Taxonomy of adversaries

card details were exposed.[6] When giving evidence, the teenager in question admitted to the court: "*I was just showing off to my mates*". This desire to be cool, to do something extraordinary, is the main driving force for naïve adversaries.

Naïve adversaries may include: naïve creators, script kiddies, as well as green- and blue-hat hackers. Naïve creators are creative individuals engaging in various hypothesis-testing activities online. Script kiddies are individuals who capitalize on information and code available on the web, testing this information and code in a variety of contexts.[7] Script kiddies do not care about coding skills. They are essentially copycat amateurs who engage in hacking out of curiosity or the desire to "*be cool*". Green hats are amateur hackers with a huge motivation and desire to grow into master hackers. They tend to spend ages in various online forums and bombard others with

---

[6]See https://www.bbc.co.uk/news/business-34743185 for more detail.

[7]Note that some script kiddies do engage in for-profit hacking, yet the majority of them tend to do this out of intellectual curiosity.

questions. Unlike script kiddies, green hats have an enormous capacity and ambition to learn. Finally, blue hats are another type of amateur hackers. They are very similar to script kiddies, except that they often have a vengeful agenda which they try to pursue with minimal (rather traditional and not very innovative) hacking tools.

Ethical actors usually include individuals who either explore vulnerabilities out of intellectual curiosity but report them to the potential victims, or who are tasked to perform security tests on systems by a public body or a business. Ethical actors usually include white hats and red hats. White hats are the "good guys" on the Dark Web who explore vulnerabilities in the system, aiming to inform potential victims and help them protect themselves. Red hats also explore potential vulnerabilities, yet they differ from White hats in their ruthless pursuit of the cybercriminals instigating the attacks. Specifically, instead of simply reporting vulnerabilities, they mastermind vigilante cyberattacks on cybercriminal penetrators.

But if white hats and red hats are good guys, how come they are listed in the topology of adversaries? It is true that both white hats and red hats are well intentioned, but good intentions do not necessarily guarantee that white hats always do "the right thing" or act ethically. When white hats are commissioned by business or the government to do "controlled experiments" on security systems, their impact is undeniably positive: they do useful things and help identify otherwhile unanticipated threats. Yet, white-hat hacker enthusiasts can, if operating in an uncontrolled environment, damage business reputations and even endanger lives.

In 2015, security researcher and self-proclaimed ethical hacker Chris Roberts was removed from a United Airlines flight. Roberts states that he hacked into the thrust management computer of the Boeing 737 through the inflight entertainment system and attempted to do a live "pen test" of the plane mid-air. Roberts claimed that he managed to alter the plane's movement and temporarily steer it off the intended course. The event sparked many debates, with many reputable security experts commenting on the impossibility of the claim. Yet, two brands—Boeing and United Airlines—found themselves in the middle of controversy which, to date, is unresolved. It remains largely undiscovered whether and to what extent one can actually hack into airplane systems from the passenger seat. However, the potential dangers of such testing are widely known.

It does not mean, however, that all enthusiasts are necessarily a cause of potential harm. Recall Kamil Hismatullin, a notorious Russian white hat, who discovered vulnerability in the YouTube system and showed that any video could be deleted. Instead of exploiting his discovery, he reported the bug to Google, which paid him a $5000 reward. The point of all these stories is that ethical hackers may be both a driving force for any cybersecurity innovation, as they are very efficient in discovering zero-day vulnerabilities, and also a source of potential threat, in that they act without stakeholder authorization and in an uncontrolled environment. One of the big problems is that ethical hackers' discoveries and tests often surface in the public domain. This could cause unintended damage to various organizations as, if anything, it may also give cybercriminals new ideas. Vulnerability discovered in one area with one particular company, community, or even a state can in many cases be applied to other contexts. Think of all those active cyberwar examples when techniques and even publicly available code developed by ethical actors were then utilized on the Dark Web with very bad intentions.

Goal-oriented actors are probably the most heterogeneous group. By "goal-oriented", we mean actors who do not engage in cybercriminal activity with a desire to earn money but those who pursue a broader goal. Goal-oriented actors are not interested in monetary reward. Their actual goal may be benign or evil. They can also be motivated by revenge or have mixed goals (e.g., whistle-blowers may be motivated by revenge and/or benign goals such as disclosing unethical practices within an organization). In pursuit of their goal, they may cause financial damage or even make money, but money is never the intended purpose of their activity.

Think of the hacktivists: they often have a broad civic or social agenda. They believe they are acting "for the greater good" of individuals, community, country, etc. They always have a cause or agenda, which they clearly articulate. They are essentially activists operating in cyber space. Even though private companies rarely become the targets of hacktivists, they may incur collateral damage if their business interests get in the way of a hacktivist. Many remember the story of Aaron Swartz, an American hacktivist and the mastermind behind Creative Commons, Reddit, and many other important tech inventions of the early 2000s. He came into the limelight when he founded the group Demand Progress, which led a campaign against the Stop Online Piracy Act. In 2011, Swartz was arrested and charged with two counts of wire fraud and 11 violations of the Computer Fraud and Abuse Act after the MIT police linked him to an MIT guest account which had been set up on a computer placed in an unmarked and unlocked closet at MIT and set to systematically download content (mostly academic articles) from the academic online publication repository JSTOR. Facing 35 years in prison and multiple penalties, including a $1 million fine, Aaron Swartz committed suicide. He was 26 at the time. Even though he did not leave a suicide note, in the *Guerrilla Open Access Manifesto*, he clearly explained his motivation: "*Information is power. But like all power, there are those who want to keep it for themselves. The world's entire scientific and cultural heritage, published over centuries in books and journals, is increasingly being digitized and locked up by a handful of private corporations.*"[8] Clearly, Aaron Swartz had a much broader agenda and his actions were not targeting the online academic storage giant JSTOR specifically. Yet, his attempt to bulk-download JSTOR content was a manifestation of his belief that information, especially academic research, should be free for all, which inevitably infringed upon the JSTOR business model. To date, there is no unified view on this controversial and tragic case. While representatives of large publishing houses have discussed the dangers of copyright infringement online, many of Swartz's supporters celebrate his heritage. Posthumously, Swartz became a recipient of numerous awards celebrating the freedom of information and speech, recognizing his contribution to the fight for unlimited access to information.

Rebels are goal-oriented individuals who are interested in attracting public attention to an important "protest" message. In 2000, Rafael Gray (aka Curador), an 18-year-old teenager from Wales, stole and published over 26,000 credit card numbers which he had obtained by compromising several e-commerce websites. His goal was not to profit from the operation but to expose the lack of cybersecurity concerns by businesses who store personal data. In an interview to pbs.org, he said: "*There are a lot of people out there who won't even safeguard their own safety, let alone the safety of their customers. At the end of the day, it's the fault of these companies. The buck does stop with them ... But they're not even trying to protect their own business from that.*"[9] Gray did not receive any jail time as a result of his actions but had to get psychiatric treatment. Another interesting rebel adversary is Kimberley Vanvaeck (aka Gigabyte), a Belgian hacker, born in 1985, who became a feminist legend after she wrote a number of viruses in response to sexist comments made by Graham Cluley, a representative of Sophos cybersecurity company, who insisted that virus writers were always male. Vanvaeck wrote such viruses as Coconut-A, Sahay-A, and Sharp-A (reportedly, the first virus ever written using C#). Vanvaeck did not benefit from the viruses but posted them openly on her website as a "*proof-of-concept*", which enabled others to make use of them. Belgian authorities detained Gigabyte, confiscated

---

[8]See https://archive.org/stream/GuerillaOpenAccessManifesto/Goamjuly2008_djvu.txt for more detail.
[9]See https://www.pbs.org/wgbh/pages/frontline/shows/hackers/interviews/curador.html for more detail.

her computer equipment and deleted her website. Yet, she was released in 24 hours. In an interview to silicon.com, Vanvaeck revealed that her actions were motivated not only by the feminist agenda, but had a broader message: "*Actually, yes, [Cluley's] sexistic comments [are] a reason why I don't like [him] but that's not everything ... Except for that, he also continues talking shit about virus writers in general, saying we're pizza-addicted, sex-starved, ugly teens who never get outside. It's always the same yet, I think, fairly unrealistic.*"[10]

Another group with non-monetary goals are cyberterrorists. There are many definitions of cyberterrorism [1]. For example, the FBI defines cyber-terrorism as "*premeditated, politically motivated attack against information, computer systems, computer programs, and data which results in violence against non-combatant targets by subnational groups or clandestine agents*".[11] It is, however, obvious that cyberterrorists do not necessarily have political goals. They could be ideological or religious. Due to the potential variety of these non-pecuniary goals, some definitions concentrate on the way in which these goals are achieved. While these definitions are very different, they gen-erally agree that terrorists achieve their goals through the use of *intimidation* (i.e., "terror") and target vital infrastructures and systems or pose a signifi-cant threat to human lives. For example, one of the early definitions of cyber terrorism by the Director of the National Infrastructure Protection Center (NIPC), Michael Vatis, postulates that cyberterrorism is "*the use of cyber tools to shut down critical national infrastructures (such as energy, transportation, or government operations) for the purpose of coercing or intimidating a government or civilian population*" [2]. Dorothy Denning, a renowned information secu-rity scholar, once defined cyberterrorism as "*a computer-based attack or threat of attack intended to intimidate or coerce governments or societies in pursuit of goals that are political, religious, or ideological. The attack should be sufficiently destructive or disruptive to generate fear comparable to that from physical acts of terrorism*" [3].

While cyberterrorists are a different group compared to hacktivists, both groups share a motivational similarity: they have underlying non-pecuniary incentives [4]. You may say that cyberterrorists often do pursue targets for monetary gain. Indeed, they might, yet money is just a "means to an end". In other words, they might sometimes resort to gainful cyberattacks, yet they intend to use these attacks as part of their broader agenda, which is primarily political, ideological, or religious. While cyberterrorists are often

---

[10]See https://www.zdnet.com/article/hacker-gigabyte-angered-by-stereotypes/ for more detail.

[11]See https://www.fbi.gov/investigate/cyber for more detail.

united in organizational structures, the unique characteristics of cyber space make it possible for one person to achieve a significant impact and cause a lot of damage. The first person charged with both computer hacking and terrorism was Kosovan hacker Ardit Ferizi. In 2015, Ferizi (aka Th3Dir3ctorY) broke the database of an online retailer and obtained personally identifiable information for over 100,000 customers. He was able to identify 1351 federal employees and active military personnel from the stolen data. He then provided federal and military personal data records to a member of the Islamic State of Iraq and the Levant group (ISIL), Junaid Hussain (aka Abu Hussain al-Britani), who published these records on Twitter and encouraged ISIL members and supporters to target the identified individuals. Even though Ferizi was believed to be the leader of a Kosova Hacker's Security (KSH) group which had instigated cyberattacks on over 20,000 various targets in Serbia, Ukraine, Israel, etc., it appeared that in this case he acted alone.[12] In 2016, he was arrested in Malaysia, extradited to the USA, and sentenced to 20 years' imprisonment.

Another different and, probably the most unpredictable, group are malicious insiders and whistle-blowers. They might be motivated by perfectly individualistic reasons, such as the desire to avenge a back-stabbing boss, rebel against something they perceive as unjust at their workplace (amount of monetary compensation, task allocation, etc.), or, in fact, pursue a more social agenda, such as disclosing irregularities, discrimination, or the unethical actions of a particular company. Notice that in the Goal-oriented category, we do not consider "contracted" malicious insiders—for example, employees who act as hired help for personal financial gain (e.g., think of insiders who leak information to competitors). Goal-oriented malicious insiders and whistle-blowers pursue non-monetary goals.

In 2000, Vitek Boden, a disgruntled former employee of the Maroochy Shire waste treatment plant in Queensland, Australia, broke into the plant's computer system and released 264,000 gallons of raw sewage, affecting local river, parks, and the property of a nearby Hyatt Regency hotel.[13] Hunter Watertech Pty Ltd., owner of the plant, and the Maroochy Shire Council spent an equivalent of more than US$500,000 and US$176,000, respectively, to deal with the aftermath. It emerged during the investigation that Boden left Hunter Watertech on a bad note and then failed to secure a job at the Maroochy Shire Council. In an attempt to "pay back" both Hunter

---

[12]See https://www.justice.gov/opa/file/896326/download for more detail.

[13]See http://web.mit.edu/smadnick/www/wp/2017-09.pdf for more detail.

Watertech and the Council, he used equipment he stole from his former workplace to issue radio commands while he drove around the plant area on at least 46 occasions. As a result of this infrastructural sabotage, the sewage released caused significant environmental damage in the area. Boden received a two-year jail sentence for 30 counts of computer hacking, theft, and environmental damage.[14]

Whistle-blowers are another group. In cyber space, the most widely known cases of whistle-blowing relate to either governmental or military data (think, for example, of Edward Snowden and Chelsea Manning). Yet, in some cases, private businesses become centers of the whistle-blowing scandals. Probably the most notorious recent case of whistle-blowing is the Cambridge Analytica case. Christopher Wylie, a behavioral strategist, revealed the alarming practices of Strategic Communication Laboratories (SCL) and its satellite company, Cambridge Analytica, which used controversially obtained data to psychologically profile people for targeted political and private-sector advertising. Wylie revealed that SCL had a contractual agreement with Global Science Research, a company owned by Alexandr Kogan (also known by his married name Dr Spectre), who harvested millions of Facebook profiles (according to different estimates, the figure fluctuates between 50 and 80 million) and sold them for profit to Cambridge Analytica. SCL and Cambridge Analytica then used the information to target voters with the aim of manipulating votes. Currently the target of major investigations on both sides of the Atlantic, both companies are believed to have been major vote manipulators in the recent Brexit vote as well as the American presidential election of 2016.

According to Wylie, Kogan used a well-known trick in data harvesting—online psychological quizzes—to obtain the data. Kogan developed a series of quizzes and collected responses through MTurk as well as Qualtrics online survey platforms which participants filled out in exchange for small monetary rewards. In the surveys, he asked participants to provide access to their Facebook pages. While around 320,000 people agreed to give Kogan access to their Facebook information, what they did not know was that their Facebook friends' profiles were also harvested. In other words, each respondent gave access to the profiles of at least 160 other people who had not consented to their data being accessed or used.[15] After Wylie provided

---

[14]See http://www.isssource.com/classic-hacker-case-maroochy-shire/.

[15]See https://www.theguardian.com/news/2018/mar/17/data-war-whistleblower-christopher-wylie-faceook-nix-bannon-trump for more detail.

the information to *The Observer* correspondent, the University of Cambridge released a response in which they revealed that Kogan initially applied through the university for approval to conduct Facebook data harvesting for research purposes but that the application was rejected by the ethics committee. It is, therefore, not clear whether Kogan had ethical approval to collect the data for research purposes at the time when the data collection happened. Kogan claimed that the app which he created to harvest the data ("thisismydigitallife") was clearly labelled as a commercial product and was not associated with research he did at Cambridge. As we write this book, the investigation into these matters is still ongoing.

This case teaches us many lessons, yet there are two ways in which we can look at it. There is a philosophical and ethical prism which clearly shows how the unethical use of data can backfire and have drastic societal consequences. There is, however, another, more pragmatic, prism. We can have endless discussions about how Cambridge Analytica exploited the data of millions of unsuspecting individuals and undermined the trust in data science research for many years to come. Yet, let's face it—before the whistle was blown, Cambridge Analytica was running a viable and highly profitable business which ceased to exist after Wylie broke his silence. And this is another side of the story relevant for us when we consider the risk to business. Clearly, if you don't want to end up like Cambridge Analytica, do not do dodgy deals. However, corporate responsibility and the border between ethics and business interests is an extremely context-dependent issue. The same practice considered in one situation, in a particular industry, under special set of circumstances may seem reasonable, while in a different industry or under a different set of circumstances, it may be completely ethically wrong. Under these circumstances, whistle-blowers and malicious insiders become perhaps the most uncertain elements of the equation. If you are holding data that could be monetized, if your business depends on computer systems, you can probably map the scope of potential threats. Yet, predicting an unhappy and impulsive response from a current or former employee is very hard. When we talk about goal-oriented malicious insiders or whistle-blowers, there is virtually no pragmatic incentive for an employee to do something like that. Their motivation is often emotional: they feel that something was done wrong either to them personally, to other employees, customers, or society as a whole. After the information reaches the public domain, they become virtually unemployable. And since there is no financial or pragmatic incentive behind these decisions, malicious insider and whistle-blower effects are extremely difficult to predict.

The Mercenary is an adversary who participates in cyberthreat creation for money. Mercenaries are contracted aids who provide services for the threat masterminds. Think of a programmer writing code which then becomes an important component of malicious software, helping to break the "locks" of computer systems, etc. Mercenaries are essentially "hired help" who aid the implementation of criminal ideas. Usually, mercenaries are highly skilled hackers motivated by monetary gain who are contracted to do certain jobs either in person or remotely. They may do freelance work for other individuals, groups, and even states. Essentially, mercenaries enter a simple contractual agreement—they offer services in exchange for monetary reward.

Mercenaries could be black-hat contractors selling malicious code in response to Dark Web demand. They could be sponsored by states to infiltrate or disrupt the systems of their counterparts in cyberwar. Finally, they could be contracted malicious insiders (e.g., employees working for the benefit of competing businesses with the aim of for-profit industrial espionage). Between 2005 and 2007, hackers stole and exploited 45.6 million credit and debit card numbers by instigating a series of attacks on the TJX companies (a multinational off-price department store with headquarters in the USA and a variety of brands, including HomeGoods, TJ Maxx, Sierra Trading Post, HomeSense, Marshalls, TK Maxx, etc.). It then emerged during the course of the investigation that the scheme was much wider than just TJX and that 170 million credit and debit card numbers had been illegally obtained by the same group of conspirators. Albert Gonzalez, a cybercriminal mastermind, was convicted of planning and organizing the attacks and sentenced to 20 years in jail. Gonzalez had a number of accomplices. One of these accomplices, Jeremy Jethro, received a three-year probation sentence and was ordered to pay a fine of $10,000 for the typical mercenary work. Jethro created an exploit for Microsoft Internet Explorer and sold it to Gonzalez for $60,000.[16]

An interesting question is whether one can be a mercenary without realizing it. Specifically, is it possible to write a piece of totally legitimate "benign" code and sell it for profit and not recognize that it could be used with evil intentions? While in principle nothing is impossible, in practice it is highly improbable. Most malicious code is written with particular

---

[16]See https://www.wired.com/2010/03/jethro-sentencing/ for more detail.

systems in mind, so it does not take much deduction to realize what could be the consequences of applying the code in practice. So, while there are, of course, exceptions to the rule, not understanding the consequences is highly unlikely. There are, however, examples when mercenaries were not paid in cash or bitcoin but worked for other potential benefits. Stephen Watt (aka Jim Jones, Unix Terrorist) wrote a "sniffer" program which allowed Gonzalez's group to monitor and record information transferred across the TJX network. Before getting caught, Stephen Watt had great career prospects in programming and a shiny job first at Morgan Stanley, earning $90,000 a year as a software engineer, and then at Imagine Software, making $130,000 as a developer of trading software for finance industry.

The prosecutors did not find any evidence that Watt actually profited from the scheme. However, Watt failed to prove that he did not know how his code was used. He was Albert Gonzalez's friend and exchanged messages with him on a daily basis. After analyzing the content of those messages, the prosecution was able to show that Watt, if not fully aware of the entire scheme, had a significant degree of knowledge about it. Watt's legal counsel said in an interview to *Wired* that his client fully acknowledged "*responsibility for aiding people that he knew would commit wrongdoing*".[17]

Criminal architect actors are the guys behind the cybercriminal groups. They are the brains of the operation. They think through the whole business model of the activity and develop links between various operational nodes of the ecosystem. Criminal architects may lead a well-designed close group of conspirators who all know each other personally. Equally, they may create and lead a "distributed" ecosystem where each person plays a tiny part without knowing how big the operation actually is. If you have never heard of a "distributed" criminal ecosystem, the 1968 movie *The Thomas Crown Affair*, with Steve McQueen and Faye Dunaway, provides a great example of how "distributed" criminal operations can work. In the film, millionaire Thomas Crown designs and orchestrates a distributed "*proof of concept*" bank robbery operation, recruiting five individuals to commit the crime. The five never see Crown and don't know who hired them. They also do not meet each other, and are not even aware that they are participating in a crime before the start of the operation. Arriving at the bank on the day of the robbery, they suddenly realize that they have to work together and co-operatively steal over

---

[17]See https://www.wired.com/2013/04/stephen-watt-stalked-by-past/ for more detail.

$2,660,000 for Crown, who collects all the proceeds and remains undetected. Distributed cybercriminal structures work in much the same way: they may involve dozens or even hundreds of people, each doing a small part for monetary rewards of varying size, while it is the criminal architects who ultimately receive the lion's share of the criminal proceeds.

Criminal architects can be roughly divided into two categories: Black-hat entrepreneurs and Visionaries. The difference between the two lies in the level of their technical expertise. Black-hat entrepreneurs are very technically skillful people (black-hat hackers) who engage in designing and masterminding various operations. They often lead the operation with a very hands-on approach, frequently engaging personally in the creation of malicious code, the exploration of vulnerabilities, and even the execution of the attacks. Albert Gonzalez is a good example of a criminal architect of the black-hat entrepreneur type. Criminal visionaries are qualitatively different—they often do not possess advanced technical skills but have enough understanding of the landscape to design and organize successful attacks. They do not produce a single line of code and have only a rudimentary knowledge of programming, but they are extremely skillful in masterminding fraudulent schemes and are very good at understanding human psychology.

The other type of adversaries are organizations. Both private and public organizations may be behind cyberattacks. On the **Private** side, we have Organized Criminal Groups (e.g., cybergangs), Hacker Groups, Terrorist Groups, Extremist Groups. On the **Public** side, Nation-state Hackers, Cyberwar Units, and Intelligence Units.

Private organizations may have a broad range of motives for engaging in cyberattacks. For example, Organized Criminal Groups are criminal organizations acting in cyberspace. Their main purpose is to engage in gainful activity by means of cybercrime. Hacker Groups usually have different motives. Usually, by hacker groups we mean goal-oriented organizations with a non-monetary agenda. While there are many prominent hacker groups, the most well known is probably Anonymous, which targets governmental websites, state services and agencies, large corporations, and even religious organizations (Anonymous are particularly known for their attacks on the Church of Scientology) [5]. Terrorist Groups use intimidation techniques to put pressure on governments, nation-states, the civilian population, or international community in pursuit of political, ideological, or religious goals. One of the first documented attacks by a cyberterrorist group was on Sri Lankan embassies, planned and executed by the Tamil guerrillas in 1998. The goal of the attack was to paralyze the digital communication of the embassies, which throughout the two-week period of the attack received 800 email messages a day. All the messages had the same content: "*We are the Internet Black Tigers and we're doing this to disrupt your communications*" [6]. Extremist Groups are radical goal-oriented groups using cyber means to target governments, corporations, and the international community. In 2007, the official web resource of the Ukrainian president Viktor Yushchenko came under attack. In the aftermath, the Eurasian Youth Movement, an extremist nationalistic youth group, claimed responsibility for the attack. The group had an anti-European agenda and instigated the attack to channel dissatisfaction with Yushchenko's pro-EU policies.

Public adversaries are very blurred. States rarely (if ever at all) take responsibility for cyberattacks. Even when they do, there is much uncertainty as to which governmental entity is behind a particular attack, while Nation-state Hackers, Cyberwar Units, and Intelligence Units can be involved. On November 24, 2014, Sony Pictures Entertainment studio was hacked. As a result of the attack, large amounts of data, including the identity information of Sony Pictures employees and their families, unreleased motion pictures, as well as other information, were stolen. The attack also set in motion wiper malware, which deleted and damaged much of Sony's digital records. A group which identified itself as Guardians of Peace (GOP) claimed responsibility for the attack and demanded Sony Pictures withdraw *The Interview*, a comedy motion picture about an attempt to assassinate Kim Jong-un, the North Korean leader. Sony Pictures withdrew the movie from broad theatrical release, opting instead for a digital release as a result of the attack. Even though to date there is no agreement among scholars as to the adversaries responsible for the Sony Pictures hack of 2014, many experts believe that it was planned, sponsored, and executed by North Korea. North Korea has officially denied any responsibility.[18]

As you can see, adversaries are extremely varied and each type can cause significant monetary and non-monetary (e.g., reputational, environmental, psychological) damage. They also exhibit a wide variety of motives, from intellectual curiosity, thrill, a desire to highlight important issues, to blunt mercantile goals like theft.

---

[18]See https://www.cnbc.com/2018/09/06/north-korean-hackers-will-be-charged-for-sony-pictures-wannacry-ransomware-attacks.html for more information.

Cybercriminal Ecosystems and Business Models

Our taxonomy of adversaries (Fig. 3.2) shows that the motivation of many adversaries (e.g., mercenaries, cybercriminal architects, organized criminal groups) targeting business or personal information is financial. This is also in line with our analysis of the direct speech of individual adversaries (hackers) when they talk about their motivation (see Fig. 3.1). If this is correct, then for-profit cyberattack actors should form ecosystems and operate well-designed business models. The general structure of an ecosystem for for-profit attacks usually exhibits the structure depicted in Fig. 3.3.

While specific ecosystems may or may not have all elements, all systems have a mastermind and a victim or victims. On the one hand, if we are talking about a solo hacker who implements their own for-profit ideas, then we observe a

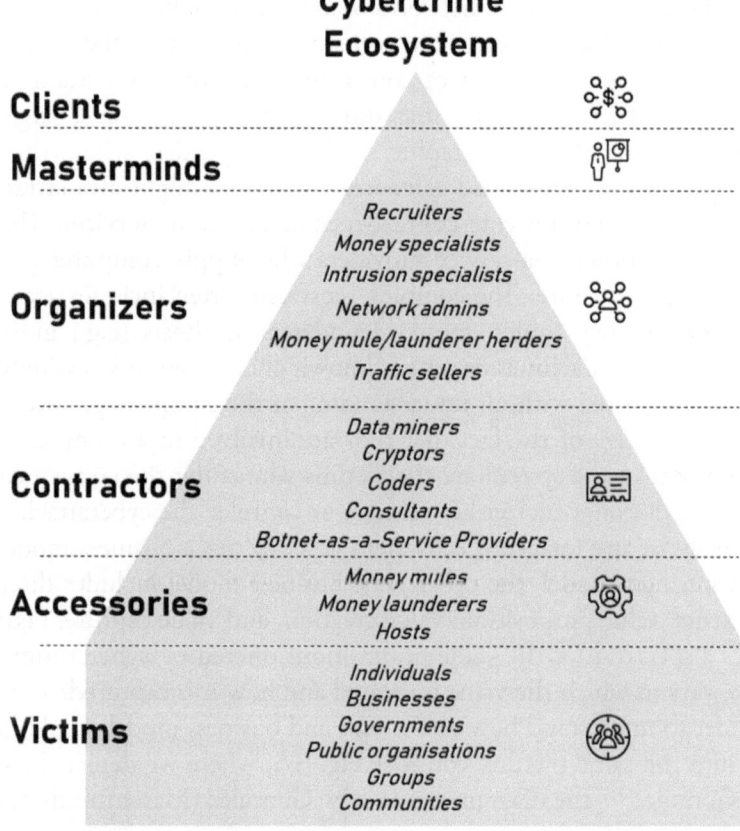

Fig. 3.3 Cyberattack ecosystem

mastermind designing and implementing an attack. On the other hand, the most sophisticated structure may have a client who "orders the attack" and either pays the mastermind or offers valuable information or resource for developing the attack, with a view to receiving a share of the criminal proceeds. The mastermind is a criminal architect who designs the attack and leads the operation, receiving the lion's share of the profit. The mastermind usually engages a number of organizers who help to channel and centralize specific tasks.

Organizers often include recruiters, who are responsible for attracting contractors with the required technical skills who are capable of supplying the necessary services: money specialists who analyze monetary streams and design business models (i.e., compile precise plans about how the value from the activities can be created and captured); intrusion specialists who scan the main vulnerabilities of targeted systems and identify sets of skills necessary to implement a successful attack; network administrators who manage a large number of compromised systems spreading spam, malware, etc.; money mule/launderer herders who provide access to networks of individual money mules and money launderers; and traffic sellers who are in charge of arranging traffic services.

Organizers work with a net of contractors, including, for example, data miners who collect data, often harvesting personal data on a large scale, cryptors who provide cryptographic services, and coders who write useful bits of programming code and software. Organizers might also attract consultants, who usually provide context-specific advice or services. They also might engage botnet-as-a-service providers who supply computer power by offering botnets for hire. The complex ecosystem often includes accessories: for example, money mules, money launderers, or hosts (e.g., individuals hosting malicious machines or servers knowingly or even unknowingly) who aid the scheme often without understanding of the complete picture or even without knowledge of the fact that they are involved in a criminal activity. At the bottom of the system are the victims who suffer the consequences of an attack. It does not matter how simple or complex the cyberattack ecosystem actually is, any for-profit ecosystem is set to run a business model. And like any business model, the cybercrime business model includes three basic components: value proposition, value creation, and value capture. Figure 3.4 captures a spectrum of the value propositions offered by cybercriminals and lists the ways in which the value is created and how it is captured.

In order to understand how ecosystems and business models could be integrated into the same picture, consider Fig. 3.5, where we depict the case of Albert Gonzalez.[19] The diagram shows how Gonzalez (Mastermind) managed

---

[19]This diagram is constructed based on James Verni's (2010) depiction of the case published in the *New York Times* magazine: https://www.nytimes.com/2010/11/14/magazine/14Hacker-t.html.

Business Model of Cybercrime

Value Proposition	*Value Creation*	*Value Capture*
Nudging	Demand Shaping	Ransom
Creativity	Customer Service	Contracts
Uniqueness	Cost Reduction	Blackmail
Manipulation	Payment Plans	Harassment
Access to Information	Data Brokerage	Commissions
Personalized Service	Software Development	Sale of Goods/Services
Customized Offering	Software Hacking	Property/Money/Data Theft
Behavioural Expertise	Hardware Hacking	Black Market Facilitation
Specialized Resources	Vulnerability Identification	Resource Exploitation
Anonymization	Network Architecture	Money Laundering
Reputation Shaping	Asset Recruitment	Cryptocurrency Mining
Expertise	Mule Herding	Shared Knowledge
	Defamation	Monetization
	Training	Selling Code
	Hosting	

Fig. 3.4 Business model spectrum of cybercrimes

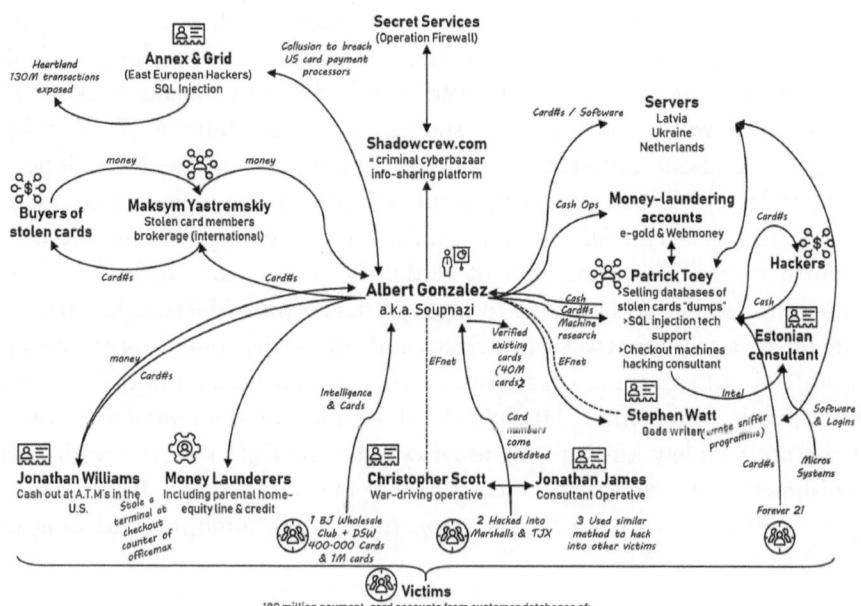

Fig. 3.5 Cybercriminal ecosystem and underlying business models for Albert Gonzalez case

his cybercriminal empire, using a large network of operatives (Organizers, Contractors, and Accessories) to cause harm to many victims. His case was also complicated by the fact that he co-operated with the US Secret Service in uncovering the shadowcrew.com (a cybercriminal multisided market platform) and had an opportunity to study the behavior of law enforcement officers in order to better understand the gaps in cyberdefense systems.

So far, we have talked about the many potential motivations of cyberattack actors, from simple intellectual curiosity and thrill to ideological, political, and religious goal-oriented agendas. We also specifically considered the for-profit motivation and business models of cybercriminals. Yet, maybe another important aspect we have so far overlooked is the cost-benefit considerations on the part of adversaries.

What About Costs Versus Benefits?

A few years ago, the New York City Crime Commission ran a very powerful campaign against illegal guns. "Got an illegal gun? Next stop prison"[20] or "All illegal guns in NYC come with 3½ year guarantee"—messages like these appeared all over the NYC subway. Notice that these messages are very clear: illegal actions (i.e., possession of an illegal firearm) will have real negative consequences, with specific clear numbers attached to each reckless or deliberate act. Yet, the complexity and variety of cybercrimes make it extremely difficult to develop and articulate "standardized" punishments [7–9]. While we can talk about different varieties of cyberthreats (as we have done in Chapter 2), each cybercrime is different and needs to be evaluated on a case-by-case basis [10–12]. All this creates difficulties in the application of law.

Furthermore, the probability of getting caught remains quite low. Even though it is sometimes possible to trace particular individuals, it is extremely difficult to attribute attacks to private and, especially, public organizations (unless, of course, these organizations take responsibility for these attacks using public statements). Historically, if we look at the convictions of 44 of the most widely known individual cybercriminals,[21] we can see that the punishment was extremely heterogeneous: many individual hackers managed to get away with no actual prison time, while some received long jail sentences (see Fig. 3.6).

---

[20]http://www.nycrimecommission.org/pdfs/guns-prison-campaign.pdf.

[21]We omit the case of Captain Zap from the analysis as he was convicted on theft charges, and start with the case of Wondra (from the 414s), who were convicted for phone phreaking.

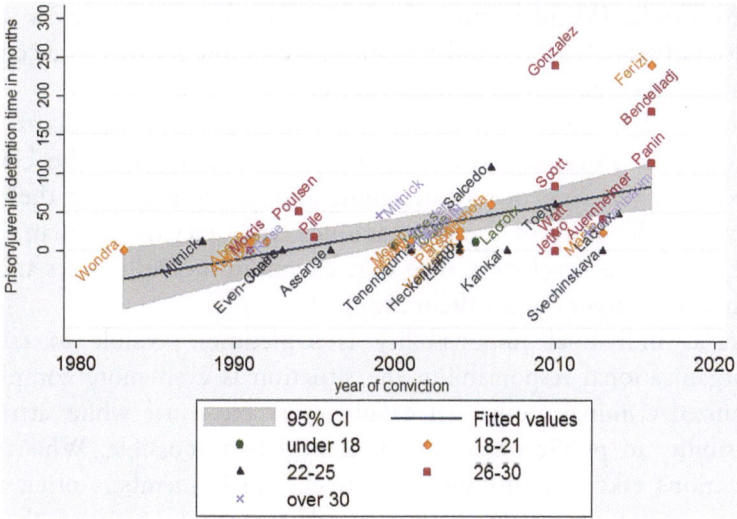

Fig. 3.6 Prison time by age of a cybercriminal

Looking at these 44 convictions, we see that the majority of convicted cybercriminals are, on average, slightly older than 24 (24.7 years of age to be precise). Furthermore, the majority of these convictions (28 of 44) involve individuals 25 years old or younger at the time of sentencing. However, the data considered does not appear to show the trend towards harsher punishment for older cybercriminals: cybercriminals in the over-30 group do not seem to receive significantly higher jail sentences.[22]

Even though this sample is rather limited, if we try to fit a simple regression line to the data, we will see that between the 1980s and 2018, the punishment for cybercriminal activities became progressively harsher (this trend is statistically significant at $p < 0.1\%$ level and has a high coefficient of 3.61). However, if we look at Fig. 3.6 in more detail, the more severe punishments are associated with large-scale for-profit criminal activity (as in the case of Gonzalez); with an ideological underpinning of the act (Bendelladj and Panin[23]); with engagement in cyber terrorism (Ferizi); or result from

---

[22]Obviously, potential conviction is not the only cost for cybercriminals. Time and the complexity of the target are also important factors. We will consider these factors later in the book.

[23]Hamza Bendelladj (aka BX1, Smiling Hacker) and Alexander Panin (aka Gribodemon) attacked over 50 million computers globally with the RimiG33k virus, which allowed them to steal banking information from infected computers. As a result of their activities, $280 million from compromised accounts were transferred to a number of Palestinian NGOs.

repeated felonies (Mitnick and LaCroix[24]). Therefore, it is not clear whether we indeed observe harsher punishment, or we simply see that in recent years cybercrimes become more and more severe.

There is also considerable heterogeneity in prosecutions across countries: recall the story of David L. Smith, who was tried in the USA and received a ten-year sentence for designing and setting in motion the Melissa virus, versus the story of Reonel Ramones and Onel de Guzman, alleged ILOVEYOU virus developers, who were caught in the Philippines and eventually had all charges against them dropped.

Whereas individual responsibility is sometimes possible to establish, with organizational responsibility the situation is even more complicated. If organized criminal groups get caught every once in a while, attributing responsibility to public organizations is next to impossible. When private organizations take responsibility for attacks, their members often remain anonymous, leaving no direct evidence that the links between them and those organizations exist. State-sponsored activities are even more difficult to prove. Even when activities can be traced to individual people (as in case of North Korean hacker Park Jin Hyok, the alleged state-sponsored hacker behind the attacks on Sony Pictures Entertainment, a series of attacks targeting large financial institutions, as well as the global WannaCry ransomware attack),[25] in the absence of hard evidence, it is very easy for states to deny any involvement in cybercrimes.

All this leads us to the conclusion that the chances of getting caught are quite low and, statistically, the punishments (with several recent exceptions) remain rather mild. But how does that compare with the potential gain from cybercriminal activity? Estimates of how much profit one can make from such activities vary. For example, the study of Palo Alto Networks and the Ponemon Institute published in 2016 reports an average figure of just over £20,000 per year (around $26,000 per year according to the 2016 exchange rate).[26] This number seems incredibly low and quite

---

[24]Cameron LaCroix (aka camo, cam0, camZero, cmuNNY) is a repeatedly convicted felon who was first detained as a teenager on hacking charges and sentenced to 11 months in a federal juvenile detention facility in 2005. He is primarily known for hacking into the telephone of Paris Hilton, as well as breaking into the systems of LexisNexis.

[25]There are 42 hackers on the FBI's most-wanted list https://www.fbi.gov/wanted/cyber.

[26]See https://media.paloaltonetworks.com/lp/ponemon/report.html for more detail.

unrealistic considering the alternative remuneration offered to technically skilled staff by the industry. If we look at the felons convicted for for-profit cybercrimes, we observe a completely different picture, with hackers taking and sharing if not multimillion-dollar scores, then certainly profits of hundreds of thousands of dollars (e.g., the Albert Gonzalez credit card fraud case). It is clear, however, that the gain from cybercriminal activities primarily depends on the relative position of the individual in the ecosystem. The lower the level occupied by an actor in the ecosystem pyramid, the higher the probability of getting caught and the lower the financial remuneration.

Apart from the probability of getting caught, attacks are time-consuming for the adversary. Yet, there is little data on how long, on average, the attacks take and to what extent an additional hour added to the hacking task affects an adversary's willingness to engage. The aforementioned Ponemon study reports that most attacks take about a day to program and that 20 more hours of effort time would completely discourage a hacker from the attack; yet, considering that the study is based on the opinions of self-reported hackers, it is not clear whether and to what extent this information is accurate for a wide variety of adversaries. It seems that if the target is important and financially viable enough, then the adversaries would be prepared to invest a large amount of time into the attack.

Coming back to our original analogy, the overwhelming majority of contemporary cybercriminals, as well as cybercriminals of the future, are *"younger, better, more experienced"*, and incredibly motivated. Many of them are after money and many after something else (thrill; excitement; political, ideological, or religious goals; revenge; etc.). As the chances of getting caught remain relatively low and potential benefits tend to be relatively high, it is unlikely that in the near future we will see a decrease in cybercriminal activity. Even though the legislation related to cybercrimes becomes more and more detailed and offers more severe punishment year by year, it is still very difficult to attribute[27] attacks to specific agents and even more difficult to prosecute them.

---

[27]See https://www.internetgovernance.org/research/is-it-time-to-institutionalize-cyber-attribution/.

References

1. Gross, M. L., Canetti, D., & Vashdi, D. R. (2016). The psychological effects of cyber terrorism. *Bulletin of the Atomic Scientists, 72*(5), 284–291.
2. Vatis, M. A. (2000). Statement on Cybercrime before the Senate Judiciary Committee, Criminal Justice Oversight Subcommittee and House Judiciary Committee, Crime Subcommittee. Washington, DC: US Department of Justice, 29.
3. Denning, D. (2001). Is cyber terror next? *Understanding September, 11*, 191–197.
4. Denning, D. E. (2001). Activism, hacktivism, and cyberterrorism: The internet as a tool for influencing foreign policy. *Networks and netwars: The future of terror, crime, and militancy* (pp. 239, 288). Santa Monica: RAND Corporation.
5. Coleman, G. (2014, November 4). *Hacker, hoaxer, whistleblower, spy: The many faces of anonymous.* London and New York: Verso Books.
6. Denning, D. (2000, Autumn). Cyberterrorism: The logic bomb versus the truck bomb. *Global Dialogue, 2*(4). Archived from the original on 27 June 2013. Retrieved 20 August 2014.
7. Holt, T. J., & Schell, B. H. (2010). *Corporate hacking and technology-driven crime: Social dynamics and implications* (p. 146). Hershey: IGI Global.
8. Parikka, J. (2007). *Digital contagions: A media archaeology of computer viruses* (p. 145). New York: Peter Lang.
9. Salomon, D. (2005). *Foundations of computer security* (p. 43). London: Springer Verlag. https://doi.org/10.1007/1-84628-341-8.
10. Bocij, P. (2006). *The dark side of the internet* (p. 57). Westport, CT: Praeger.
11. Szor, P. (2005). *The art of computer virus research and defense.* Reading: Addison-Wesley.
12. Holt, T. J., & Schell, B. H. (2013). *Hackers and hacking: A reference handbook* (p. 31). Santa Barbara: ABC-CLIO.

4

Wake Up: You Are the Target!

So far, we have talked about the types of threats one could encounter in cyberspaces, as well as the main motivations and business models of cybercriminals. We also touched on the differences between threat, vulnerability, and risk in cyberspace. Yet, in many cases, individuals and businesses have numerous misconceptions about cyberthreats and significantly underestimate their propensity to become the victims of cybercrime. Let us first look at some of these misconceptions.

Popular Cybersecurity Misconceptions

Misconception 1: I am too insignificant to be targeted. Many individuals and businesses believe that they are "too small" or they have "nothing to steal" to be targeted. In the contemporary world, there is no such thing as a system which is not of interest to cybercriminals. No matter how little money you have, no matter how small your business is, if you store or handle some information, it is highly likely that this information can be monetized, and probably in many different ways. Even if the information you hold is only of interest to you or your business and there is no other party on this planet that would ever be interested in it, it still makes sense to steal it and sell it back to you for a ransom. Therefore, it is important to understand that anybody can become a target. Unless you are prepared to take all of your operations offline and not store any data in the digital form (which, in the overwhelming majority of cases, is equivalent to business suicide), there is always a positive probability of being targeted.

© The Author(s) 2019   **55**
G. Pogrebna and M. Skilton, *Navigating New Cyber Risks*,
https://doi.org/10.1007/978-3-030-13527-0_4

In 2018, thousands of individuals and businesses became the target of a ransomware attack which spread through spam emails around the globe. Adversaries mostly targeted business email accounts which could be easily obtained in the public domain. The spam email exercised what is called an "extortion phishing" technique. The email titled "You should be ashamed of yourself", "You are my victim", or "Concentrate and don't get angry" read: "*Hi, victim. This is my last warning. I write you because I put a malware on the web page with porn which you have visited ...*" The senders then claimed that they had obtained personal data and infected the victim's computer with a virus which allowed them to shoot compromising videos of the victim watching porn. The email demanded a payment in bitcoin in exchange for the destruction of the compromising videos. The phishing email was sent to a large number of untargeted email addresses (i.e., apart from the actual online porn consumers, many other people received the message). As a result, the attack had an effect not only on individuals who frequented the porn websites but also on those who never visited such sites and, yet, were still concerned that their webcams could have been hijacked. So, ransoms were paid not only by those to whom the threat could have been relevant, but also by those who simply were concerned about privacy. The attack had particularly severe consequences in Australia, where the police and the Australian Competition and Consumer Commission had to deal with multiple reports and complaints.[1] This example shows that even when people think they have nothing of interest to the cybercriminals, they still may become the victims of various scams.

Misconception 2: Technology is the main weapon of cybercriminals. It is certainly true that technology is an important tool for cybercriminals, but looking at the types of threats and their history, we see that many of the currently used threats (with several notable exceptions, such as the block-chain-related attacks or AI-informed attacks discussed earlier in this book) existed in the 1960s, 1970s, and 1980s. So, what we observe now (with several exceptions) are often unlikely to be new types of threats; these are essentially old threats "on steroids". But the increased impact of these threats is mostly due not so much to the development of technology—although the technological component does play a role—but rather to the increased use of hybrid scams, where social engineering and psychological impact are the main methods employed by cybercriminals.

---

[1]See https://nexusconsultancy.co.uk/blog/email-scam-ashamed-of-yourself/ and https://www.news.com.au/technology/scammers-catch-porn-users-with-8217ransomware8217/news-story/b328a238d3e5e7d-ca4219833749150fb for more detail.

With over 90% of successful breaches worldwide starting with a phishing email,[2] it is clear why cybercriminals concentrate on the psychological tools for planning and implementing the attacks. With technological advances in the area of cybersecurity becoming more and more sophisticated, humans remain the weakest link.

In 2012, a renowned film director, Jake Schreier, released *Robot and Frank*, a film based on Christopher Ford's screenplay, in which Frank (Frank Langella), an ex-jewel thief, takes his artificial intelligence (AI) healthcare robot on a heist. The pair target the most expensive house in the neighborhood which seems to have the most sophisticated security system. Yet, Frank explains to his AI companion that "*Every security system is designed by security companies, not thieves. It's not the question of if a thief can break in, it's how long. They place all the heavy systems where their customers can see them. They're selling the feel of security.*" Frank then explains that one can spend weeks preparing for the robbery trying to decipher the highly advanced security system and making attempts to disable the alarms. Yet, wouldn't it be much easier just to ring the doorbell and wait for someone to open the door?

In Chapter 2, we discussed the major cybersecurity threats and even tried to summarize them in a table (see Table 2.1). Let us consider various cybersecurity threats and how they depend on human (victim) psychology. In Fig. 4.1, we present the psycho–technological matrix of cybersecurity threats discussed earlier. The vertical axis displays the technological component necessary to ensure the success of a certain cyberthreat. This technological component might rely on physical systems, digital (cyber) systems, or may exist in both. The technological component is mapped versus the psychological component, which captures the degree of the threat's reliance on the "co-operation" of human victims. In other words, the psychological component depicts whether and to what extent tricking people into doing something as a result of social engineering is necessary for the threat to succeed. The psychological component is presented on the horizontal axis and shows that, at one extreme, a cybersecurity threat's success can be completely independent of human psychology; at another extreme, human involvement may be essential for the threat to succeed. There is also a space in between where certain threats can be either independent or very dependent on the "co–operation" of humans.

---

[2]See   https://www.darkreading.com/endpoint/91--of-cyberattacks-start-with-a-phishing-email/d/d-id/1327704 for more detail.

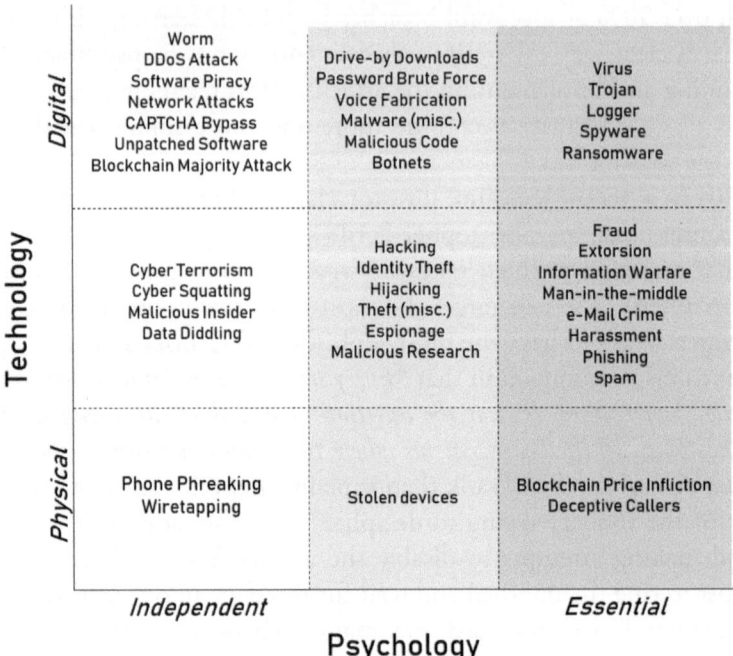

Fig. 4.1 Psycho-technological matrix of cybersecurity threats

For example, phone phreaking in theory can work without any involvement of human psychology and can operate in the physical rather than digital domain. At the same time, a distributed denial-of-service (DDoS) attack requires digital technology but does not rely on human psychology. Threats like cyber terrorism in principle may not rely on human psychology and can use either physical or digital tools. For a range of threats, the psychological component is often needed, although it is not essential. For example, in the physical domain, stealing a device may involve playing tricks on a particular individual but can also be done without their involvement. In the digital domain, an individual's password can in theory be broken simply using password brute force, yet it often helps to know something about this individual or even trick them into revealing sensitive information which would help the hacker to guess the password. Identity theft may be accomplished physically (by making a simple telephone call) or through digital means, but it often requires at least some human co-operation.

For a number of threats, human psychology is a key component which ensures success. In order to manipulate prices for various bitcoins (blockchain price infliction), one has to influence market price expectations. This can be achieved primarily by physical rather than digital means, particularly through convincing the impactful media to channel "fake news". Threats like viruses use digital means but require human involvement as the user has to open an email attachment, click on a link, or go to a website in order to set them in motion. Threats such as phishing may use physical or digital tools but rely heavily on social engineering.

Note that of the nine areas of the psycho-technological matrix of cybersecurity threats, only three do not involve human psychology, while six either may to some extent rely on human psychology or have human psychology as a key factor. This shows that social engineering is an important component for the majority of successful attacks, making the weak spots of human psychology the major weapon utilized by cybercriminals.

Misconception 3: It can only happen to me once. In behavioral science, we often talk about a paradox which we call the "*law of large numbers*". What it boils down to is a very simple psychological phenomenon: most people believe that "*probability or chance has memory*". Imagine that you are playing a game where each coin toss gives you $1 if you are right and nothing if you are wrong. Let's say, for the sake of argument, that for some reason you prefer betting on heads and you have just played five rounds of the game where heads were turning up on every coin toss, and you won $5 as a result. Now you have an opportunity to place the next bet. Will you bet heads or tails? In this situation, many people would choose tails. Why? They just observed heads come up five times out of five, so they think that getting heads on the next coin toss becomes less probable. This, of course, is a psychological paradox. The chances of getting heads or tails is 50–50 and these chances remain the same no matter how many times you toss the coin.

When we talk about cybersecurity, this paradox is even more prevalent. Once hit by cybercriminals, business owners think it will not happen to them again. This is especially true in the case of ransomware attacks. There is a widespread view that once the ransom is paid and the data is returned, the adversaries will now leave the systems in peace and will not target the same business with a similar attack again. This, of course, is a wrong attitude. Adversaries share information and often disclose targets and code to each other. Therefore, becoming a victim of a cyberattack does not mean that it will not happen to your business again. In fact, it probably makes you a more likely target in the future, as adversaries talk to each other and you might get hit again with very similar tools in a very similar way. In September 2018, British Airways revealed that the personal and financial details of 380,000 customers had been stolen. In October 2018, the same company admitted that 185,000 more customers who made reward bookings using payment cards between April and July 2018 may also have been compromised.[3]

Misconception 4: I have the best technology on the market to protect me. Many business owners we talked to during the preparation of this book told us that they outsource security issues to a contractor, who takes care of their system, or that they expect that company, along with Microsoft, Apple, IBM, Google, or other large tech providers, to take responsibility in case of a cybersecurity breach. There are, however, several important caveats here. First, any technological solution, like any sophisticated lock, can be broken. We often talk about using sophisticated technology, such as AI, for detecting threats and preventing adversaries from getting into systems. However, we often forget that adversaries are also using technology and they have exactly the same (if not better) set of tools available to them. Recall that in Chapter 3 we introduced the concept of "zero-day vulnerability"— an unknown gap in the system. This vulnerability is not visible to the security system designers (despite all the tech they are armed with), yet it may become visible and, ultimately, used ("exploited") by adversaries.

Furthermore, as we explained above, technology is not everything where cybersecurity is concerned. In his 2017 public talk at Google, Frank Abagnale, a former con man turned security consultant whose story inspired Steven Spielberg's movie *Catch Me If You Can* (2002), explained that most cybersecurity breaches result from someone in the organization "*doing something they ARE NOT supposed to do*" or "*failing to do what they ARE supposed to do*" [1]. Under these circumstances, it does not matter how amazing your technological solutions are and how many hundreds, thousands, millions of dollars you are spending on buying the next technological wonder or engaging the next technological wizard to fix things for you. What is important is how likely your staff are to do what they ARE NOT supposed to do or fail to do what they ARE supposed to do.

Misconception 5: I am very careful, so I cannot be tricked. One of the most popular misconceptions is that being careful or cautious somehow decreases the chance of being targeted. The truth is, unfortunately, that it

---

[3]See https://www.bbc.co.uk/news/uk-england-london-45440850 for more detail.

does not matter how careful or careless you are. Even if you are very careful and surrounded by the best cybersecurity minds in the country, there is still a very good chance that a strong enough adversary will succeed in compromising your data or systems.

One would have thought that the US Democratic Party has pretty good cybersecurity and that their staff are well versed in the potential dangers of cyber breaches. After all, most of these people have worked in politics for years and understand not only the responsibility associated with handling and transferring confidential information, but also the reputational consequences of losing such information. Yet, we all know that Hillary Clinton's presidential campaign in 2016 was sabotaged by a series of breaches later labelled as "Russian influence on" or "Russian involvement in" the elections due to the alleged links to 12 Russian intelligence officers [2]. How do you think the hackers got into the emails and data of some of the most guarded people in the USA? Simple. They used "good old" phishing techniques!

In March 2016, John Podesta, the Clinton campaign chairman, along with other campaign staff, received a spear-phishing email. The adversaries made the email look like a security notification from Google and invited the email recipients to click on the embedded link and change their password (a "spoofing" technique). As a result of this simple trick, the adversaries were able to gain access to John Podesta's account as well as obtain information on over 50,000 emails mostly belonging to the members of the Democratic Congressional Campaign Committee (DCCC), the Democratic National Committee (DNC), as well as employees and volunteers involved in the Clinton campaign. This information, along with data obtained from social media as well as from other spear-phishing attacks, allowed the adversaries to hack into the accounts of senior members of the Democratic campaign staff team.

In April 2016, the adversaries sent another spear-phishing email which appeared to be a message from a trusted member of the Clinton's campaign team to all Clinton campaign staff members. The email contained a link to an Excel document titled "hillary–clinton–favorable-rating.xlsx". Recipients who clicked on the link (and there were many who fell for this trick!) were directed to the website allegedly created by a Russian intelligence organization (GRU[4]). The website was created with the aim of harvesting further personal data from Democratic Party staff.

---

[4]The same organization is alleged to be responsible for the "Novichok" poisonings in Salisbury, UK, in 2018.

The aftermath of this attack had dramatic consequences for the US Democrats. The adversaries published correspondence of the DNC members through WikiLeaks. This correspondence showed a complete absence of impartiality during the Democratic Party preliminaries in 2016. Thousands of embarrassing messages revealed the efforts of many officials to aid Clinton's campaign and damage the campaign of Bernie Sanders, Clinton's main opponent. As a result of the controversy, the chairperson of the DNC, Debbie Wasserman Schultz, resigned. To date, many experts believe that this series of events, which started with a spear-phishing email, by and large determined the outcome of the 2016 US presidential elections as it significantly damaged Hillary Clinton's chances of becoming president.

Why Do We Have Misconceptions About Cybersecurity?

So far, we have looked at five major misconceptions about cybersecurity. The natural question is—why do we have those misconceptions? Unfortunately, the problem is a lot deeper than cybersecurity and the way we, as humans, perceive it. It is related to the fact that digital environments are very new to humanity and we simply have not developed enough understanding of those environments. In other words, we do not have a culture of navigating digital spaces. In physical spaces, by contrast, we feel more confident and seem able to estimate potential risks quite well. For example, those of us who live in urban areas know that wandering around some parts of the city after dark is probably not a very good idea. Yet, in cyber spaces, we do not know which areas are crime-ridden, which are safe, and which are dangerous. As a result, people are quite reckless about everything they generate or do in digital spaces.

Think, for example, of our personal data. On a daily basis, we generate large amounts of data, most of which we give away for free. As a result, a few large tech players are benefiting from collecting, packaging, and monetizing the personal data of a large numbers of individuals. People generally pay very little attention to their personal data and privacy and often cannot tell the difference between safe activities and risky places online. Have you ever thought, for example, what permissions you give to the various apps you have on your smartphone, or which data is accessible to the various online platforms and services you use? We have conducted many tests in which we asked people about their level of awareness about these issues. For example, using a representative sample of British users (534 individuals),

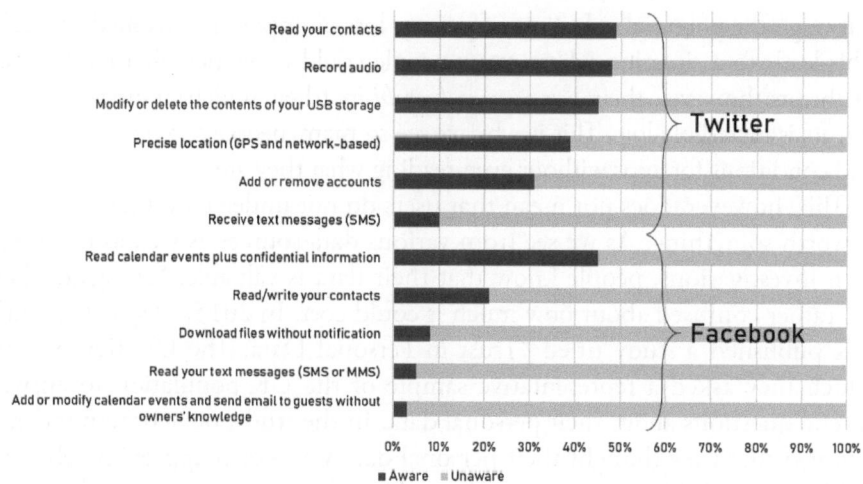

Fig. 4.2 Percentage of UK users aware and unaware about a menu of Facebook and Twitter permissions

we asked whether people understood some of the privacy settings of popular social network apps. Looking at just Facebook and Twitter (see Fig. 4.2), our analysis revealed shocking results.

Almost none of respondents (3%) knew that Facebook had access to their events calendar—i.e., that the app could add or modify calendar events and send emails to invitees without the calendar owner's knowledge. Only 5% and 8% of respondents realized that Facebook could read their text messages and download files without notification, respectively. About a fifth of respondents (21%) knew that Facebook could read and write their contacts, whereas 45% were aware that Facebook could view their calendar and other confidential information. With Twitter permissions the situation was slightly, though not massively, better. Specifically, 10% of users understood that Twitter had access to their text messages; 31% knew that Twitter could add and remove accounts; 39% realized that Twitter could track their location; 45% understood that Twitter could modify or delete the content of their USB storage (e.g., use USB storage to cache photos); 48% knew that Twitter could record audio using their smartphone; and 49% were aware that Twitter could read their contacts. Notice that all these percentages are below 50%.

This illustrates that most people are simply not concerned with the issues of security, safety, and privacy as long as they believe that the benefits of using a particular digital service (in the case of a social media app, we are talking about the ability to share information and get access to information posted by others) outweigh the potential risks (loss of privacy, loss of important private data, etc.). This leads to a situation where many people could be vulnerable to a number of threats; however, their *perceived vulnerability* (their understanding) of these threats is incredibly low. This is why we see so many people accepting the terms and conditions for apps without even reading what they are.

This, however, does not mean that users do not understand that their data is worth something. As we see from various data sources as well as from our own investigations, people know that their data is valuable. Yet, again, they are rather confused about how much it could cost. In 2015, Digital Catapult UK published a study titled "Trust in Personal Data: The UK Review", in which they asked a representative sample of the UK population to answer several questions about their personal data. In the study, 60% of respondents revealed that they thought their personal data was worth approximately £30 ($39) per week [3]. The Digital Catapult study measured users' willingness to accept (or WTA): users were asked how much money they were *willing to accept* in exchange for selling one week's worth of their personal data.

We have conducted a more comprehensive study in the UK, in which 526 participants (a representative sample of the British population) were asked to estimate the worth of their personal data in two ways and for different types of data (Fig. 4.3). We asked participants to indicate their WTA (the amount of money they were willing to accept to sell one week's worth of their personal data), as well as their willingness to pay, or WTP (the amount of money they were willing to pay to protect one week's worth of their personal data). In other words, WTA is the price people were willing to accept to sell their data; while WTP is the amount of money they were willing to pay (say, to insurance) to make sure that no one will ever have access to their data. This simple test revealed surprising results. Even though, just as in the Digital Catapult UK report, for many types of data individual users, on average, gave WTA values close to £30 (Internet Search data, Digital Communications via Skype, WhatsApp, Viber, etc.; Social Networking data, Online Purchasing History, Internet Browsing data, Digital Communication via Social Media, Loyalty Cards, and Physical Location data), yet, for four types of data these estimates were a lot higher.

For example, users said that, on average, they would be willing to sell their Bank Statements data for £73 ($95); Digital Communication data for £251 ($328); Demographic data for £300 ($392); and Health Records for £505 ($660). Furthermore, the data revealed interesting disparities between WTP and WTA estimates for the same types of data. It is usual to expect WTA to be higher than WTP, however, for some types of data the difference is surprisingly high (e.g., Health Records data), while for others it is surprisingly low (e.g., Physical Location).

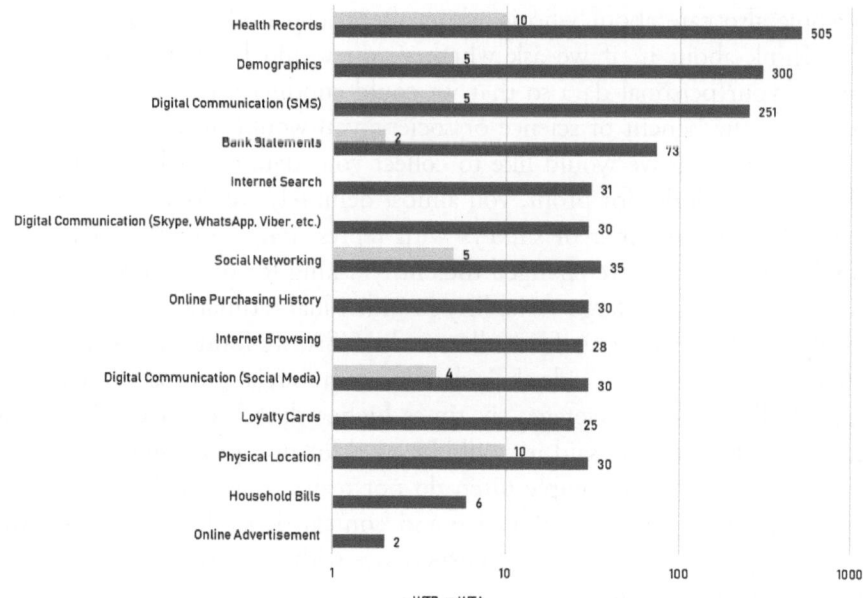

Fig. 4.3 Weekly amount of money in British Pounds which UK users are willing to accept to sell their data (WTA) and willing to pay to protect their data (WTP)

On the one hand, all of this is surprising for the following reasons. First, people often give away many of these types of personal data for free (e.g., Social Networking, Internet Browsing, Internet Search, Physical Location, Loyalty Cards data, Demographic Data, etc.). Second, they are not even trying to protect many types of data, yet they still believe their data is worth something.

On the other hand, these results are quite explainable. High WTA estimates for health records and bank statements data can be explained by the fact that the data in these categories is likely to be very sensitive to individuals. High WTA estimates for demographic data can be rationalized because one week or one year of demographic data is equally valuable (demographic data does not change much with time, or it changes in a very predictable way—e.g., every year you simply become one year older). Therefore, people believe that one week's worth of demographic data is equivalent to a lifetime's worth of demographic data and put a large asking price on it. Overall, we observe that people are very confused about the precise price of their data as this price is (i) highly context-dependent to them (you are likely to feel different about your data dependent on what has happened to you in a particular week), and (ii) they do not have experience or a good reference point as to how companies determine the price of personal data. Hence, it is incredibly difficult for individuals to come up with precise numbers.

People also care about who is asking them to provide personal data and why. Think about it: if we ask whether you would be willing to provide some of your personal data so that we could conduct a non-profit research project for the benefit of science or society, you would probably agree. Yet, if we tell you that we would like to collect your data and sell it to the top private-sector bidder for profit, you almost definitely would say "no". When we conducted a number of surveys with representative samples of the US population, in which we changed the entity asking for the data and the reasons why, we found a large variability in individual estimates. Specifically, in a study of 606 participants from all over the USA, we found that when individuals were asked to provide their data for commercial purposes, the asking price (WTA) was, on average, six times higher than the price (WTA) for the same data when we said it would be used for non-profit research. These results confirm that (i) people often do not realize how much their data is worth, as this is a highly subjective and context-dependent issue; and (ii) people simply do not have enough experience with cyber spaces to be able to understand what a "safe space" is.

Unfortunately, the same is true for businesses. Many businesses, especially small and medium enterprises, have little clue about the market value and worth of the data they hold, which also stems from the fact that even very sophisticated and mature business communities have scant information about the underlying business models of cybercriminals and, as a result, have little idea of the total cost of their data. The Internet offers a wide variety of estimates about the potential losses which various cyberthreats could bring. A simple search will give you hundreds of websites offering numbers and infographics. Yet, it is often not clear how these estimates were obtained and whether and to what extent any of these numbers are reliable.

Another important consideration we need to keep in mind is that any estimate released into a public domain becomes immediately accessible and is likely to be absorbed by the adversaries, who may use this information to obtain their own reference points. One of the most notorious examples of this is an estimate of business costs associated with the loss of personal data provided in the EU's General Data Protection Regulation (GDPR), which came into effect on 25 May, 2018 and concerned not only companies with headquarters in the EU but also global corporations which operate in the EU or engage with EU customers (see Fig. 4.4). The GDPR highlighted many important problems with corporate responsibility and introduced new human rights applicable to the digital domain, such as privacy by design, right to be forgotten, right to action, breach notification, etc. At the same time, it estimated that the damage to customers from the loss of personal

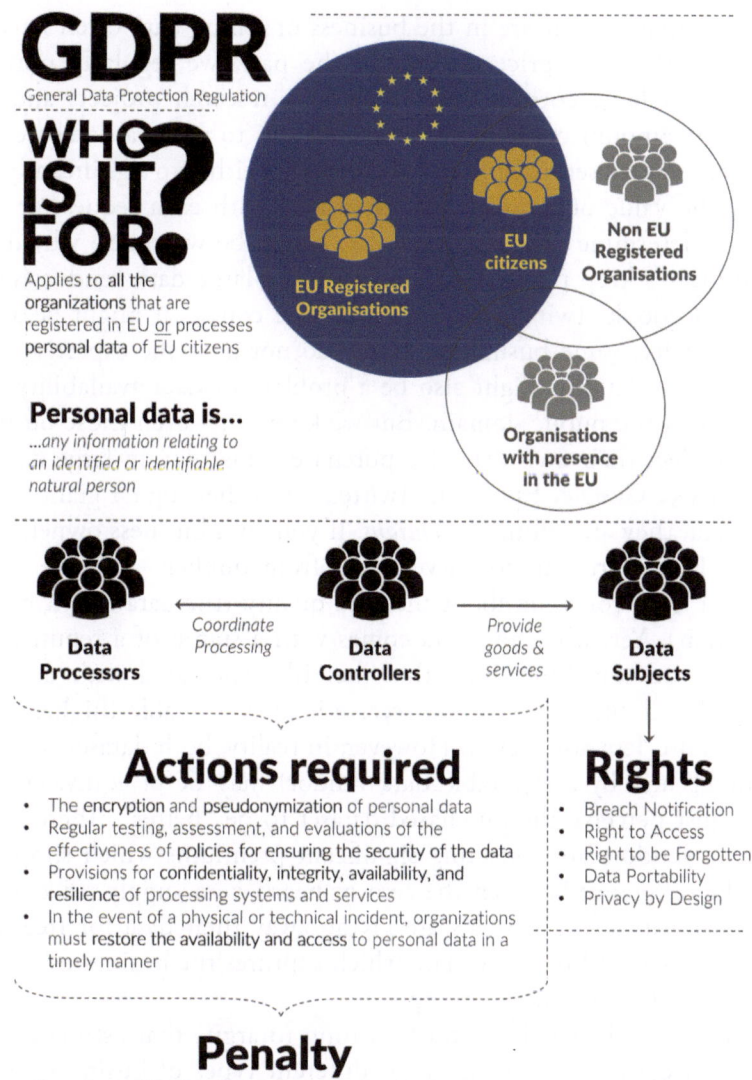

Fig. 4.4 Summary of the General Data Protection Regulation

data when it is proved that a particular business has failed to protect the data is 4% of the worldwide turnover of this business, capped at €20 million (over $23 million). Now imagine that you are a cybercriminal thinking of stealing customer data from a particular business for ransom. How much ransom should you charge? Even if you had no idea before May 2018, you now have a good reference point from a reputable source …

Even companies that are in the business of selling data often have very arbitrary methods of price setting. In the past, we regularly purchased datasets from large corporations for various research projects and, considering the amount of time and effort it takes to make a database query and produce a dataset, the pricing model seems either to significantly overestimate the value of human labor associated with each request or rather arbitrarily determine how much the data might be worth. So why do various businesses keep purchasing data from the large data vendors such as Google, Facebook, Twitter, among others? Of course, it might be a problem of capacity: some businesses simply do not have the expertise to collect their own data. It might also be a problem of data availability: some data is not in the public domain. But we know that even those businesses who do collect their own data also purchase datasets from large data vendors. You see, Google, Facebook, Twitter, and other digital giants are not selling data, they are selling *perceptions*. If you, as a business owner, simply ask your IT department to harvest data from publicly available sources, you might have concerns about the data quality (the data might be noisy or irrelevant). Yet, when the data comes with a stamp of a reputable digital giant, you somehow think that the risks associated with data quality are reduced and the data you receive is more valuable (higher quality, more relevant, less noisy, etc.). However, in reality, both datasets (collected by your IT and by a reputable data vendor) may be of equivalent quality: you just perceive the purchased dataset to be "better". Therefore, the large data vendors are collecting significant premiums which simply represent the difference between the zero or nearly zero supply price for data (as the majority of individuals are giving away their data for free) and a rather large demand price for data which captures the businesses' desire to "de-risk" the data they are working with.

Having said all that, it would be wrong to argue that estimates of the value and worth of various data for different types of businesses should not be made. Estimates are very useful to develop effective cybersecurity architecture, understand the costs and benefits of various cybersecurity measures, and determine whether your business needs to outsource cybersecurity issues or purchase cybersecurity insurance policy. All we are trying to say is that caution should be exercised when using such estimates to make sure that they are (i) built based on some rational principles and not arbitrarily; (ii) based on transparent and verifiable methodology; and (iii) presented in ways which would complicate their use by adversaries.

Cybersecurity Statistics and Most Costly Threats

Despite the great variety of literature offering cybersecurity statistics, it is hard to understand the relative cost of various cybersecurity threats as sources of information about cybersecurity and the underlying methodology for conducting various measurement exercises are rarely revealed. In the UK, the Department for Digital, Culture, Media and Sport releases an annual Cyber Security Breaches Survey.[5] In its 2018 edition, the survey included answers from 1519 UK businesses (with the exception of sole traders; agriculture, forestry, and fishing businesses) as well as 569 third-sector organizations (charities). According to the survey, 43% of businesses and 19% of charities admitted that they have experienced a cybersecurity attack during the 12 months preceding the survey. 49% of businesses and 24% of charities revealed that they outsourced their cybersecurity to a third-party vendor. The survey also established the most common threats. Phishing comes firmly in first place and splits between two types of activities: fraudulent emails or redirection to fraudulent websites, which represents the lion's share of adversarial impact (75% in businesses and 74% in charities), and spear-phishing attempts (28% and 27% in businesses and charities, respectively). Viruses, spyware, or malware attacks represent 24% of breaches for businesses and charities. 15% of breaches for businesses and 10% for charities are ransomware attacks, while DoS attacks represent 12% and 13% of experienced threats for businesses and charities, respectively. Brute force attacks such as hacking online bank accounts are infrequent, totaling 8% and 3% for businesses and charities, respectively. Unauthorized use of computing power, networks, and servers by insiders (staff) is related to 7% of breaches targeting businesses and 6% targeting charities. Other types of threats are associated with 5% and 6% of attacks on businesses and charities, respectively. Additionally, 48% of businesses and charities admitted that phishing attacks were the most costly and caused the greatest disruption to their organizations. In terms of monetary costs, the estimates varied greatly between different types of organizations, with large businesses spending, on average, £15,300 ($19,635) to address the problem associated with the harmful outcome of a breach; while medium businesses, small businesses, and charities

---

[5]See https://assets.publishing.service.gov.uk/government/uploads/system/uploads/attachment_data/file/702074/Cyber_Security_Breaches_Survey_2018_-_Main_Report.pdf for more detail.

spent £12,100 ($15,528), £1190 ($1527), and £678 ($870), respectively. Yet, at the same time, estimates revealed that only 11% of their cybersecurity investment went into protecting staff and systems, and only 20% of businesses had cybersecurity training for staff.

Reliable and traceable statistics on US cybersecurity breaches are harder to obtain than those for the UK as the majority of published results come from private entities and large cybersecurity providers. Data in the USA is mostly provided by private cybersecurity surveys. For example, IDC[6] conducted a survey of US businesses and released a report in 2018 suggesting that 77% of surveyed American businesses were victims of cyberattacks in the 12 months prior to the survey. In February 2018, the Council of Economic Advisers published a report titled "The Cost of Malicious Cyber Activity to the US Economy",[7] which cited several sources, including the Ponemon Institute, and highlighted that, due to the lack of centralized statistical records, the estimates of the cybercriminal impact on businesses are likely to be biased or inaccurate because they are primarily based on survey data and often highlight the most notorious or publicly available events. The Council conducted its own analysis, using 290 events in the 2013/2014 financial year covering mostly large businesses, and estimated the effect of cyberattacks on market capitalization of the victim companies. Their analysis revealed that businesses in their sample lost, on average, $494 million per event. For comparison, Ponemon came up with a different estimate of $21 million per year using a similar sample of companies. The Council's report does not provide a comprehensive breakdown of costs by threat, leaving us to rely on other sources. Yet, the landscape seems to be somewhat similar to the UK, as 56% of "1,300 surveyed IT security decision-makers" in the CyberArk Global Advanced Threat Landscape Report 2018 named phishing attacks as the most challenging threat.

The Measurement Problem

Of course, any business owners need to know not only how much various cybersecurity threats might cost on average, but also what is the actual risk and cost associated with each potential threat to their business. Recall that in Chapter 2 we explained the difference between "threat", "vulnerability", and "risk", and argued that all three are measurable "in principle" or "in theory".

---

[6]See https://www.idc.com/topic/security for more information.

[7]See https://www.whitehouse.gov/wp-content/uploads/2018/03/The-Cost-of-Malicious-Cyber-Activity-to-the-U.S.-Economy.pdf for more detail.

Yet, theory and practice are two different things. The main problem is that in practice the measurement is very difficult. While we do not aim to list all the reasons why the measurement of cyberthreats, vulnerabilities, and risks maybe difficult, we do provide a subset of these reasons below.

Issues with threat measurement are primarily associated with four main difficulties. First, threats are multiple (see Table 2.1) and for a regular risk management exercise it is often very costly to consider all possible threats. Second, even though the majority of threats we observe today are not new, every once in a while an innovative technique would emerge, and it is extremely hard to anticipate such techniques before they are executed. This primarily concerns attacks executed by AI, machine learning (ML), or deep learning (DL) algorithms. Third, the information sharing and communication of experienced threats between businesses, within businesses, between businesses and consumers, as well as between businesses and policy- makers, is broken. Since the harm from various cyber events is uncertain, information about executed attacks are often reaching the relevant parties too late, thereby providing the adversaries with a competitive advantage as some threats remain undiscovered for a long time. The EU GDPR tried to address this challenge by making the reporting of every instance of a breach relating to consumer data compulsory. Yet, it is too early to say whether the regulation will work and what consequences will be seen in the next few years. Finally, what we seem to observe more and more often are "hybrid" threats, where several threats from our Table 2.1 are mixed, matched, and deployed by adversaries.

Issues with vulnerability measurement relate to several factors. First of all, vulnerability diagnostics is closely related to the diagnostics of potential threats. Therefore, if one cannot be done systematically and reliably, the other cannot be done either. Second, exploring vulnerabilities efficiently requires putting yourself into the adversaries' shoes. Yet, not many businesses have enough experience and "maturity" (strategic and expertise readiness) to perform such exercises. Finally, and most importantly, even when the business is mature enough and has a good understanding of the underlying vulnerabilities according to a particular methodology, there is always a possibility that a "zero-day vulnerability", an unknown and underexplored gap in the system, may exist which still could be exploited by cybercriminals.[8]

---

[8]Of course, there are several methods in which zero vulnerabilities can be understood. In subsequent chapters, we discuss some of these methods, such as engaging ethical hackers, having broader conversations with the staff and the general public, etc.

All these issues with threat and vulnerability measurements bring us to the difficulties associated with risk measurement.

Issues with risk measurement are primarily associated with the fact that it is often not possible to obtain the exact probability measure of cybersecurity risk. The purpose of any traditional risk assessment exercise is to provide exact risk measurement in a form of some discrete value (probability, percentage chance, etc.). Yet, very often it is not possible to pin down the exact probability of some adverse event happening. Naturally, it relates not only to the difficulties in cyber space threat detection and imprecision in vulnerability analytics, but also to the fact that due to the complexity of the cyberspace, traditional tools used for risk detection and management are no longer adequate and need significant revision to effectively address the cybersecurity risks.

In what follows, we expand on this point looking at existing tools to measure and alleviate cybersecurity risks as well as discuss the threats and risks we are likely to face in the future. We will also explore how these new risks could be addressed using a variety of tools.

References

1. *Frank Abagnale: "Catch me if you can"* | *Talks at Google.* https://www.youtube. com/watch?v=vsMydMDi3rI.
2. Indictment. *United States of America v. Victor Netyksho, Boris Antonov, Dmitriy Badin, Ivan Yermakov, Aleksey Lukashev, Sergey Morgachev, Nikolay Kozachek, Pavel Yershov, Artem Mayshev, Aleksandr Osadcguk, Aleksey Potemkin, and Alatoliy Kovalev.* https://int.nyt.com/data/documenthelper/80-netyk-sho-et-al-indictment/ba0521c1eef869deecbe/optimized/full.pdf?action= click&module=Intentional&pgtype=Article.
3. Digital Catapult UK. (2015). *Trust in personal data: The UK review* (The Digital Catapult Report).

Part II

Existing Solutions and Cybersecurity
for Business

5

Existing Solutions Summary

So far, we have painted a rather gloomy picture, suggesting that in circumstances when much data and systems are digitized, the adversaries seem to be, if not winning, then getting significantly ahead in the cyber game. Yet, is it really as gloomy as we might think? Let us now explore what solutions are available to businesses and how well these solutions are addressing various cybersecurity risks.

Wouldn't it be great to have one universal solution for all cybersecurity issues? Imagine that you could apply a simple tool to estimate all your potential cybersecurity risks and, as a result, the tool would give you a set of concrete recommendations about what you should do to protect yourself and your business against those risks. Unfortunately, the world is much more complex than that. We saw in the previous sections that cybersecurity threats are multiple, vulnerabilities are not easy to anticipate and risks are difficult to estimate. Therefore, the solutions we apply to cybersecurity issues should also be multifaceted. When we talk about cybersecurity for business, three types of solutions exist: Technology-driven approach (or "patching with technology" [1, 2]); Human-centered approach (or "patching with people" [1, 2]); and Canvas approach (or "patching with frameworks and architectures"). In what follows, we first consider the Canvas approach, and then turn to the discussions of Technology-driven and Human Centered approaches.

Canvas Approach

Canvas approach is represented by general frameworks and architectures for cybersecurity. They sit on top of technology-driven and human-driven approaches as they incorporate "patching with technology" and usually include

© The Author(s) 2019
G. Pogrebna and M. Skilton, *Navigating New Cyber Risks*,
https://doi.org/10.1007/978-3-030-13527-0_5

"patching with people", at least to some extent. Apart from frameworks and architectures, canvas approach also incorporates risk management methods aimed at approximating and measuring the most relevant cybersecurity risks. Usually, canvas approach is discussed separately and not included in the description of solutions; however, for the purposes of our explanation, we decided to include it as a separate category because it helps to understand the way in which various cybersecurity solutions are organized at a strategic level, while "patching with technology" and "patching with people" operate at a tactical level.

It is important to understand the differences between frameworks, architectures, and risk management tools for cybersecurity. Even though all three are aimed at decreasing and managing cybersecurity risks, they are not the same. Frameworks refer to a set of non-compulsory or voluntary guidelines, recommendations, best practices, and standards aimed at helping businesses to strengthen their cybersecurity and to alleviate cyber risks. Architectures explain how business systems (including computer systems, technological systems, human systems, supply-chain systems) should be designed in order to reach business cybersecurity goals. Risk management tools include risk assessment, risk identification, risk analysis, risk evaluation, and risk mapping techniques which help to estimate the probability of harm associated with various adverse cyber events, understanding the nature of these events and what countermeasures could be applied to address them.

Frameworks are very widespread cybersecurity canvas tools used by many businesses. Even though approximately 250 different security frameworks exist globally,[1] according to the survey conducted by Tenable and released at the beginning of 2018,[2] there are four frameworks which are most widespread.

- Payment Card Industry Data Security Standard (PCI DSS) is used by 47% of surveyed organizations;
- ISO 27001/27002 is implemented by 35% of surveyed organizations;
- Center for Internet Security Critical Security Controls (CIS) is adopted in 32% of surveyed organizations;
- National Institute of Standards and Technology (NIST) Framework for Improving Critical Infrastructure Cybersecurity, known as NIST Cybersecurity Framework (NIST CSF), in place at 29% of surveyed organizations.

---

[1]See https://originit.co.nz/the-strongroom/five-most-common-security-frameworks-explained/ for more information.

[2]See Trends in Security Framework Adoption Survey (2018) https://www.tenable.com/whitepapers/trends-in-security-framework-adoption.

Table 5.1   Most widely used cybersecurity frameworks in the USA

PCI DSS (47%)	ISO (35%)	CIS (32%)	NIST CSF (29%)
Plan ↓ Design ↓ Implement ↓ Operate ↓ Optimize	Initiate ↓ Define ↓ Assess ↓ Develop ↓ Readiness	Basic controls / Foundational controls / Organizational controls	Identify ↓ Protect ↓ Detect ↓ Respond ↓ Recover

The quoted percentages do not add up to 100% because even though 84% of surveyed organizations revealed that they were using some type of framework, 44% explained that they were using more than one framework. Tenable reported that there was a high level of the frameworks' adoption among organizations of different sizes: 90% of large organizations with 10,000 employees and 77% of relatively small organizations with 1000 or fewer employees operate using a cybersecurity framework.

Even though frameworks allow cybersecurity to be viewed from a strategic level, it is hard to estimate their practical value to organizations. They seem to offer the general flow of strategic actions for cybersecurity (i.e., explain "what" should be achieved), yet it is not clear from the frameworks which particular actions should be taken to reach favorable cybersecurity outcomes (i.e., "how" or "in what way" the strategic "what"s could be attained is not clear). Of course, much of this is driven by the underlying generality and universal appeal of frameworks, as it is implied that they should be useful for a wide variety of organizations, operating in different countries, working in different industries, and facing various contexts. Yet, at the same time, it is hard to avoid noticing that the most popular frameworks look very similar (see Table 5.1 and Fig. 5.1).

Specifically, three of four frameworks (PCI DSS, ISO, and NIST CSF) include five components which detail the strategic flow of activities aimed at preventing and responding to various cybersecurity risks. The CIS framework offers a layered approach, splitting activities into Basic, Foundational, and Organizational, capturing different levels of strategic thinking. Yet, in its essence, it also offers a high-level plan, although it suggests that all components should work simultaneously rather than sequentially.

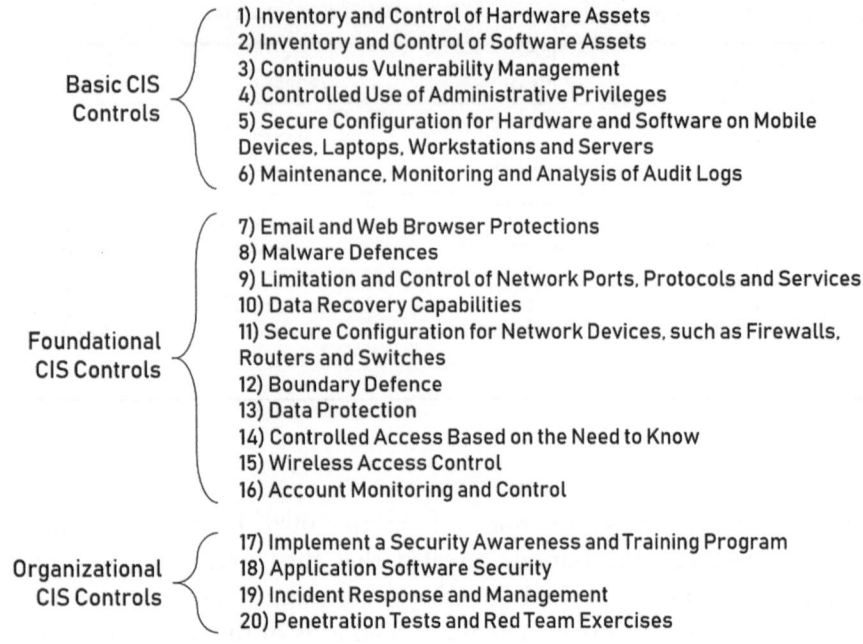

Basic CIS Controls
1) Inventory and Control of Hardware Assets
2) Inventory and Control of Software Assets
3) Continuous Vulnerability Management
4) Controlled Use of Administrative Privileges
5) Secure Configuration for Hardware and Software on Mobile Devices, Laptops, Workstations and Servers
6) Maintenance, Monitoring and Analysis of Audit Logs

Foundational CIS Controls
7) Email and Web Browser Protections
8) Malware Defences
9) Limitation and Control of Network Ports, Protocols and Services
10) Data Recovery Capabilities
11) Secure Configuration for Network Devices, such as Firewalls, Routers and Switches
12) Boundary Defence
13) Data Protection
14) Controlled Access Based on the Need to Know
15) Wireless Access Control
16) Account Monitoring and Control

Organizational CIS Controls
17) Implement a Security Awareness and Training Program
18) Application Software Security
19) Incident Response and Management
20) Penetration Tests and Red Team Exercises

Fig. 5.1 CIS framework explained

In other words, while frameworks seem to provide a nice starting point for those not familiar with cybersecurity and new to the field, it is hard to distill from frameworks how one should go about tackling various types of cybersecurity risks.

Architectures offer more concrete instruments to ensure cybersecurity. Cybersecurity architectures are usually very specific to businesses operating digital systems and depend on a wide variety of factors: the industry in which the business operates, its size, its supply-chain features, the characteristics of its business-to-customer and business-to-business relationships, the context in which the business operates (e.g., political, geographical, economic, legal factors which impact day-to-day operations), etc. Providing general advice on how architectures should be constructed is extremely difficult as they need to be designed on a case-by-case basis and take into account security goals as well as the needs of specific businesses. Nevertheless, some general principles are offered by governmental bodies. For example, the UK's National Cyber Security Centre (NCSC) released four basic goals[3] for good cybersecurity architecture design. According to the NCSC, any cybersecurity architecture should pursue the following security goals:

- Robustness: the system should be difficult to penetrate and compromise (*"make initial compromise of the system difficult"*);
- Resilience: the system should be designed to minimize adversarial impact so that it can effectively and quickly recover and survive this impact (*"limit the impact of any compromise"*);
- Agility: the system should be flexible to quickly adapt to changes in the environment so that it is difficult to disrupt (*"make disruption of the system difficult"*);
- Traceability: the system should allow for quick and efficient detection of compromises (*"make detection of a compromise easy"*).

We can easily see how, in theory, or in an ideal world, reaching or at least aiming to reach all four goals should be the purpose of any cybersecurity architecture. Yet, several practitioners have highlighted the impossibility of accomplishing all these goals simultaneously, as (i) they appear to be mutually exclusive, and (ii) they may pose serious cost limitation problems if businesses try to achieve them all at the same time [3, 4]. There are structured mathematical arguments which could be applied to prove the impossibility of overlap between the four goals. However, let us follow a simple logical argument.

In the real world, of all the four goals, the hardest to achieve is Robustness. You might use the most sophisticated technology to try and stop the adversaries in their tracks; you might make it really hard to penetrate the system and, that way, seriously increase the time which is needed by adversaries to compromise your business. Yet, if you have something really valuable to steal, it does not matter how thick the wall is which separates you from the cybercriminals. If the adversaries understand that there is a highly monetizable asset behind this wall, they will just get better and find a way to drill a hole in that wall, dig a tunnel underneath it, or go around the wall and avoid it altogether. In other words, stronger, bigger, more sophisticated barriers will only attract smarter, better, and more experienced adversaries. Despite this, billions of dollars, pounds, euros, etc. are spent every year trying to make the

---

[3]See https://www.ncsc.gov.uk/blog-post/how-ncsc-thinks-about-security-architecture for more detail.

systems robust to attacks. And yet, all this investment is not making systems secure because on a daily basis we hear about new cases of highly reputable businesses being compromised. You might wonder why. In some sense, it is clear that we want to do is let the cybercriminals in but then throw them completely off track (away from valuable information or assets), compromise their virtual private networks (VPNs), collect forensic evidence about them, lead them to something completely useless and worthless and make them give up, thereby rendering your business unattractive to them as a target. It is true that some companies try to engage in such activities; however, the over-whelming majority of businesses concentrate on Robustness.

Philosophy offers some possible answers to this. Security is a social con-struct and, as a society, we feel very strongly about some security targets more than others. For example, philosopher Jonathan Wolff argues that the UK tends to spend a lot more on railroad security compared to motorway security precisely because we would feel incredibly ashamed as a society if a major railroad accident occurred; by contrast, we are used to hearing about motorway accidents and collisions and do not feel the same sense of shame when they happen [5]. Similarly, many businesses feel very strongly about Robustness: imagine a leading bank or financial institution in any country in the world declaring that cybersecurity Robustness is not their top prior-ity. This would lead to a major scandal as customers and regulators, as well as the general public, would automatically regard this organization as being reckless with cybersecurity. The reputational damage would be devastating. However, despite all the declarations about Robustness, none of the sys-tems operated by banks or financial institutions in the modern world are "unbreakable", in the sense that under certain circumstances, with a certain menu of available resources, cybercriminals may succeed in compromising even the most sophisticated systems.

Recently, practitioners called for a shift in the architectural paradigm to concentrate more on Resilience rather than Robustness [3, 4]. Indeed, it is extremely important to make sure that the impact of the adversarial act is minimized and that all systems can be up and running as quickly as possible. If we agree that it is impossible or almost impossible to pre-vent an adversarial event from happening, then it is clear that Resilience is a lot easier to achieve than Robustness. There are many ways in which Resilience can be accomplished. One way is to keep important data assets and records backed up on different independent platforms. For example, it is no secret that the National Health Service (NHS)—a publicly funded healthcare service provider in the UK—has been compromised by cyber-criminals many times. Yet, despite all these attacks and leaked records, the system was relatively quick to recover. The reason for this is that the

NHS runs a large number of different platforms in parallel, where copies of recorded data exist completely independently. That way, if one part of the system (one platform) is compromised, the other can quickly provide a copy of missing or maliciously encrypted data. The NHS runs branches of its systems which are powered by the Microsoft Windows platform and Linux Ubuntu (i.e., NHSubuntu),[4] as well as usually keeping printed copies of all patient records. Therefore, despite not being the most secure organization in the world in terms of Robustness, it is reasonably resilient as multiple backups allow the NHS to recover after an adversarial impact.

Another way is to quickly get the information into the public domain. Think of Adobe. Adobe was hacked on multiple occasions, but every time the software giant was honest about the attacks and quickly released the information to customers, urging them to change their passwords. In 2013, over 38 million Adobe accounts were compromised, yet Adobe quickly released the information they had about the breach even though initially the company thought that 2.9 million customers had been affected.[5] Nevertheless, the company recommended that all customers change their passwords not only for Adobe but on other websites where they used the same login details.[6] Adobe recovered from the breach relatively quickly.

Yet, it is worth noting that this path might not be optimal for all companies. There are many factors influencing this, one of which could be whether security is essential to the core value proposition of the company to the customer. For example, if hackers go after McDonald's and steal a handful of credit card numbers, McDonald's will suffer. Yet, it will not suffer as much as, say, PayPal in a similar situation. The reason for this is that McDonald's main value proposition is to feed the customers quickly, whereas PayPal's value proposition is to offer a secure and fast way of electronic payment. This is why sometimes we are surprised when we go to https://haveibeenpwned.com/ (a website which allows you to check whether any of your current email accounts have been compromised) and discover that some of our emails have been subject to a data breach even though no public announcement was made about the breach. The EU GDPR now requires all businesses dealing with EU customers to release any breach information into the public domain as soon as it becomes available to the company. Nevertheless, we have yet to see how this regulation is going to be enforced and whether it will lead to higher numbers of reported breaches.

---

[4]See https://www.theregister.co.uk/2017/06/30/nhsbuntu_nhs_revolution/ for more detail.

[5]See https://www.bbc.co.uk/news/technology-24740873 for more detail.

[6]See https://theblog.adobe.com/important-customer-security-announcement/ for more detail.

Agility, or flexibility, of the system is also a goal which is hard to achieve, though, again, probably not as hard as attaining Robustness. The main issue with Agility is that there is considerable heterogeneity in understanding what it might mean for different systems. If we consider Agility as an ability of the cybersecurity system to adjust to the environment, then the main challenge Agility poses to the architectural design is similar to the challenge which potential customization or personalization poses to many products and services if the underlying flexibility needs to be achieved purely by technical means. It is possible, for example, to make a car fully customizable or even personalizable, yet there is a trade-off between customization and the cost of the car: i.e., the more customizable it is, the more expensive it will be to produce. Likewise, to make the cybersecurity architecture Agile using technical means, one has to consider a long list of possible threats, vulnerabilities, and risks and make sure that the system is ready to face them. All these actions are costly if businesses are aiming to achieve them using technology. Yet, it is possible to decrease the costs if human-centric measures are applied. We will consider human-based solutions below.

Finally, Traceability is something many organizations struggle with. Recall Google's recent announcement about the closure of their Google+ service in 2018. The vulnerability in Google+ was only discovered by Google in 2018 but could have been there since its launch date (June 28, 2011). Even though Google made statements that they had no reason to believe that the discovered vulnerability was exploited by adversaries, the uncomfortable truth is—there is no way to know for sure whether someone was able to get in and out of the system undetected before the vulnerability was discovered. This example illustrates that even the most sophisticated companies with the best cybersecurity architects cannot avoid unexplored vulnerabilities and, in many cases, will not see if something goes wrong until it is too late. Usually, the more sophisticated the cybersecurity system is, the more difficult it is to spot problems as there are too many places where they may appear.

So, it appears that each of the goals in isolation is hard to achieve. However, the real challenge is to make sure that these goals could be combined. Robustness seems to be in conflict with Resilience and Agility; Traceability with Agility, etc. [3, 4].[7] This means that achieving all four goals simultaneously is utopian, even if two of the four goals could coexist harmoniously in the same architecture.

---

[7]For a more detailed discussion on the impossibility of overlap between Robustness, Resilience, and Agility, see Taratine, B. (2018) "How can we build an agile robust resilient (cyber)security defence system?" LinkedIn article, https://www.linkedin.com/pulse/how-can-we-build-robust-agile-resilient-cybersecurity-boris-taratine/.

Frameworks and architectures are supported by the **risk management tools**. Any risk management exercise starts with risk assessment or understanding, estimating and measuring the probability of potential harm from various threats. Risk assessment can be conducted using qualitative and/or quantitative methodology. Qualitative methodology allows us to assess potential cybersecurity risks using interviews, discussions, focus groups, or other non-numerical methods, such as considering the strengths, weaknesses, opportunities, and threats (SWOT) of the cybersecurity system. There are also numerous quantitative methods for assessing risk. Since there is a lot of literature dealing with risk assessment tools and algorithms [6–8], we will provide several examples for illustration only. For example, a hazard model could be used to generate a vulnerability versus risk curve which maps loss versus the temporal probability of adverse events. Where the path-dependence of adverse events is common (i.e., when one adverse event is likely to lead to another), event-tree analysis is usually used. The main attraction of this method is that it provides a clear mapping of how one adverse event is linked to another and by this associative thinking allows us to calculate the probability of each subsequent adverse event. The Risk Indicator-based approach allows us to map multiple indicators related to threats, exposures, vulnerabilities, and capacities of the organization and then use scoring and weighting procedures to obtain a Threat Index and Vulnerability Index. The overlap between the two indexes yields the Risk Index, which is then used to formulate responses and design solutions. The most commonly used and popular approach, however, is the Risk Matrix approach. If your business has a risk assessment or risk management unit, it is highly likely that you have previously seen and worked with risk matrixes. The matrix maps the frequency of the adverse events versus their impact or consequences. Both frequency and impact usually include three (Low = Green; Moderate = Yellow; High = Red) to five (None = White; Low = Green; Moderate = Yellow; High = Orange; Very High = Red) color-coded levels and offer a useful tool which allows us to clearly systematize the risks and prioritize responses. By looking at the risk matrix, you usually know that a system is risky if the majority of events are red, and mostly safe if the majority of events are green.

Yet, the main issue with using quantitative risk assessment is that historical data or live data on risks is not readily available. There are many reasons for this: data on cybersecurity is not centrally accumulated; information about cyber risks is not only not shared between organizations but even within the same organization; even when it is possible to confirm that the adverse event has taken place, its consequences remain unknown or uncertain. Therefore, measurement of risk using traditional quantitative risk assessment is not straightforward. This leads to a situation where traditional quantitative risk assessment techniques offer little help to cybersecurity architects. We are, of course, not trying to suggest that these techniques are useless; however, without reliable and accurate historical data, it is hard to expect that the outcome of these techniques can lead to valuable predictions. In later chapters, we look at alternatives to traditional risk assessment and risk management tools which help mitigate at least some of the problems we face when trying to measure and quantify cybersecurity risk.

As we explained above, modern cybersecurity canvas solutions incorporate both technology-driven and human-centered approaches to identify a set of tools, methods, and solutions for tackling potential adversarial impact. Let us look closer at those solutions.

Technology-Driven Approach

"Patching with technology" [1, 2], to date, represents the most widespread way of dealing with cybersecurity threats. A cybersecurity "patch" refers to a set or series of technological measures, changes or alterations of programming code, supporting data, underlying algorithms, or programming system logic aimed at improving the system's security, fixing existing bugs, addressing vulnerabilities, and updating defense mechanisms. A Technology-driven approach can be split into two main subcategories: Reactive and Active. Reactive approaches deal with the problem of how to react to a particular threat and how to prevent threats from happening by designing robust systems which are difficult to infiltrate; whereas Active approaches address issues around designing mechanisms which allow us to anticipate cybersecurity risk, effectively detect attacks, as well as mislead and catch adversaries.

Reactive technological tools currently represent the main frontier of cyberdefense. Since most businesses outsource their cybersecurity issues to a range of large digital giants or smaller and specialized cybersecurity companies, any discovered gap in the system (i.e., vulnerability), whether exploited or unexploited, is usually fixed by applying a technical "patch". For example, such "patches" are applied by Microsoft when companies spot loopholes in the Microsoft Office or email systems. While technological patches are very effective, the main issue is that they cannot be applied before the vulnerability is discovered. Therefore, in many cases, patches are applied after the harm has already materialized.

Firewalls are another popular security measure. In the contemporary network security, firewalls usually represent the first line of defense as they separate networks with restricted access and valuable information or data from publicly accessible cyber spaces. While in the past it was rather obvious where firewalls were located in the cybersecurity architectures, contemporary systems allow for the use of firewalls which are not connected to the Internet-powered networks (i.e., "invisible" on the Internet). This creates an illusion that such firewalls are "unbreakable" or impossible to attack. It is certainly true that such measures as taking firewalls off the Internet make it more difficult to spot and compromise systems. Yet, it is important to remember that even the most sophisticated firewall, even if it is invisible on the Internet, offers only a temporary protection. In other words, while a firewall can definitely slow down a motivated adversary, if you have something very valuable to steal, it will not stop this adversary.

We have recently been called to consult a company which suffered an unprecedented breach of a "physical" firewall. While, for confidentiality reasons, we cannot describe the particulars of this company's cybersecurity architecture, we will, nevertheless, explain the principle behind this firewall. Imagine that you have a highly secure building with two floors. Each floor operates a separate intranet network (not connected to the outside world) and there is a "physical firewall", in the sense that the two floors are physically separated from each other and operate independent (unconnected) networks. Therefore, in order to infiltrate the two networks, one has to physically go to a particular floor and "plug" into the network. The building has very sophisticated entry requirements and both floors are filmed 24/7. What if we told you that, despite all these precautions, it was possible for adversaries (who are not malicious insiders) to infiltrate such a system? This is what we mean when we say that a firewall is only a temporary measure capable of slowing down but not stopping the adversary.

Antivirus is also a popular measure which many companies as well as individuals believe protects them from malware. Yet, again, considering the level of sophistication with which attacks are currently executed, it is highly unlikely that antivirus will offer you adequate protection. For example, if previously viruses were delivered to personal computers using email attachments, currently your computer can be infected by you simply accepting a malicious calendar invite sent as a part of a spear-phishing campaign.

Multifactor authentication has recently become a new norm. When logging in to your email from a new device for the first time, you are usually asked to verify your identity by typing in a code which is sent to you as a text message on your mobile phone. However, considering that mobile phones are also infiltratable, or keeping in mind that your mobile device can simply be stolen or hijacked, multifactor authentication does not really offer a reliable defense. Although, by any standard, it is hard to disagree with the fact that adopting a multifactor authentication does offer an additional layer of protection.

Technical measures also include (among many others) backups, zero-trust, and device solutions. Backups are generally a good idea. However, it is important to remember that cloud backups can easily be accessed from a compromised device. Therefore, it is important to keep several copies of your data files on an external drive or a CD not connected to the Internet. It is also a good idea to encrypt those offline files. Zero-trust refers to a security model where any attempt to access an organizational security system is treated as not trustworthy. Zero-trust systems have recently gained momentum due to their "never trust, always verify" principle which implies having multiple checks of access and movement points. Yet, even such systems can be abused and loopholes for infiltration can be found. Finally, device solutions are also not the best way of dealing with cybersecurity problems. Speaking at a cybersecurity debate at The Alan Turing Institute in September 2018, Cal Leeming, formerly the youngest hacker prosecuted for cybersecurity crimes in the UK at the age of 12 and currently a cyber-security consultant, maintained that Chromebooks were relatively secure compared to other devices. It is true that Chromebooks are not very easy to compromise. However, by moving all your files to Chromebook, (i) you are placing all your security into the hands of Google, and (ii) we have recently seen a live demonstration from a white-hat hacker who apparently infiltrated and extracted valuable data from a Chromebook in a matter of minutes.[8]

Active Cyberdefense (ACD) technological solutions, unlike Reactive measures, are usually designed to proactively lure and mislead cybercriminals in order to collect forensic data on them as well as find out who they are. This is an exciting new direction in cybersecurity. Yet, as Pete Cooper, a cybersecurity expert puts it, "*ACD is not about hacking back*". It is about a systematic approach to understanding the criminal mind [9]. Currently, the most widespread methodology used for ACD is the creation of a sophisti-cated net of so-called "smart honeypots", or traps, on the network which are intended to attract cybercriminals. The honeypots are usually machines on the network which look very attractive to an adversary but do not contain

---

[8]See https://www.youtube.com/watch?v=KIrrA1-O6LE for more detail.

any valuable or interesting information and, most importantly, do not act as a gateway to anything important. By hitting these pre-set targets, cyber-criminals waste their time and compromise their forensic data, allowing the cybersecurity team to track them and, with luck, even identify them.

There are, however, several issues with this approach. First of all, engaging in ACD is not a route for all businesses. This path requires a great deal of "maturity" (i.e., an understanding of the issue at a strategic level), resources, and technical capability from the organization. Second, recent advances in AI offer cybercriminals a variety of ways to detect honeypots on the system, thereby destroying the whole purpose of setting them up in the first place. Obviously, AI technology is available to both sides, and several savvy busi-nesses have responded by using AI to set up smart honeypot nets. However, like any technological solution, it is only a matter of time before a motivated set of adversaries will find a way to detect and avoid smart honeypots if the method used to set them up is determined purely on algorithmic logic. This is because any system set up purely by mathematical logic can be infiltrated by employing a mathematical counter–logic.

As we can see, technological solutions on their own are unlikely to solve the cybersecurity problems of businesses as they primarily focus on the Robustness goal, and it is next to impossible to make a system robust. It is highly likely that despite all the technology available to an organization, sooner or later highly motivated adversaries will find their way in. Under these circumstances, it is important to shift the cybersecurity paradigm from "patching with technology" to "patching with people" [1, 2].

Human-Centered Approach

"Patching with people" [1, 2], a term coined by Debi Ashenden, Professor of Cybersecurity at the University of Portsmouth, incorporates a set of human-centered solutions which allow us to ensure the Agility and Traceability of the system as well as support Resilience in a way that tech-nological solutions cannot. Businesses often talk about "the human firewall", referring to the ability of human beings within the organizations to effectively detect, report, and alleviate major cybersecurity risks. Yet, the mechanisms for creating the human solutions are not in place in the majority of organi-zations. There are several reasons for this. It is obvious that in circumstances where many companies outsource their cybersecurity, there exists a rather large bias towards technological fixes as opposed to human-centered solutions. Cybersecurity is perceived within organizations as an incredibly "dry" topic requiring significant technical expertise. At the same time, the overwhelming majority of cybersecurity companies offer technological or algorithmic solutions which seem to offer a convincing panacea from all cybersecurity troubles. Yet, as our earlier quote from *Robot and Frank* suggests, the "*perception of security*" which these solutions create do not equate to actual security. No matter how good your cybersecurity consultant is, and no matter how awesome their product, unless you see cybersecurity issues as *hybrid* (anthropotechnological) problems, this product is unlikely to save you from a harmful attack.

Looking back at the UK 2018 Cyber Security Breaches Survey,[9] we also spot a rather alarming paradox. Even though over 70% of surveyed organizations in the UK admit that cybersecurity issues are their top priority, only 20% of them have cybersecurity training for staff. This is incredibly low considering our earlier conjecture that social engineering is widely used by cybercriminals to compromise organizational cyber systems. Even though efforts have been made to develop new human-centered solutions, they are still very scattered and, in many cases, counterproductive. Let us consider several examples.

Staff compliance with the cybersecurity policies of the company is probably one of the most common ways in which cybersecurity human-related issues are addressed within businesses. Many companies have a set of rules with regard to their computer and data systems. For example, while some companies are very relaxed about taking data outside the company premises, allowing employees to work from home, others are extremely cautious about this, requiring staff to use dedicated internal drives or internal clouds for all operations with data; whereas some businesses allow free unencrypted communication, others heavily restrict the way in which communication happens and even insist on encrypting all externally faced emails. With respect to compliance, three aspects are particularly worth mentioning: policies with regard to device ownership, USB port usage, and passwords.

With regard to devices, businesses tend to operate one of two models: "bring your own device" or "in-house device" policy. "Bring your own device" implies that company employees are allowed to bring and use their own devices (laptops, iPads, etc.) to fulfill their duties; whereas an "in-house device" policy refers to a situation where each employee has to use devices and systems provided by the company. There are pros and cons associated with each model. Generally, an "in-house device" policy serves a Robustness

---

[9]See https://assets.publishing.service.gov.uk/government/uploads/system/uploads/attachment_data/file/702074/Cyber_Security_Breaches_Survey_2018_-_Main_Report.pdf for more detail.

goal, whereas "bring your own device" is more focused on Resilience. Specifically, many large organizations (with several notable exceptions in the technology industry) prefer to have a single supplier of personal computers and limit themselves to one operational system (say, Microsoft Windows). This is primarily due to the fact that the majority of employees are not technically savvy and rely on IT services to manage and fix problems should any arise: be it an issue with a particular PC or with the digital security of the organizational system as a whole. This is why such systems are built with technical solutions in mind and are designed to minimize human interactions with the fragile segments or areas of a system's elements and networks.

At the same time, the "bring your own device" policy is often exercised in smaller and more technically aware organizations. It is true that individual devices might have a higher probability of being compromised in those organizations compared to "in-house device" organizations; however, the fact that different employees operate not only different systems, but also different versions of those systems, makes it very difficult for adversaries to infiltrate such organizations. For example, many research institutes allow staff to bring their own devices to work. Under these circumstances, you are likely to see people coming to the office with different devices and working in a wide variety of operating systems: e.g., HP computers may coexist with Macs on the same office floor and operate not only different versions of Windows and MacOS but also different distributions of Linux. Therefore, even if adversaries compromise all users of Windows, users of other operating systems are likely to sustain the attack and the organization will be able to quickly recover. Yet, of course, "bring your own device" creates issues in day-to-day systems' management as it requires an IT department capable of working with multiple systems and devices.

USB ports' usage represents another interesting aspect of compliance policy. The nature of academic work implies that we give invited talks in many different organizations throughout the year. Even when those organizations position themselves as tough on cybersecurity, very often they ask external speakers to bring presentations on USB sticks. In fact, of all organizations where we have given external talks within the last 12 months, only three required us to send presentations to the organizers by email in advance. This simple example is extremely characteristic of a major gap in the compliance policies of many organizations: even though it is clear that a major cybersecurity threat could be delivered to the system via an infected USB stick, employees are often left in charge of their own USB ports as well as USB ports of network computers placed in various parts of their office spaces.

However, internal policies with regard to passwords often supersede all other policies in terms of precision and severity. And yet, these policies often lead to unintended consequences. If you recall the passwords we used for various online accounts in the 1990s, you will remember that there were no particular restrictions on them. They could have consisted of letters only, or numbers only, and their length was not regulated. Now think of your email password at work. It probably has to contain no fewer than eight characters, with both capital and small letters, and at least one number and one special character. Considering that the system also prohibits use of your name or common word phrases, all this makes it very difficult for any individual to remember the password. Another major problem for many of us is that we have to change our password regularly to keep accessing the systems (it is a requirement in most organizations to change email passwords at least every three months). Karen Renaud (Professor of Cybersecurity at Abertay University, Professor Extraordinarius at the University of South Africa, Fullbright Scholar, and Honorary Research Fellow at the University of Glasgow), who has conducted many experiments and written extensively on this subject, argues that current policies leave many of us with no choice but to write down passwords because we, as humans, have a limited capacity to memorize letter and digit sequences of the form required by the current cybersecurity systems [10, 11]. Our own experience and the anecdotal evidence we collected in preparation for this book tell us that Professor Renaud is right. We have recently come across a CEO of one of the largest corporations in the UK who kept his multiple passwords on a sheet of paper attached to the desk lamp in his office. We have also talked to a reputable cybersecurity professor from a major US university who told us that for one of his projects he has to use a different password for a data storage cloud every week throughout a year. His team of research assistants needs frequent access to the cloud and it is next to impossible to memorize the 52 complicated passwords required for the whole calendar year (as there are 52 weeks in a year). Furthermore, even if one could memorize them, it would be very easy to confuse the week when a particular password should be used. Therefore, the professor in question has no other choice but to print off those passwords on a sheet of paper and attach the list to the bottom of his desk drawer… Clearly, this is hardly the smartest way to handle security. Apart from writing down our password, another strategy which many of us use when we need to set up a complex password is making the browser remember that password. This is also far from optimal.

Obviously, the fact that we write down passwords or make the browser remember them in many ways destroys all the good will created by the complicated and hard-to-break passwords in the first place. Karen Renaud tested several solutions to the problem. For example, in an experimental study, she showed that users can be incentivized to create more sophisticated passwords. When setting up a more complex password was associated with a longer delay before a replacement was required, users were more likely to set up harder-to-break passwords [10]. Their efforts to come up with a more sophisticated password were rewarded by not having to think of another one for the next six months. Yet, as we have already seen above, this does not mean that users were necessarily "safer" in terms of their password behavior as they could have used their browser to remember the new passwords.

In another study, Karen Renaud showed that users who have a hard time setting and remembering passwords are better off using password managers [11]. Indeed, password managers are very useful tools. They allow a user to set up and remember only one "master" password while keeping passwords for all accounts encrypted. They even have built-in random password generators. By using a password manager, you can synchronize all online accounts requiring passwords in a single system, create sophisticated 16-character passwords for every login, and simply revoke those passwords by typing in a "master" password instead of the account password every time you need to log in. Of course, like any technical solution, password managers are not unbreakable. yet, using a password manager is indeed a lot better than trying to remember multiple passwords, write them down, or even ask the browser to remember them.[10]

Stick rather than carrot measures are usually employed when businesses apply human-centered strategies in cybersecurity. In many large organizations we have spoken to in preparation for this book, IT departments exercise the practice of creating benign bogus attacks (most often phishing attacks) and trial these attacks on their staff. There are also rather severe punishments in place for those who fail to spot the threat or attack, to the extent that those members of staff who do not perform well in the test lose some functionality of their computers. For example, we have talked to a PA in one large organization whose job was to schedule meetings, prepare documents, and liaise externally and internally on behalf of her manager. This PA failed to spot a fake phishing attack two times in a row and, as a result, faced internal IT sanctions: she lost the capacity to send any emails for two weeks. Can you imagine the effect these sanctions had on this person's productivity (as she had to fully rely on telephone communication to fulfill her duties) and, more importantly, on her psychological ability to treat her organization as

---

[10]There are many password manager tools available to any user. Some of them are commercial, others are free. For a recent comparison of password managers, see https://uk.pcmag.com/password-managers/4296/the-best-password-managers.

a trusted entity? We also talked to a member of staff in a large corporation who revealed that monetary fines are imposed for doing poorly in cybersecurity "surprise" tests in his organization and that once he paid out over a third of his monthly salary in related penalties.

All these examples illustrate an important trend: many companies seem to be using negative reinforcement mechanisms in order to incentivize their staff to pay attention to potential threats. Yet, very often this leads to negative results: people become overly suspicious, panicking over simple emails, and fail to constructively address potential problems because they do not know how they will be viewed by the management. Such measures also tend to create an erosion of trust. Many corporate employees we have talked to about cybersecurity issues told us that they were unlikely to inform their IT department of a potential problem (e.g., if they clicked on a link in a malicious email, for example) simply because they thought this might have a negative impact on their promotion opportunities, salary, reputation, etc. Obviously, by introducing such measures, organizations often underestimate the potential consequences of negative reinforcement as their goal is to subject their staff to potential threats and help them gain experience in recognizing risks. Yet, it appears that instead of gaining experience, employees tend to become anxious about cyber issues when negative reinforcement is used. It would seem that positive reinforcement (bonuses, praise, etc.) would work a lot better than punishment where staff training is concerned as it would allow organizations to encourage staff to participate in cybersecurity tasks by avoiding unnecessary blame and negative feelings. We will come back to this point later when we discuss future human-centered cybersecurity solutions.

Overloading people with cybersecurity information is another major problem for many organizations. It seems that many businesses believe that the more information they provide to their staff and customers, the less human-related risk their cybersecurity system will face. Unfortunately, systematic measurements reveal that too much information about cybersecurity leads to the completely opposite result. People who are overwhelmed with cybersecurity information become more risk-taking in cyberspace [12]. We believe this might be because the constant reminder of potential risks makes them overconfident or overoptimistic in this space, leading to a situation where they fail to spot rather obvious threats.

The concept of overconfidence was introduced by Ola Svenson, a psychophysicist from Sweden, who conducted research on road safety in the 1980s. Svenson noticed that the overwhelming majority of car drivers in his survey sample believed that their driving ability was above average; while, statistically, this could only be true for only half of his sample [13]. He concluded, therefore, that people tended to exhibit overconfidence about their relative ability and underestimated the abilities of others. We seem to observe a similar phenomenon in cybersecurity: people who receive large amounts of information about cyber risks and cyberdefense, and who operate in highly regulated environments, tend to significantly overestimate their ability to detect and avoid cybersecurity threats [12]. This, in turn, leads to risk- taking rather than risk-averse behavior in cyberspace.

Gamification is currently one of the in-vogue "patching with people" measures which seems to be gaining momentum in many different industries. Many cybersecurity vendors offer interfaces where company staff can engage in cyber risk detection exercises and earn points. Some companies use those points as "citizenship" tokens, which then could either be publicized or used as a basis for promotion assessment. Although we have not heard examples of this in interviews, in principle, gamification of the space could also be used to offer monetary rewards or annual bonuses to the staff.

There is, however, a major caveat which one has to remember about gamification. It is incredibly difficult to keep the momentum going where games are concerned. Remember how almost the entire planet was excited about *Pokémon Go*? On the day of its release, millions of people were out wandering the streets in search of the cute artificial characters. Yet, very soon the enthusiasm died down and, apart from a handful of fans and enthusiasts, it is impossible to imagine anyone being interested in catching pokémons now. The same is true for most games, including cybersecurity games: unless these games are updated and changed regularly, it is hard to see them succeeding as long-term measures. Another problem with gamification is making sure that incentives to play games during the work time do not outdo the incentives to work. It is important to remember that every member of staff has a set of duties and, while we know from research that short distractions during the working day boost productivity, too many distractions may be detrimental to it [14–16].

Conversation is another promising direction of human-centered approach. Debi Ashenden's Centre for Research and Evidence on Security Threats[11] at the University of Portsmouth pioneered the technique of *Cybersecurity Conversation*. Researchers from the Centre noticed that people at different layers of organizational structure (who may be working in completely

---

[11]See https://crestresearch.ac.uk/ for more detail.

different areas than IT) felt they had a lot of ideas to contribute to enhancing cybersecurity in their organization. Yet, they are never asked to contribute to the conversation about cybersecurity. By facilitating these useful discussions, the Centre showed the value in listening to different opinions about cybersecurity within the organization. By creating an open and inclusive environment, conversations often lead to "out-of-the-box" solutions and allow staff to exercise their digital and physical citizenship within organizations.

References

1. Ashenden, D., & Lawrence, D. (2013, December). Can we sell security like soap? A new approach to behaviour change. In *Proceedings of the 2013 Workshop on New Security Paradigms Workshop* (pp. 87–94). ACM.
2. Ashenden, D., & Sasse, A. (2013). CISOs and organisational change: Their own worst enemy? *Computers & Security, 39*, 396–405.
3. Taratine, B. (2018). *How can we build an agile robust resilient (cyber)security defence system?* LinkedIn article. https://www.linkedin.com/pulse/how-can-we-build-robust-agile-resilient-cybersecurity-boris-taratine/.
4. Snowden, D. (2011). *Risk and resilience.* https://www.youtube.com/watch?v=2Hhu0ihG3kY.
5. Wolff, J. (2006). Risk, fear, blame, shame and the regulation of public safety. *Economics and Philosophy, 22*, 409–427.
6. Ralston, P. A., Graham, J. H., & Hieb, J. L. (2007). Cyber security risk assessment for SCADA and DCS networks. *ISA Transactions, 46*(4), 583–594.
7. Cherdantseva, Y., Burnap, P., Blyth, A., Eden, P., Jones, K., Soulsby, H., & Stoddart, K. (2016). A review of cyber security risk assessment methods for SCADA systems. *Computers & Security, 56*, 1–27.
8. Hughes, J., & Cybenko, G. (2013). Quantitative metrics and risk assessment: The three tenets model of cybersecurity. *Technology Innovation Management Review, 3*(8), 15–24.
9. Cooper, P. (2016). *Cognitive active cyber defence: Finding value through hacking human nature* (MSc dissertation). Cranfield University.
10. Renaud, K., & Zimmerman, V. (2018, February). Nudging folks towards stronger password choices: Providing certainty is the key. *Behavioural Public Policy*, 1–31. https://doi.org/10.1017/bpp.2018.3.
11. Alkaldi, N., & Renaud, K. (2018, October 2). Encouraging password manager adoption by meeting adopter self-determination needs (Extended Version). Available at SSRN https://ssrn.com/abstract=3259563.

12. Kharlamov, A., Jaiswal, A., Parry, G., & Pogrebna, G. (2018). *Heavy regulation and excessive information about cybersecurity makes people risk taking in cyberspace* (Alan Turing Institute Working Paper).
13. Svenson, O. (1981). Are we all less risky and more skillful than our fellow drivers? *Acta Psychologica, 47*(2), 143–148.
14. Friedman, S. E., Musliner, D. J., & Rye, J. M. (2014). Improving automated cybersecurity by generalizing faults and quantifying patch performance. *International Journal on Advances in Security, 7*(3–4), 121–130.
15. Jenkins, D., Arnaud, J., Thompson, S., Yau, M., & Wright, J. (2014). *Version control and patch management of protection and automation systems.* Paper Presented at the 2014 12th International Conference on Developments in Power System Protection (DPSP), Copenhagen, Denmark, 31 March–3 April.
16. Kilber, J., Barclay, A., & Ohmer, D. (2014). Seven tips for managing Generation Y. *Journal of Management Policy and Practice, 15*(4), 80.

6

Cybersecurity Business Goals and Stories Around Them

The Question of Rationality

There is a small 4-star hotel in Austrian Alps called Seehotel Jägerwirt. On the one hand, there is nothing special about this hotel—it is a small gem located on Lake Turracher close to Klagenfurt and owned by the Brandstätter family. Yet, it is famous for being hacked for ransom by cyber-criminals not once, not twice, not three times—it was hacked four times![1] Cybercriminals used vulnerabilities in the hotel's computer system to lock the hotel guests out of their rooms. The ransom message was hidden in a Telecom Austria letter and Christoph Brandstätter (the owner) paid the ransom in bitcoin. There are several interesting aspects to this story. First of all, it shows us again that no business is "too small" to be the target. Second, this story is often cited as a showcase of business irrationality: indeed, from the outside it seems rather silly to become the target multiple times and pay the ransom. But is it really irrational?

The question about whether it is irrational or not depends heavily on several factors. First of all, when a business is trying to build a "safe" space, what is the meaning of "safe"? Second, in doing so, what is the ultimate business goal—is it to really be safe or to be compliant with the latest cybersecurity regulations? Finally, what characteristics of the system are the most important for the business? Is it "robustness", "resilience", "agility", "traceability", which we have already considered earlier in this book, or is it something

---

[1]See https://www.bbc.co.uk/news/business-42352326 for more detail.

© The Author(s) 2019
G. Pogrebna and M. Skilton, *Navigating New Cyber Risks*,
https://doi.org/10.1007/978-3-030-13527-0_6

else? What might seem rather stupid if the ultimate goal is a Robust security system may make perfect sense if the ultimate goal is Resilience. In fact, paying ransoms might not seem such a bad idea if you want to quickly put your business back on track. Fair enough, the Seehotel Jägerwirt's case is a bit extreme, but imagine yourself in Christoph Brandstätter's shoes? You are running a hotel and you know a lot about the hospitality business (confirmed by a 4.5 start rating on TripAdvisor)[2] but not much about computers and computer systems. One day, you find all your guests locked out of their rooms. Naturally, as any business owner who puts customers first, your main concern is how to reassure your customers and fix the situation as soon as possible to avoid reputational and financial losses. So, for Christoph Brandstätter it was perfectly rational to put the system back on track as soon as possible, even at the cost of paying the ransom. It is important to note that despite suffering all these attacks, the hotel is doing fine. It has now gone back to physical instead of the digital key system (i.e., the hotel is now using traditional metal keys) to avoid being compromised for ransom in the future.

Compliance Versus Security

The story about Seehotel Jägerwirt is important because it highlights that where cybersecurity is concerned, business goals are key [1–3]. Therefore, it is extremely important to determine at the beginning of your journey as a business what exactly your security system is trying to achieve. In the overwhelming majority of cases, business owners face a trade-off between compliance and security. By compliance we mean adherence to the regulatory norms and laws. So, being compliant implies being careful with systems and data not to break any regulations or laws. In contrast, being secure means minimizing the actual risk of cybersecurity breaches.

You have probably already guessed that compliance is a lot easier to achieve than security. There are several reasons why this is the case. Compliance is a very certain phenomenon. There is a set of regulations, laws, and regulatory practices which clearly specify where and how responsibility is assigned to various actions. In other words, the legal systems tell us precisely that if something is not done to ensure the security of the system, your business will be automatically liable *by law*. Obviously, the aim of the law is to make systems more secure, yet (i) since the law usually offers rather

---

[2]As of September 25, 2018.

general guidelines for a broad variety of actors, it is interpretable in various ways and (ii) like any mechanism rooted in our culture, it triggers a set of predictable responses which are mostly related to the *perception of security* rather than to the *actual security*. For example, if the law regulates that an organization should protect customer data using all possible means and best practices, the easiest response from any organization holding customer data is to say that they purchased the most sophisticated algorithmic solution from a reputable cybersecurity provider. Does it comply with the regulation? Yes, it does. Does it mean that this organization really did everything in its power to secure customer data? No, it does not.

Unlike compliance, security, as we saw in all our previous arguments leading up to this, is a very uncertain phenomenon. Whether a system is really secure depends on many factors and, most importantly, on an organizational ability to anticipate threats, discover vulnerabilities, and approximate risks. We are not trying to suggest that there is something wrong with trying to be compliant rather than trying to be secure. After all, if you believe that "perception is everything", compliance is exactly what you should be targeting. We are saying, however, that it is important to define what you are really after before investing in any cybersecurity measures because your goals will in many ways define your strategies.

On the Definition of "Safe" and "Secure"

The definition of "safe" and "secure" when it comes to cybersecurity is also not very clear-cut. As we have discussed earlier, for many businesses, "safe" and "secure" primarily means "Robust". Under these circumstances, their main efforts are concentrated on building higher cyber fences and investing in more sophisticated cyber door locks. Yet, again, as we saw earlier, when it comes to cybersecurity, unless an organization applies a multilayered (catering to different behavioral types of adversaries) and hybrid (anthropotechnological) approach, its systems become highly vulnerable.

Furthermore, for different countries, political systems, even industries, safety and security will mean different things and will be defined in different ways. What is good enough for the cybersecurity of transport may not be good enough for the cybersecurity of cities. What can be considered a cyber "safe" space in the catering industry is not enough to qualify as "safe" in fintech. In this sense, it is incredibly important to define the concept of "safe" and "secure" for your organization before you move on to considering how various cybersecurity risks could be identified and addressed.

False Flags?

The question of false flags is also central to defining business goals with regard to cybersecurity. Our colleague, a medieval war history professor, told us a very interesting fact about medieval battles. It turns out that when knights fought against each other in a major battle, they used their military flags (or standards) as *reference points* to help them co-ordinate their actions. Here is how this worked.

Imagine that you are in the middle of a medieval battle. You are wearing armor. It is heavy and the visibility inside your helmet (sallet) is incredibly low. It is also very noisy around and you are riding a horse, which adds yet more uncertainty to the entire operation. So, in principle, you are operating in an incredibly uncertain environment with almost zero visibility. How can you possibly know (i) how well your troops are doing and (ii) how to co-ordinate with others in common actions? This is where the standard-bearer comes in. Since you cannot hear or see much, your best bet is to locate the flag. That way you can tell whether your side is winning, losing, or needing to regroup.

In the medieval age, since the standard-bearer had almost no means to defend himself, he was usually the first target for the enemy troops as capturing the standard not only had a symbolic meaning, but left the enemy practically disoriented on the battlefield. The beauty of the battle standard as a reference point was that it revealed to those in the middle of the battle the real state of affairs.

In cybersecurity, we also determine a set of reference points (flags) which *should* help us to trace the compromises or attacks. We are deliberately using the word *should* because the fact that these flags exist does not mean that they are real. For example, if your organization has a system of firewalls (or if you are applying a perimeter-free zero-trust approach, as system of verification and validation points), they could act as flags. Yet, it is possible to compromise the system without even touching the firewalls (or verification and validation points). In this case, the flags which you have set up and identified are useless for the formulation of an effective and agile cybersecurity strategy. In this sense, our perception of security often operates in a system of false flags. False flags are often a product of *context dependency neglect* (i.e., the inclination to adopt universal solutions rather than solutions tailored to a specific context) as well as psychological biases (e.g., these biases could come from previous experiences where being a subject of a particular attack alters your perception of the likelihood of a similar attack in the future). Therefore, it is incredibly important to constantly test a set of flags determined by your organization to see whether these flags still matter and to what extent noticing them helps you to reach your cybersecurity goals. Coming back to our firewalls example, it would be silly to invest large amounts of money into firewall solutions if major cybersecurity risk for your organization comes from phishing or spear phishing. But to identify the waste in your cybersecurity system and to realize that your flags might be false, you have to constantly question these flags.

Cost Versus Benefit

Cost versus benefit is another crucial consideration when making decisions about cybersecurity. Understanding the costs of adverse cyber events combined with the cost versus benefit of various cybersecurity measures allows you to learn which system is "*good enough*". What does "*good enough*" mean for your business? Considering the complexity of cyberspaces and multiplicity of potential threats, some of which may match your organization's zero-day vulnerabilities, it becomes obvious that it is impossible to avoid cybersecurity risk altogether. Therefore, to a certain extent, risk should be taken. Yet, at the same time, it is necessary to ensure that this risk does not lead to catastrophic consequences. This, of course, is a lot easier said than done.

The main issue is understanding the process of estimating costs versus benefits. Traditional quantitative risk management techniques (discussed in the previous chapter) would dictate considering all possible types of threats (e.g., from our periodic Table 2.1) and then, based on the historical data on each threat, estimating the precise probability with which each type of risk is likely to occur. The issue, of course, is that the overwhelming majority of businesses will not have historical data on all threats. Moreover, the variability of publicly available statistics from different private and public sources creates an additional confusion, offering little guidance to enterprises. Under these circumstances, it is clear that a different approach would be more appropriate. Instead of applying a backward induction approach by trying to consider all possible threats and "guestimate" or "backward-engineer" the propensity with which your business might be vulnerable to those threats, it would make a lot more sense to use a forward-looking methodology, putting yourself in the adversaries' shoes and thinking of all the "digital valuables" you have which might be of interest to them (see Fig. 6.1).

This process starts by a business or organization listing and understanding all the digital valuables it possesses. Digital valuables may include: consumer personal data; consumer financial data; digital access to important know-how

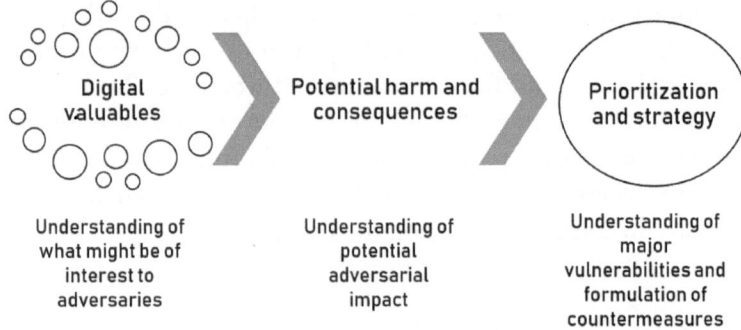

Fig. 6.1 Valuables-based forward-looking cost–benefit analysis procedure

or intellectual property; digital access to physical assets (such as money or infrastructure), etc. Each of these valuables, if lost, will lead to a set of consequences for a business which may include *legal* consequences, *operational* consequences, and *reputational* consequences. Legal consequences refer to the legal responsibility which results from adversarial impact. For example, under the EU's GDPR, there are a number of legal costs and even a potential fine of up to 4% of annual global turnover, or €20 million (whichever is greater), for violating personal data rights and new digital privacy rights of EU citizens. Operational consequences are related to costs resulting from the immediate disruption of service or regular flow of work within the organization. For example, in the case of a DDoS attack, it is highly likely that the routine delivery of services between a particular business and its consumers will be interrupted and there will be costs associated with putting the usual processes back on track. Reputational consequences are associated with costs which lie more in an ethical domain, but may, nevertheless, impact on business. For example, recent scandals associated with lack of privacy and social engineering on Facebook have already contributed to, and continue to impact, younger users of the social media platform, who are switching to other platforms.[3] While reputational concerns do not necessarily lead to direct and immediate financial consequences, they may cause consumer erosion of trust in the brand and lead to a decline in profits over a period of time.

By associating each digital valuable with a set of consequences, your business can then come up with a hierarchy of measures which you need to invest in and map those measures into a "prioritization chart" for

---

[3]See https://www.theguardian.com/technology/2018/feb/16/parents-killed-it-facebook-losing-teenage-users for more detail.

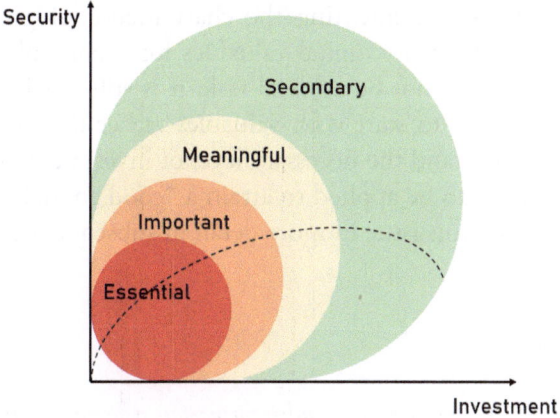

Fig. 6.2 Cybersecurity investment prioritization chart

investments in cybersecurity (Fig. 6.2). This prioritization chart allows us to classify valuables into *essential* (the loss of or serious harm to such valuables threaten business survival); *important* (the loss of or serious harm to such valuables threaten relevant or crucial operations and processes with immediate and irreversible effect but do not threaten business survival); *meaningful* (the loss or serious harm to such valuables threaten relevant operations and processes with lagged and potentially reversible effect); and *secondary* (the loss of or serious harm to such valuables cause temporary and fully recoverable damage to business operations).

The chart also allows us to map the level of investment relative to the expected return on investment captured in the form of the level of "security". The dashed curve on the chart captures the nature of investment relative to the type of valuable. For essential valuables, each monetary unit (dollar, pound, euro) of investment yields higher security. For important valuables, the relationship between investment and security is still increasing but at a lower rate compared to essential valuables. For meaningful valuables, the relationship is almost flat—i.e., each additional monetary unit of investment increases the level of security only slightly or even does not make much difference. For secondary valuables, each additional monetary unit of investment yields a diminishing return. It is important to note that the chart assumes that the ultimate goal of a particular business is a higher level of security rather than compliance, as return on investment in the chart framework is measured by security level.

The main trick in implementing the chart methodology in practice is, of course, to list and classify digital valuables for a particular organization. Even though this might not be a trivial task, it is still much easier from the practical point of view to start with valuables rather than potential threats when trying to understand the necessary level of investment and the types of measures which need to be applied to attain a "good enough" level of cyber-security. We consider this issue in more detail in subsequent chapters.

References

1. Morgan, T. (2002). *Business rules and information systems: Aligning IT with business goals*. New York: Addison-Wesley.
2. Tobin, D. R. (1998). *The knowledge-enabled organization: Moving from "training" to "learning" to meet business goals*. Amacom.
3. Chmielecki, T., Cholda, P., Pacyna, P., Potrawka, P., Rapacz, N., Stankiewicz, R., et al. (2014, September). Enterprise-oriented cybersecurity management. In *2014 Federated Conference on Computer Science and Information Systems (FedCSIS)* (pp. 863–870). IEEE.

7

Communication, Communication, Communication

Why Is Communication Important?

We saw in the previous chapters that understanding the threats, vulnerabilities, and risks associated with cybersecurity is complicated. Part of this complication is that while for non-cyber risks most companies have data about previous cases where things went wrong (in other words, there is data about threats which materialized into harmful events in the past), there is no such data for cybersecurity risks. For example, we know quite well the probability of being injured in a car crash or the probability of being robbed in different parts of the city because we have *historical information* or *data* about the number of car crashes and robberies. This data is collected from verifiable sources and recorded officially by reputable public or private entities. Furthermore, anyone who wants to know these numbers can obtain this information in a few seconds from governmental databases or the databases of global international organizations (such as the OECD).

Unfortunately, the nature of cybersecurity events is such that collecting publicly available and verifiable datasets on cyber risks is a highly complex task. Information about possible threats and vulnerabilities is isolated in different private and public sources and this "siloed" information is not accumulated, not cross-checked, and not verified. Even if an adverse event is confirmed and reported by a particular organization, there is often no way of knowing how harmful it was and it might not be possible to exactly identify the victims. Again, the uncertainty with regard to the victims comes from the fact that (i) harm from an adverse cyber event is not always certain;

© The Author(s) 2019
G. Pogrebna and M. Skilton, *Navigating New Cyber Risks*,
https://doi.org/10.1007/978-3-030-13527-0_7

(ii) victims need to spot the harm to be able to report it; and (iii) even when victims can identify the harm, they often do not have an incentive to report it.

In other words, the probability and level of harm from an adverse cyber event is not easy to measure. This is why quantitative risk measurement tools as we know them, which are very helpful to us in physical spaces, usually cannot be applied to cybersecurity issues (at least not directly, without being significantly modified). This mostly occurs because information- sharing mechanisms fail at several levels simultaneously: at business-to-regulator, business-to-consumer, within business, and business-to-business levels.

Whom Do You Call If You Are Compromised?

Imagine that you log in to your computer and suddenly spot something weird. For example, you notice a bunch of sent emails to unknown address-ees which went out from your email address. Does it mean that you are under attack? And if so, what are you going to do about this? Whom do you call?

We have conducted a series of questionnaires with representative sam-ples of the US, UK, and German population and discovered a very alarming trend. It turns out that the majority of people often do not even realize they have experienced an attack. Specifically, using a sample of 1234 people from the USA (450 individuals), UK (450 individuals), and Germany (334 indi-viduals), we first asked them a very simple question: "*Have you been a victim of a cyberattack in the last 12 months?*" If a respondent replied "Yes" to that question, we would ask them to briefly describe the event. If they answered "No", we would ask the respondents a series of questions to test whether they could have been subjected to an adversarial action without their knowl-edge. In our survey, 28% of US, 27% of British, and 29% of German respondents said they had been a victim of a cyberattack. So, over 70% of individuals from each country reported that they had not experienced a cyberattack in response to our direct question. Yet, in the subsequent ques-tionnaire, it became obvious that the majority of those who replied "No" to our first question (equating to over half in each country) actually were vic-tims of some type of an attack without realizing it. Furthermore, over 55% of people in all countries did not know whom to call and where to report cybersecurity issues; and about 30% in each country said they would first call their Internet provider, irrespective of the issue.

Unfortunately, the situation with businesses is not a lot better. We have recently been in contact with a company where a CEO noticed that several

	Businesses	Cybercriminals
Information sharing	Trusted parties	Community
Platform	Proprietary (if it exists)	Public (Dark Web, Forums)
Visibility	Identifiable	Anonymous
Attack management	Individualistic	Collaborative
Goals	Competing	Common
Technology	Ownership	Shared
Tool sharing	Partnerships	Multi-sided Market
Innovation	Ownership	Shared
Expertise	Outsourced	Elite
Operations	Centralized / Outsourced	Centralized / Decentralized
Training	Limited	Advanced

Fig. 7.1 Information sharing: businesses versus adversaries

things had gone wrong with his laptop login. He did not pay much attention to this and simply recounted the story about the problem as an anecdote to his friend, who happened to be a police officer. Luckily, this friend advised the CEO in question to call cyber police unit asap, and they helped the company to uncover a major cybersecurity threat and prevent a cyberattack. Though this story ended well, it is very characteristic of the current state of affairs in the private sector. Even when an attack or potential start of an attack is spotted, businesses often do not know how to react and whom to call.

Why Do Information Sharing and Communication Fail?

It is obvious that while businesses fail at information sharing, cybercriminals excel in it. Recall our example of the Austrian hotel which was hacked four times. The reason why cases like this happen is that adversaries have very efficient channels of information sharing, so different groups of cybercriminals are sharing intelligence about business vulnerabilities and the tools which could be used to exploit them. Figure 7.1 summarizes the main reasons why adversaries manage to effectively share and communicate information while businesses do not.

First of all, while information sharing in the business environment is only possible among trusted parties, adversaries operate a community system where anonymity allows them to openly transfer and obtain information. Businesses often share information through proprietary platform channels (accessible to trusted parties only), whereas adversaries have an opportunity to share information through the open sources of the Dark Web. Businesses have to operate openly and, therefore, can always be identified or traced when they share information, whereas adversaries are hiding behind aliases.

While businesses often face attacks individually and can only count on their own expertise and resources when dealing with a threat, adversaries work collaboratively. This stems from the fact that adversaries have a common goal while going after the digital valuables of certain actors, whereas businesses have competing goals, or at least *perceive* their goals to be competing, when operating in cyber spaces.

Businesses also often operate proprietary technological systems, while cybercriminals openly share technological know-how and intellectual property. Even when businesses share technological tools or human-centered methodologies, they do so within a circle of partners, whereas adversaries operate in a multisided market environment where they share information, expertise, and where any actor, no matter how small or insignificant, can get in direct contact with any other actor (even when that actor is large and powerful). In the business world, innovations are subject to ownership and patenting, while adversaries effectively share innovations. As we saw earlier in this book, cybersecurity expertise is often outsourced when we talk about businesses; whereas adversaries are in possession of unique ("elite") skillsets which allow them to directly engage in attacks at different levels.

Cybersecurity operations within businesses are either outsourced or centralized, dependent on the level of technological and strategical maturity of the business, while adversaries often operate decentralized systems (centralized operations are also possible when we talk about organized criminal groups). Finally, as we have discussed earlier, while the average level of technical and attack-recognition training in businesses is very limited, most adversaries have an advanced understanding of the field.

Academic research shows that the main reason fueling deficiencies in information sharing and communication is a common view among the business community that barriers of information sharing outweigh its benefits [1–3]. Usually, eight groups of barriers are identified [3]: (1) *legal* barriers are associated with potential disclosure of private information; (2) *technological* barriers reflect a lack of synergies and comparability between sharing the systems of different businesses; (3) *informational* barriers include the availability of excessive, irrelevant, or even misleading information; (4) *collaborative* barriers refer to a lack of trust between businesses; (5) *managerial* barriers comprise risk aversion due to concerns of being potentially subjected to uncontrolled risk, disagreement about trusted channels through which information should be accumulated and shared, etc.; (6) *organizational* barriers reflect a lack of operational capability and, sometimes, a lack of expertise to process cybersecurity information; (7) *performance* barriers are associated with the potential reputational costs and loss of profit should undesirable information surface in the public domain; finally, (8) *cost* barriers are the associated investment needed to increase information-processing capabilities and create the systems associated with them.

At a business-to-consumer level, communication and information sharing fails primarily due to business inability to effectively deliver information to the targeted audiences. In circumstances where the overwhelming majority of attacks start with a phishing email,[1] it is very important to equip customers with useful information, allowing them to spot cybersecurity threats. Many businesses devise information campaigns to warn their customers of potential risks. However, like any social marketing campaigns, they are "one-size-fits-all" tools. Yet, we know that people have a different propensity to detect cybersecurity risks and engage in risky activities in cyberspace.

Within businesses, we often observe either (i) no investment in cybersecurity training or (ii) the supply of too much "one-size-fits-all" information to staff about cybersecurity issues. The former is equivalent to buying the best defense systems to fight the war but not training the population to use those systems. The latter is equivalent to providing the same information about flu to a highly anxious, nervous person and a laid-back person. Clearly, both of these strategies are suboptimal.

At business-to-business and business-to-regulator levels, the information-sharing channels are also broken, although recently the trend towards establishing better systems of communication has started to pick up in many industries. For example, the MISP platform (https://www.misp-project.org) positions itself as "*a threat intelligence platform for gathering, sharing, storing and correlating Indicators of Compromise of targeted attacks, threat intelligence, financial fraud information, vulnerability information or even counter-terrorism information,*" and seems to be making steps in the right

---

[1]See https://www.darkreading.com/endpoint/91--of-cyberattacks-start-with-a-phishing-email/d/d-id/1327704 for more detail.

direction. There are also interesting moves in the same direction within particular industries where businesses understand that if a particular threat hits their competitor today, it might hit them tomorrow as well. Yet, again, very often information sharing within industries happens among a circle of partner organizations, fueled by trusted personal relationships between CEOs, CIOs, and cybersecurity architects, rather than within an open and multisided platform.

How Can We Aid Information Sharing?

There are many ways in which information sharing could be improved, especially if we consider the fact that it is highly dependent on establishing trustworthy relationships between various actors within and outside organizations. For example, there is a significant amount of work in cybersecurity which offers framework solutions to these issues [4]; these framework solutions often have information technology, operations management, or strategy concepts at their core and overlook behavioral aspects of information sharing. Yet, understanding organizational and human behavior in cyberspace may offer significant benefits and suggest ways in which existing barriers to information sharing can be alleviated or event eliminated [5]. Despite the multiplicity of tools which could potentially be applied here, we would like to highlight one method as a good contender for solving the issue of information sharing to ensure (i) that historical data for various types of risks could be accumulated, and (ii) that traditional quantitative risk management methodology could be applied to cybersecurity issues.

Specifically, behavioral science can contribute to the improvement of information sharing, including: understanding information flows through the prism of behavioral theories; modeling risk associated with information sharing; development of algorithmic solutions for information sharing rooted in behavioral science models. It can also provide *behavioral segmentation* tools to solving information-sharing problems. Behavioral segmentation, in particular, is a simple approach used to group individuals or organizations according to a menu of common behavioral characteristics into "types" and then use these "types" to (i) predict, (ii) understand, and (iii) influence a wide range of behavioral outcomes. Behavioral segmentation can contribute to optimizing information-sharing behavior in business-to-consumer; within business; as well as business-to-business and business-to-regulator layers in the following ways.

Table 7.1 Behavioral segments of population according to CybeDoSpeRT in the USA and the UK as elicited by Kharlamov et al. (2018a) [6]

Behavioral type	Country	
	USA (%)	UK (%)
Relaxed	29	16
Anxious	34	45
Opportunistic	12	17
Ignorant	25	23

Behavioral segmentation for business-to-consumer information sharing: In 2018, a team of behavioral scientists proposed a Cyber Domain-Specific Risk-Taking (CyberDoSpeRT) instrument in order to measure individual risk attitudes in cyber spaces [6]. This instrument consists of 30 activities split into five domains (Security, Personal Data, Privacy, Negligence, and Cybercrime) which may or may not result in potential harm to an individual. For example, "*Using the same password on multiple devices/websites*" is one of CyberDoSpeRT activities within the Negligence domain. The instrument then allows us to elicit Risk-Taking (how likely an individual is to engage in a risky activity) as well as Risk Perception (how risky an individual thinks a particular activity is) on a scale from 1 (not at all likely/not at all risky) to 7 (extremely likely/extremely risky). By totaling up all Risk-Taking and Risk Perception scores and mapping Risk-Taking against Risk Perception for each individual, the instrument allows us to understand the Cyber Risk Attitude of a particular individual. Furthermore, it allows us to divide the population into four types: Relaxed (people who underestimate cybersecurity risks and often engage in risky activities); Anxious (people who overestimate cybersecurity risks and avoid engaging in risky activities); Opportunistic (people who understand cybersecurity risks but still engage in risky activities); and Ignorant (people who underestimate cybersecurity risks but rarely engage in risky activities) [6]. the results of this research (see Table 7.1) show that the British population is characterized by the prevalence of Anxious types (45%), while the US population has almost equal percentages of Anxious (34%) and Relaxed (29%) types, both forming about a third of the US population, followed by Ignorant types (25%).

CyberDoSpeRT suggests that consumers are likely to be of different types when it comes to cybersecurity risk attitudes. Since consumers of different types comprehend and process information about cybersecurity risks in different ways, we need to design different campaigns for each group instead of using the same campaign for all groups.

Our research also shows that heavy cybersecurity regulation as well as excessive information do not solve the problem as both measures make people more risk-taking in cyber space. Specifically, the Chinese population has predominantly Opportunistic types due to the high level of cybersecurity regulation in the country [7]. Equally, large UK companies who create an overflow of cybersecurity information for their customers create a false sense of security and overconfidence, increasing the percentage of Opportunistic types in their customer base [7]. This tells us that providing too much information about cybersecurity risks is just as damaging as providing no information at all. Our ongoing work in this area is currently looking at how these types are associated with other observable behavior (e.g., social media behavior, spending behavior, etc.)

Behavioral segmentation for within business information sharing: Combining CyberDoSpeRT behavioral type information (e.g., Opportunistic, Ignorant, Relaxed, Anxious) with organizational role information (CEO, board member, manager, employee, etc.) and designing targeted information campaigns and information exchange mechanisms can also significantly decrease human-centered risks within organizations. In other words, behavioral segmentation for information sharing within organizations allows us to (i) measure the cyber risk attitudes of people within different layers of the organization and model their types; (ii) based on the obtained topology, algorithmically model human-centered vulnerabilities and risks; and (iii) propose solutions based on (i) and (ii).

Behavioral segmentation for business-to-business and business-to-regulator information sharing: Behavioral segmentation is also valuable for business-to-business and business-to-regulator information sharing. Even though modeling informational exchanges between businesses and, more generally, between organizations is more complex than looking at individuals and their behavior in cyberspace, the behavioral segmentation approach allows us to identify how the actual risks which organizations are facing in cyberspace are mapped onto how these risks are perceived by the key decision-makers in the organizations. Highlighting the mismatch between the two creates opportunities for alleviating or even significantly diminishing many existing barriers for information sharing. In order to obtain the behavioral profile of a particular organization, the following components are taken into account: (i) the underlying business modeling approach (understanding the value creation, value proposition, and value capture of a particular organization); (ii) the underlying organizational structure (horizontal or hierarchical, etc.); (iii) the mapping of cybersecurity risks onto the underlying business modeling approach (understanding how various cyber-security risks can damage the value creation, value proposition, and value capture of a particular organization); (iv) comparing where current efforts and investment are concentrated with where they should be concentrated. For a group of businesses, the behavioral segmentation approach allows us to measure and highlight (a) the cyber risks and vulnerabilities which businesses *perceive* to be important versus (b) the cyber risks and vulnerabilities which businesses *are* most likely to suffer from based on (i), (ii), and (iii). By highlighting the inconsistencies between the two measures and finding the overlap in these inconsistencies for a range of businesses (i.e., concrete-use cases where information sharing benefits the business models of all partic-ipating parties), we can show how the benefits of information sharing can outweigh the barriers.

In later chapters we will offer an algorithmic example of how a mul-ti-attribute model rooted in behavioral science could work in practice. We will also discuss further how cybersecurity risk assessment can be under-stood within the frame of the underlying business model of a particular organization.

References

1. Aviram, A., & Tor, A. (2003). Overcoming impediments to information sharing. *Alabama Law Review, 55*, 231.
2. Dressler, J., Bowen, C. L., Moody, W., & Koepke, J. (2014). Operational data classes for establishing situational awareness in cyberspace. In *2014 6th International Conference on Cyber Conflict (CyCon 2014)*, (pp. 175–186). IEEE.
3. Koepke, P. (2017). *Cybersecurity information sharing incentives and barriers* (MIT, Working Paper CISL# 2017-13). http://web.mit.edu/smadnick/www/wp/2017-13.pdf.
4. Kadobayashi, Y. (2010). Cybersecurity information exchange framework. *Computer Communication Review, 40*(5), 59–64.
5. Cooper, P. (2016). *Cognitive active cyber defence: Finding value through hacking human nature* (MSc dissertation). Cranfield University.
6. Kharlamov, A., Jaiswal, A., Parry, G., & Pogrebna, G. (2018a). *A cyber domain-specific risk attitudes scale to address security issues in the digital space* (British Academy of Management Award-Winning Paper). https://bit.ly/2P9o990.
7. Kharlamov, A., Jaiswal, A., Parry, G., & Pogrebna, G. (2018b). *Heavy regulation and excessive information about cybersecurity makes people risk taking in cyberspace* (Alan Turing Institute Working Paper).

Part III

Future Threats and Solutions

Part II

8

Future Threats

When talking about the new frontier of human culture and creativity in the twenty-first century, the major art innovator, film director, and script writer Rustam Khamdamov once made a point about the fact that we now live in the era of "*stylists*" rather than "*inventors*". Describing creative industries of the future, he said that "*nowadays, if you have a style, you can get away with a lot*".[1] By this he meant that in the modern creative landscape, we often observe citations of what has already been written, things that have already been said, plots that have already been used, melodies that have already been composed. According to Khamdamov, in the current creative landscape, it does not matter "what" you do, but "how" you do it. He maintained: "*No one cares about content anymore. Today style is the key. Are you writing a book? Think of "how" you will be writing it. In the end, all possible subjects or what's have already been investigated and researched, and there is nothing new left to be explored for humanity except for maybe something in outer space and other galaxies. All the plots we have come from either biographies or from Shakespeare. They are all quoted from here and there but we are keen to know "how" these plots should be translated into books, movies, art, creativity in general. And when we know "how", we become stylists.*"

In the previous chapters, we have shown that many adversaries excel in creativity and, much like many creative industries, cybercrime suffers from the same deficiency. As we saw earlier in this book, the majority of contemporary cyberattacks use tools, methods, and sometimes even code which

---

[1] See https://seance.ru/blog/diamonds/ for the complete interview.

© The Author(s) 2019
G. Pogrebna and M. Skilton, *Navigating New Cyber Risks*,
https://doi.org/10.1007/978-3-030-13527-0_8

has existed since the 1960s, 1970s, 1980s, or 1990s. So, what we seem to observe today are citations of previously invented methods. Yet, new successful attacks are nothing more and nothing less than "talented" or "stylish" citations which represent a creative mix of tools and tricks used in the past.

When we look at the evolution of the fashion industry from the twentieth to the twenty-first century, we can clearly identify fashion trends from the 1920s to the early 1990s. For example, what was "in vogue" in the 1960s in terms of clothes, hairstyles, cars, etc. was drastically different from the fashion of, say, the 1980s. But from the late 1990s, all the way into the 2000s and 2010s, we see many couturiers and fashion designers simply offering a stylish and creative mix or "fusion" of previously invented fashion. In the twentieth century, it would be impossible for Brigitte Bardot and Madonna to be fashion icons at the same time, yet it is perfectly possible in the twenty-first century.

Similarly, it would be hard to imagine ransomware and phishing coexisting in the same attack 20–25 years ago, yet these two methods seem to work in tandem in many cyberattacks of the present. Therefore, what we see today is essentially the rise of an era of "stylists" and "fusion specialists" in cybercrime. Instead of carrying out the attacks locally and from one PC, adversaries now develop stylized versions of the same attack using botnets, or even employing AI. While the adversaries of the past used primarily one method to execute the attack, cybercriminals of the present have mastered the art of fusion and manage to "mix and match" various threats into different types of attacks. This trend towards "stylized" and "fusion" attacks is likely to continue as it offers cybercriminals multiple if not an endless pot of ideas and possibilities.

So, what is the new frontier of cyberthreats? It would seem that next-generation cyberthreats are likely to have the following characteristics:

Stylized Fusion Attacks

It is clear now that stylized fusion attacks will be on the rise. Moreover, in the next few years we are likely to see more and more creative fusion mixes, along with the further creative "styling" of the attacks. Instead of observing a single and isolated technique, we will also see more and more multilayered techniques which will not only combine various threats in the same attack, but also use a set of means to creatively combine these attacks into waves, where one wave will target one set of potential vulnerabilities, while the other will target a different set. Since a wide range of tools will be available to cybercriminals of the future, they will be able to combine these tools into creative citations of previously used techniques.

Social Engineering Attacks

Social engineering will continue to be one of the main components of a cyberattack and we are likely to see social engineering tools becoming more and more sophisticated. Instead of phishing attacks, we will see more spear phishing as cybercriminals become progressively more sophisticated in compromising systems, obtaining personal information, and pretending to be acting as sources trusted by the user. What many of us do not realize is that through social media we regularly give away a lot of valuable facts about ourselves. By looking at your Facebook, Twitter, Instagram, LinkedIn, etc. accounts in separation or combined, one can gain access to important information. This information, if harvested, can open many doors for cybercriminals and it is highly likely that adversaries will make more efficient use of social media in the future.

AI-Driven Attacks

The future will offer new possibilities for higher levels of automation when planning and instigating cyberattacks. Hijacked devices, bots, and botnets already create many opportunities for cybercriminals, who now can execute large-scale global operations using the minimum of human resources. Today, we can safely assume that technological solutions available to companies and law enforcement agencies are also available to cybercriminals. In a world where any teenager can go online and get precise instructions about how to execute a cyberattack in a matter of seconds, sophisticated technology can be used by different types of adversaries. We have already discussed in previous chapters how AI can be used to create "smart honeypots"—creative "traps" in the computer systems of businesses. Yet, the problem is that cybercriminals also have access to the same technology and, equally, adversaries are already using AI to predict which machines act as honeypots. Basically, we are operating in a world where both sides are very smart and there is no such thing as technological advantage as new technology becomes available to everyone quickly.

In the future, AI-driven attacks are likely to become mainstream. Apart from traditional AI-driven means such as botnets, honeypot detection, voice imitation, etc., we will see the use of AI for social engineering. In the school year 2015/2016, a Georgia Tech professor, Ashok Goel, designed a chatbot teaching assistant to take the message–answering load off his team.[2] Professor Goel noticed that his teaching team received over 10,000 online messages from students per semester. Since the overwhelming majority of questions were repetitive, they could be classified into "types", and a typical response was generated for each type of question. These typical questions and answers were fed into the AI algorithm powered by the IBM Watson technology and a chatbot teaching assistant "Jill Watson" was born. The coolest part of this story is that a computer science class had been asking Jill questions on a regular basis for six months before some students got suspicious. The suspicions eventually grew due to the systematic referral of more complex questions to human teaching assistants and due to the fact that Jill was answering questions 24 hours a day 7 days a week. Yet, the overwhelming majority of students learned about the bot from the newspapers and other media. Now, this innovative piece of technology which saved a team of academics many human hours of work can be potentially harnessed for evil purposes and used as a tool to trick people.

To date, the majority of social engineering attacks (such as phishing campaigns) have been executed by human operators. Yet, imagine if all victims' questions and communications could be collected, analyzed, and classified into "typical" queries. Then a set of most common responses could be used to create replies and cybercriminals may, in principle, "design" or "recruit" an army of AI chatbots to instigate social engineering attacks. These attacks may use email, messaging, and even telephone (voice) communication.

AI-driven chatbot attacks will happen in the future. Yet, it would be wrong to argue that such attacks will not have an antidote. Think of our example of "Jill Watson": Jill succeeded for so long because students *did not expect* to be talking to a bot. Equally, recent Google experiments which show that people cannot recognize the chatbot personal assistant making appointments for a human only work because humans do not have much experience in talking to an AI chatbot and *do not expect* to find a chatbot on the other end of the telephone line [1–3]. But as technology evolves, so will humans. We will adapt to recognize chatbots and will be able to develop behaviors to test whether we are talking to

---

[2]See https://www.washingtonpost.com/news/innovations/wp/2016/05/11/this-professor-stunned-his-students-when-he-revealed-the-secret-identity-of-his-teaching-assistant/?utm_term=.2ed1f85347e6 for more detail.

one because we will have updated our expectations. It is only a matter of time. Yet, we need to make sure that we learn and adapt quickly so that adversaries will not have an opportunity to cash in on our lack of experience earlier.

Inception Attacks

Even if you have never heard the name Maurits Cornelis Escher, you most probably know his work. Escher was a graphic visionary and artist from the Netherlands whose creative work was inspired by mathematical concepts. Long neglected by the artistic community, Escher only became known in his seventies. Throughout his career, he created a large number of geometrically paradoxical drawings. Two of these drawings—"Relativity", created in 1953, and "Ascending and Descending", drawn in 1960—are probably Escher's most famous works. Both of these drawings show an "impossible staircase". Escher started to grapple with these ideas in the early 1950s and then discovered the work of father and son scientists Lionel and Roger Penrose, who published a paper in 1958, where they described the "continuous staircase" based on the "Penrose triangle" [4]. The main idea behind the staircase was that it depicted an ascending and descending flight of steps making four continuous 90° turns in a two-dimensional space, such that a person who tried to climb the stairs would do so for ever without getting any higher. The paper provided inspiration for Escher's "Ascending and Descending". It also gave rise to many philosophical ideas and theories of multidimensionality, and even the existence of "parallel" universes and worlds, which was later echoed in popular culture (think, for example, of Christopher Nolan's *Inception* [2010] or the *Fringe* TV series [2008–2013] created by J. J. Abrams, Alex Kurtzman, and Roberto Orci).

One of the main characteristics of the "impossible staircase" is that every individual flight of stairs is possible or "correct", while the system of flights as a whole is impossible or "wrong". This feature is becoming more and more of a characteristic of the modern cyberattacks. We have already started to observe "inception attacks"—i.e., attacks where each individual part of the cybercriminal connection system seems completely legitimate, and yet the system as a whole is criminal and serving the interest of adversaries. The detection of such systems is extremely complicated and often requires the deployment of significant resources and sophisticated expertise. The main issue is that collecting forensic evidence about cybercriminals running such systems is currently next to impossible, even when cyber police units and other agencies understand the business models and actors behind them.

Only if one goes through each connection and proves that (i) the connection actually exists and that (ii) the connection which seems completely "legit" is actually part of a larger illegal system can we talk about the potential attribution of such attacks to a specific set of individual or group adversaries. In the future, we are likely to see more and more such inception systems being developed by the adversaries. The main difficulty in spotting and uncovering such attacks would be the difficulty in tracing and tracking the entire ecosystem and business model of cybercriminals as each node of the ecosystem will seem "normal", while the system as a whole will serve a criminal goal.

Attacks on Physical Systems and Human Well-Being

Another trend which we are likely to observe in the future is the shift in cyberattacks from targeting purely digital to targeting physical or cyber-physical systems. We already live in a world which offers opportunities to control important infrastructure within cities, plants, hospitals, etc., remotely. And if something can be controlled remotely, it can also be disrupted, hijacked, and sabotaged remotely. Therefore, in the future, we would need to learn how to better defend physical infrastructure within cities and organizations from cyberthreats.

Equally, we would need to understand how to better defend our own well-being. Considering that many devices for enhancing well-being are already battery-powered and remote-controlled, there is a high chance that those devices might be susceptible to a large number of cyber threats. Imagine that someone can temper with an implantable cardioverter defibrillator or artificial pacemaker of an individual in order to either remotely disrupt its function or make it look "as if" the heart is not working properly … Unfortunately, modern health-related devices are really vulnerable to such threats and could be exploited by adversaries for ransom or other criminal benefits.

Quantum Computing Attacks

It is clear that in the distant future, cybercriminals may also get their hands on quantum computing techniques. This may lead to us potentially facing sophisticated quantum machine systems which would act in an autonomous way, in the sense that their targets will be set by cybercriminals and, yet, every particular sub-step to reach the criminal targets will be machine-generated. While we do not want to expand on this issue, it is important to mention that the crucial part of winning the quantum games against cybercriminals would be to ensure that we, as a society, meet the quantum threats with an adequate set of quantum counter-responses when the time comes.

Traditional Cybercrime

"Traditional" cybercrime types are also here to stay. Two issues which we expect to remain in the future (among many others) are (i) the use of social media to implement the attacks, as well as (ii) business email compromise. Specifically, adversaries are likely to continue to use social media in order to apply social engineering techniques (described earlier in this book) and trick people into giving away sensitive information. Equally, compromising business email systems using methods, which we described in Chapter 2, will remain widespread. Importantly, problems like (i) and (ii), as well as many other cybersecurity issues, are not addressed well by many nation-states, businesses, and individuals. This happens primarily because individuals, organizations, as well as policy-makers often believe that cybercrimes are related to technical rather than behavioral problems.

References

1. Druga, S., Williams, R., Breazeal, C., & Resnick, M. (2017, June). Hey Google is it OK if I eat you? Initial explorations in child-agent interaction. In *Proceedings of the 2017 Conference on Interaction Design and Children* (pp. 595–600). ACM.
2. Augello, A., Gentile, M., Weideveld, L., & Dignum, F. (2016). A model of a social chatbot. In *Intelligent Interactive Multimedia Systems and Services 2016* (pp. 637–647). Cham: Springer.
3. Janarthanam, S. (2017). *Hands-on chatbots and conversational UI development: Build chatbots and voice user interfaces with Chatfuel, Dialogflow, Microsoft Bot Framework, Twilio, and Alexa Skills*. Birmingham: Packt.
4. Penrose, L. S., & Penrose, R. (1958). Impossible objects: A special type of visual illusion. *British Journal of Psychology, 49,* 31–33. https://doi.org/10.1111/j.2044-8295.1958.tb00634.x (PMID: 13536303).

9

Future Solutions

In earlier chapters, we have talked about three types of solutions encompassed in the Canvas, Technology-driven, and Human-centered approaches. It is, therefore, logical to suspect that, in the future, all three types of approaches will coexist.

Canvas Solutions of the Future

Considering the fact that future threats will become more and more complex, solutions also have to be complex and multi-layered. Let us for a second imagine what a "possible" idealized cybersecurity architecture of the future might look like.

Figure 9.1 represents the three layers of organization structure: Strategic, Tactical, and Operational. While access protocols may differ for various organizations, generally one can think of the Strategic layer as being accessible to a limited number of people in the organization (e.g., business owners, key decision-makers, board members, top managers, etc.). The Private layer is accessible to all members of organization (e.g., employees, managers, etc.) but not to the outside world. The Public layer is available to a wide number of users (including customers, partner organizations, as well as the general public).

These layers are overlaid with three types of front-ends: Closed, Private, and Public interfaces. Each interface has its own network and is separated from other interfaces by firewalls. In turn, layers within each interface are

© The Author(s) 2019
G. Pogrebna and M. Skilton, *Navigating New Cyber Risks*,
https://doi.org/10.1007/978-3-030-13527-0_9

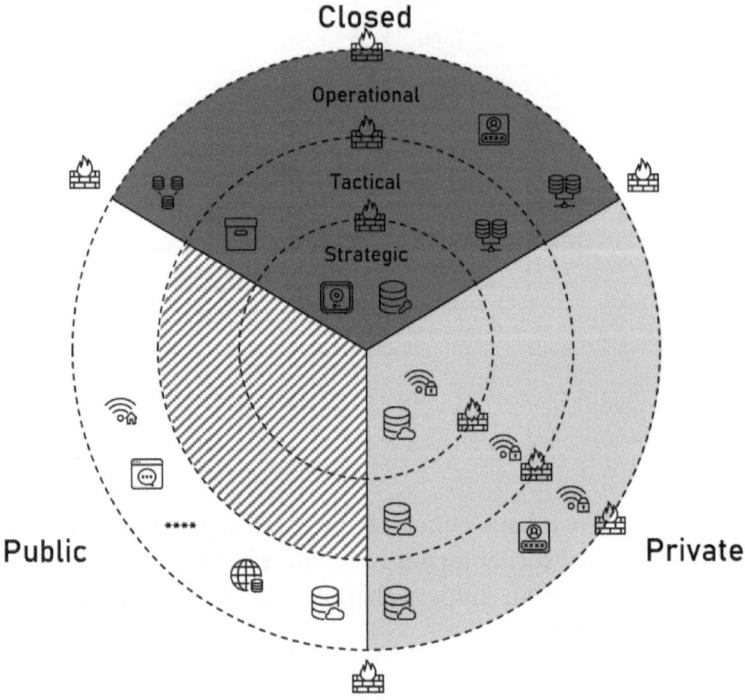

Fig. 9.1 Architecture of an idealized system

separated by secondary firewalls in order to keep the organization functioning and avoid vulnerabilities that come from the usual challenge of keeping the operational level secure due to the large number of interacting parties and agents.

The Closed interface is the most important and keeps the organization functioning at its core even if the Public and Private interfaces fall victim to cybercriminals. Relating to our previous discussion, a Closed interface is where all essential digital valuables of the organization (imperative to its survival) should be kept. This level holds the essential databases for the operational, tactical, and strategic decisions respectively. Its databases are local and some high-value data is stored physically (in vaults) without any network connection (not even ethernet) on solid-state drives or other secure medium (this data can even be paper-based). A Closed interface implies that Wi-Fi networks are forbidden. Interaction with the strategic levels must be physical since physical breaches of buildings are much harder than digital ones.

The Private interface is the one that keeps the organization running and is the largest of the three as it communicates with the management and information systems of the company, e.g., Enterprise Resource Planning (ERP) systems. This level can be the keeper of important and meaningful digital valuables and rely on cloud-based services as well as data storage to allow agility, resilience, and efficiency. Compromising the Private interface is a potential problem but it is not critical and is unlikely to have catastrophic effects for the entire organization. The focus is on traceability, rapid detection, recovery, and overall resilience. An echelon (layered) structure and firewalls ensure that breaches are contained and slow down the attack progress allowing time for countermeasures.

The Public interface does not include any Strategic or Tactical layers. It only has an Operational layer. Therefore, only secondary digital valuables could be kept within the Public interface. Its main purpose is to communicate with the public, allowing user accounts, cloud-based storage, and other web services. The focus in case of security failure is on rapid detection and recovery. The assumption is that it is not a matter of *whether* it is going to be hacked or not (the assumption is that it will be), but *when*.

The Strategic layer inside the Closed interface should be physically disconnected from the rest of the organization. The assumption is that if the Strategic Closed network is somehow connected to any other network, then it is vulnerable. Therefore, communication with this network must be restricted and controlled; any terminals able to access this network must be respectively set up, preventing any data being offloaded or uploaded without control (e.g., all USB ports should be cemented); any mobile phones or other smart devices should be removed on entry.

This, of course, is just one example of an "ideal" architecture. It may or may not fit the needs of all organizations, yet it provides a general guideline for a set of organizations operating across three layers and holding different types of digital valuables.

Note that while Fig. 9.1 may appear to summarize a possible architecture for *perimeterized* cyberdefense systems, it can easily be applied to *de-peremiterized* systems.[1] Specifically, while many cybersecurity systems are built relative to the definition of certain security perimeters (for example, internal and external systems), a security perimeter does not necessarily represent a physical or digital boundary. It could be defined in terms of the policy

---

[1]This aspect of the architecture presented in Fig. 9.1 was highlighted to us by Boris Taratine.

enforcement mechanism which is applied to different segments of the security system (e.g., in terms of layered verification and validation segments). For example, many contemporary cyberdefense systems are designed based on the so-called "zero-trust" logic. This logic has "never trust, always verify" principle at its core. In other words, instead of assuming that users located within a certain perimeter can be trusted, "zero-trust" systems abolish perimeters and assume that no one can be trusted. Such systems apply continuous verification and validation to all users. Note, that our proposed architecture can be easily adapted to "zero-trust" systems by replacing firewalls on Fig. 9.1 with verification and validation segments. Our suggested architecture adds an one more aspect to the way "zero-trust" systems could work: we propose to apply multi-layered instead of single-layered verification tools to system users. It is important to mention here that the internal logic of the "zero-trust" concept is not always entirely clear (as suggested, for example, by Boris Taratine in his recent article on the "zero-trust paradox") [1]. Yet, the conceptual architecture described on Fig. 9.1 allows us to avoid this paradox [1].

Future Technology-Driven Solutions

Now let us turn to the technological solutions of the future. Can you imagine the gap between theoretical and empirical physics? While theoretical physics already offers us "The Theory of Everything" as well as theorizes about a world full of strings and quantum constructs, empirical physics is so far behind that we won't be able to find out whether theoretical physicists are right or wrong for many decades, if not for many hundreds of years. Well, the gap between theoretical literature on cybersecurity and practice is currently almost the same as the gap between theoretical and empirical physics. However, in the future, this gap will decrease and we should be able to put many of the existing theoretical concepts to the test. Below, we discuss only a handful of such methods, each of which is equally exciting.

Scenario testing: Scenario-testing methodology implies that many organizations will reach a level of maturity which would allow them to simulate different attacks in order to understand the set of consequences which these attacks may bring. This would allow various businesses to collect simulated rather than historical data, which could then be entered into the risk assessment and risk management algorithms. To some extent, the trend towards these solutions is already observed in some industries where ethical (white-hat) hackers are recruited to explore companies' zero-day vulnerabilities.

Terraforming cyberspace: Terraforming cyberspace techniques [2] essentially represent next-generation zero-trust systems. It is implied that such systems would allow bullet-proof zero-trust networks where human errors or abuse of trust will be virtually impossible. It is envisioned that such systems will be fueled by artificial intelligence (AI) or even quantum computing. The way in which this methodology works is effectively to remove all possible human-related risks to the system. While the proponents of the terraforming methodology often comment on its efficiency, it is hard to imagine cyber systems not requiring any human input whatsoever, though it will be exciting to watch this space in the next few years.

Cryptography of the future: Theoretical cryptography has already progressed way ahead of practice, where the limitations lie in the lack of computing power and speed of encryption. Yet, with the development of new technologies, the border between theoretical and practical cryptography will eventually become obsolete. In that regard, we might be able to observe serious breakthroughs in such tools as password managers, which will become more efficient and more difficult to "break".

Zero-knowledge proofs: It is envisioned that zero-knowledge proofs—defined as "*a method by which one party (the prover) can prove to another party (the verifier) that something is true, without revealing any information apart from the fact that this specific statement is true*"—will become one of the new standards [3]. If successfully implemented, zero-knowledge proofs [4–7] will be particularly useful for ensuring human rights protection as well as privacy assurances in digital spaces of the future.

Mobile targets: Think of the way in which the US presidential security detail protects the president in case of an attack. The adopted practice is that the president should be put on a plane and his location remain uncertain and dynamic. While moving databases is, of course, costly and counterproductive, making digital valuables mobile could be beneficial and could be achieved in ways other than actually moving the data. For example, in the case of an attack where data is the target, adversaries would require not only the data itself but also the toolboxes which index the data. By making indexing mobile in the case of a suspected system compromise, it is possible to significantly complicate the job of cybercriminals.

Algorithmic active cyberdefense: Algorithmic ACD already talks about ways in which, in addition to smart honeypots, smart mazes could be designed to lure and capture adversaries. In the future, we will see more and more such systems being implemented in practice. The traps will become more sophisticated and algorithms will be more effective in capturing, diagnosing, and even predicting potential threats.

Future Human-Centered Solutions

Human-centered solutions of the future could be split into Defensive and Offensive. And within each category, we can identify quantitative and qualitative methods:

- Defensive quantitative methods include behavioral segmentation for organizations and individuals; ambiguity and uncertainty estimations; and cost–benefit analysis of human-related vulnerabilities.
- Defensive qualitative methods consist of cybersecurity hygiene methodologies.
- Offensive quantitative methods incorporate behaviorally layered active cyberdefense (ACD) mechanisms; creation of fake digital personas (chatbots) to distract cybercriminals, etc.
- Offensive qualitative methods include creativity through non-technical consultations.

Behavioral segmentation for organizations and individuals: Current behavioral science techniques allow us to segment individuals in terms of their risk perceptions and risk attitudes in cyberspace (e.g., using the CyberDoSpeRT technique described in Chapter 7). Using these segmentations, risk in the system can be anticipated and modeled using the proportions of different types in the population and making inferences about the way in which these types of individuals learn. This, in turn, could be used to design policies and measures to tackle cybersecurity risks. By treating cybersecurity as a behavioral science, new methods of risk assessment can shed light on unknown or ambiguous events.

To give a specific example, assume that using a behavioral instrument (e.g., CyberDoSpeRT), you were able to classify your customers into four behavioral types x_i, where $i \in (R, A, I, O)$: either Relaxed (x_R), Anxious (x_A), Ignorant (x_I), or Opportunistic (x_O). Since the total percentage of the customers should add up to 100%, we can safely assume that $\sum x_i = 1$. Since each behavioral type has a unique profile with regard to N potentially risky cyber activities, it is possible to obtain a relative ranking of all activities A_j, where $j \in [1, N]$, in terms of risk-taking by behavioral type $(A_j | x_i)$. Since each activity is linked to compromising a particular set of digital valuables associated with a set of related costs, it is then easy to define probability and cost correspondence for each type x_i, where for each activity one can identify probability p_j of a particular cyber risk materializing (calculated as normalized relative ranking $A_j | x_i$) relative to potential cost c_j associated with this risk. Therefore, for each x_i, you can calculate both $\alpha | x_i = \sum_{j=1}^{N} p_j \cdot c_j$ as well as identify $\beta | x_i = \max_{1 \leq j \leq N} p_j \cdot c_j$. The weighted sum of costs by behavioral type $(\alpha | x_i)$ will allow you to understand which type is most and least costly in your customer population, and coefficient $\beta | x_i$ will help you determine within each behavioral type a customer activity which poses a major risk to your business. That way, you will be able to determine how to structure a multilayered social marketing campaign in order to (i) change the relative shares of different behavioral types in your customer population, as well as (ii) to target specific costly customer behaviors.

Ambiguity and uncertainty modeling: Another option to consider is that we normally think of risk measures as some discrete values (probability, chance, etc.) But there is no reason why these measures should be discrete. For example, we have ambiguity/uncertainty models and models of stochastic choice in decision science which allow us to obtain, for example, interval measures, distribution measures, or vector measures of probability. These measures might be more informative. Specifically, if you know that a probability of a particular event is between 45 and 60%, that might be still helpful. The difficulty is that we need good communication tools to translate these theoretical measures into practical methods to make sure that they are actually informative and helpful to those working in the field.

Even though there are multiple different methods in which ambiguity could be mathematized, one of the easiest approaches (a linear model) was proposed by Daniel Ellsberg in 1961. This approach is based on the concept of Knightian uncertainty [8], which implies that in the absence of information about precise probability distribution over events, individuals form subjective beliefs about those probabilities. Ellsberg argued that these subjective beliefs instead of the actual probabilities enter into a decision-making process and could be used to calculate optimal responses [9].

Let us consider the following example. As we saw from the previous chapters, a business should be able to identify a set of digital valuables which might be of interest to adversaries and rank these valuables according to their importance to the business' survival as essential, important, meaningful, and secondary. This ranking, in turn, will help a business formulate ρ—some degree of confidence over a probability distribution y_0, which corresponds to all judgments of the relative probability distributions over a series of adverse events. If we then let $\min_x$ correspond to the minimum expected payoff from an action x (say, a new cybersecurity investment) when the probability distribution y_0 ranges over a set of Y_0; and we let $u(x)$ be an expected payoff for the business from the action x corresponding to the probability distribution of y_0, we have a decision rule according to which for each x, the business should maximize index φ_x:

$$\varphi_x = \rho \cdot u(x) + (1 - \rho) \cdot \min_x \tag{9.1}$$

Ellsberg offers an alternative formulation of (9.1), as Eq. (9.2):

$$\varphi_x = [\rho \cdot y_0 + (1 - \rho) \cdot y_x^{\min}](x) \tag{9.2}$$

where $y_x^{\min}$ is the probability vector in Y_0 corresponding to $\min_x$ for action x, associated with a vector of potential payoffs X [9]. This simple model illustrates how subjective probabilities can replace precise probabilities for determining optimal decision-making for cybersecurity.

Cost–benefit analysis of vulnerabilities: Behavioral science can also shed light on the costs and benefits associated with different threats by considering how various types of cybercriminal behaviors are associated with the underlying ecosystems and business models. That way, we can better predict where the cybercriminals are most likely to attack our systems or even increase the costs of attacking those systems (Fig. 9.2).

Cybersecurity hygiene: Current research in cybersecurity provides clues that different people have a different propensity to detect cybersecurity threats. We even know that that some people correctly identify the start of a potential attack correctly 100% of the time. By exploring the behavioral traits (personality traits, risk and ambiguity attitude, social preferences) of these people, we can identify psychological features which distinguish them from the rest. This will help us to design effective training programs for staff and customers in the future.

Behaviorally layered active cyber defense: One striking difference between the tricks adversaries are playing on us and the way we defend ourselves

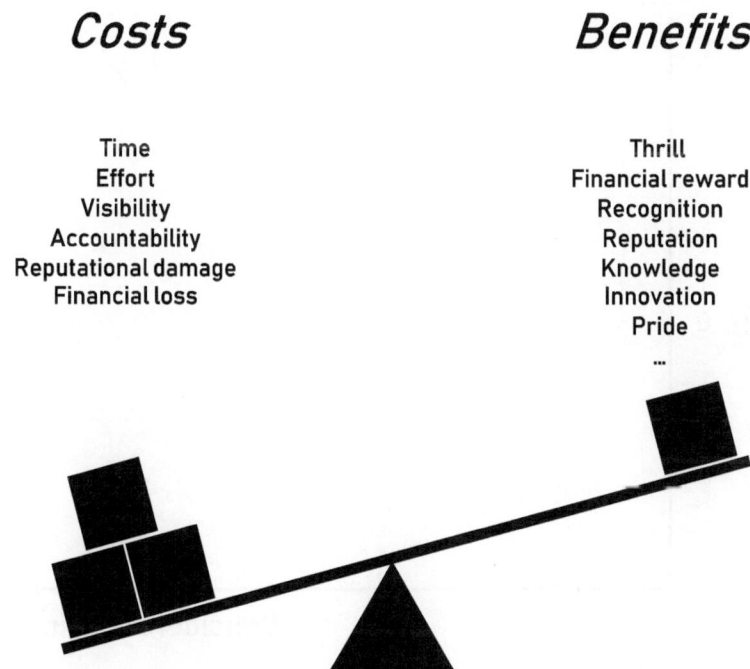

Fig. 9.2 Costs and benefits for an adversary

against cybercriminals is the fact that while they design highly personalized "services" to their victims, our defenses are built as "one-size-fits-all". By using the taxonomy of cybercriminals according to their underlying motivation (Fig. 3.2) and overlaying this taxonomy with potential business models, we can algorithmically model the propensity of each type of adversary to hit a set of organizational targets and anticipate an oncoming attack. By doing so, we can also ambush the attackers by waiting for them in the most likely places for the attack and then collecting forensic evidence in real time. Under these circumstances, recent advances in decision theory offer models like Decision Field Theory [10–12], which may be helpful in modeling adversarial behavior. Suppose the following decision problem is faced by a cybercriminal. The cybercriminal is selecting between three risk prospects (X, Y, and Z). Each prospect corresponds to a potential target within a particular business. This target is associated with a set of attributes: complexity of access, expected payoff, probability of getting caught, etc. Given potential preparation and consideration time (captured on the horizontal axis), the adversary will evaluate valences which capture the adversarial state of preference at each point in time (see Fig. 9.3). Given consideration time and random (Markov) walk, according to which different prospects might

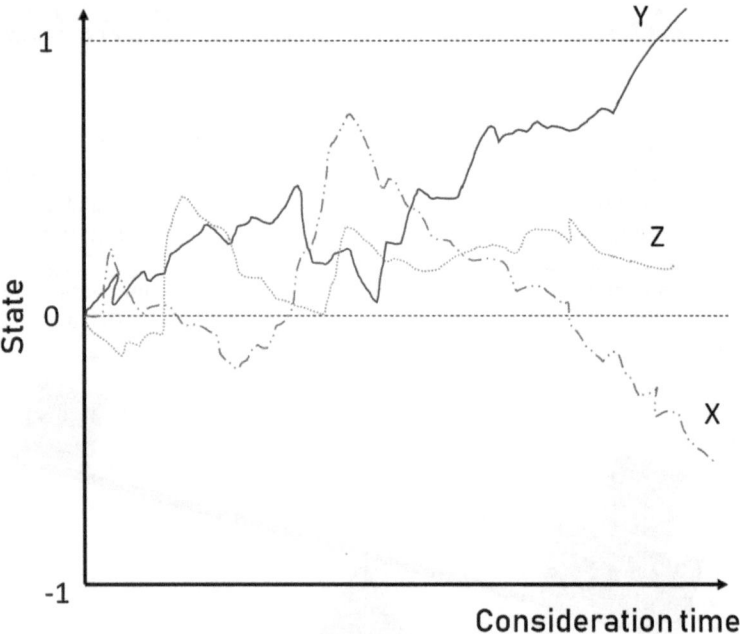

Fig. 9.3 Active cyberdefense model according to Decision Field Theory

outperform each other at different points in time, the decision to go for a particular prospect is reached when the state valence reaches a threshold of 1. In our example, prospect Y is the most attractive.

Using such a model, businesses can predict a set of prospects (targets) and form expectations about where cybercriminals are most likely to strike, creating opportunities for better defense mechanisms and evidence gathering. Note, that the model can be calibrated not only according to the different attributes of the prospects, but also according to assumptions about adversarial level of sophistication, expertise, etc.

Fake digital personas: Developments in AI already allow us to create chatbots for chatting with customers for various types of organizational tasks. We also have a number of fake digital personas present on Twitter with millions of followers. The technology which allows us to design chatbot and digital personas may also offer interesting opportunities for cybersecurity, where bots could be created to liaise with cybercriminals and prevent phishing attacks. Obviously, the same technology is available to cybercriminals. Yet, not taking advantage of this opportunity for defense purposes would be irrational.

Creativity through non-technical conversations: Obviously, the idea of having a broad conversation at different layers of organization will survive the test of the future as only with inclusive citizenship and creativity is the victory against adversaries possible.

References

1. Taratine, B. (2019). *A zero-trust paradox*. LinkedIn Article.
2. Bradshaw, J. M., Suri, N., Cañas, A. J., Davis, R., Ford, K., Hoffman, R., et al. (2001). Terraforming cyberspace. *Computer, 7*, 48–56.
3. Goldwasser, S., Micali, S., & Rackoff, C. (1989). The knowledge complexity of interactive proof systems. *SIAM Journal on Computing, 18*(1), 186–208.
4. Rackoff, C., & Simon, D. R. (1991, August). Non-interactive zero-knowledge proof of knowledge and chosen ciphertext attack. In *Annual International Cryptology Conference* (pp. 433–444). Berlin and Heidelberg: Springer.
5. Goldreich, O., Micali, S., & Wigderson, A. (1991). Proofs that yield nothing but their validity or all languages in NP have zero-knowledge proof systems. *Journal of the ACM (JACM), 38*(3), 690–728.
6. Goldreich, O., & Oren, Y. (1994). Definitions and properties of zero-knowledge proof systems. *Journal of Cryptology, 7*(1), 1–32.
7. Beaver, D. (1991). Secure multiparty protocols and zero-knowledge proof systems tolerating a faulty minority. *Journal of Cryptology, 4*(2), 75–122.
8. Knight, F. H. (1921). *Risk, uncertainty, and profit*. Boston, MA: Hart, Schaffner & Marx; Houghton Mifflin Company.
9. Ellsberg, D. (1961). Risk, ambiguity, and the Savage axioms. *The Quarterly Journal of Economics, 75*(4), 643–669.
10. Busemeyer, J. R., & Townsend, J. T. (1993). Decision Field Theory: A dynamic cognition approach to decision making. *Psychological Review, 100*, 432–459.
11. Busemeyer, J. R., & Diederich, A. (2002). Survey of Decision Field Theory. *Mathematical Social Sciences, 43*(3), 345–370.
12. Busemeyer, J. R., & Johnson, J. G. (2004). Computational models of decision making. In *Blackwell handbook of judgment and decision making* (pp. 133–154). Malden, MA: Blackwell.

10

Social and Ethical Aspects

Cybersecurity is a "social animal", in the sense that it deeply affects every facet of our digital culture [1]. In this sense, everything we do in digital spaces is directly linked to our social lives. The way we approach digital spaces is in many ways shaped by our environment. Consider, for example, such a phenomenon as privacy. Privacy in the physical and digital sense is perceived differently by the humans.

There are interesting works of modern art displayed on the walls of buildings in the London's Soho area. They form one "installation" dealing with the drawbacks of the "surveillance economy". Shaped as human noses, they were created by the artist Rick Buckley in 1997. The installation appeared on houses in Soho after the City of London installed surveillance cameras around the area. Rick Buckley wanted to show by this installation that the invasion into human privacy with 24-hour surveillance cameras is unacceptable. It is one of the most cherished and supported works of modern art in contemporary London.

Let us think about this for a moment—on the one hand, we seem to care about physical surveillance, yet digital surveillance does not appear to bother us quite so much. While we might be extremely sensitive about our pictures being taken in the street, we are willingly posting rather personal pictures on a wide variety of social networks such as Twitter, Facebook, and Instagram. Despite caring about personal privacy, social network site users may be motivated to disclose personal information as part of self-promotion, but it is suggested that online self-promotion behaviors and online vulnerability are linked [2]. For example, frequent use of social network sites has been associated with many vulnerabilities, including incidents of data misuse, online harassment, and exposure to inappropriate content [3–5].

© The Author(s) 2019
G. Pogrebna and M. Skilton, *Navigating New Cyber Risks*,
https://doi.org/10.1007/978-3-030-13527-0_10

Despite the potential risk, people continue to disclose considerable amounts of information on public social networks. The frequent use of social network sites is usually linked with such behavioral phenomenon as the *fear of missing out*. This fear is a "*pervasive apprehension that others might be having rewarding experiences from which one is absent*" [6, p. 1841] and is reflected in the form of online self-promotion in the actions of friending and information disclosure. Users experiencing the fear of missing out find themselves in a state of "self-regulatory limbo", investing significant time online and building their digital identity through sharing personal data [6, p. 1842]. Research also suggests that being on social network sites does not make the person directly vulnerable [5]. Rather, vulnerability depends on *how* the user interacts with the social network sites; and the degree of vulnerability is highly dependent on practices such as self-disclosure and having a presence on many sites [6, 7].

We also observe significant cultural differences in these perceptions. For example, the amount of digital surveillance in China is vast, yet the population is willing to conform to this situation. It is expected that Singapore will enhance its video surveillance in the next few years. However, it is hard to imagine the same situation in the countries of the EU.

It is not clear whether there is a link between psychological vulnerability and online vulnerability [8]. However, if a user was subjected to a number of digital vulnerabilities, this is likely to influence their psychological well-being [9, 10]. Research also finds that increased use of social network sites is associated with greater anxiety in cyber spaces [11]. All this suggests that social interactions in the digital domain have a direct impact on how individuals perceive and think about cybersecurity.

There are also different expectations with regard to responsibility for cybersecurity-related issues which are rooted in social norms. For example, it emerged in April 2018 that Martin Lewis (the MoneySavingExpert owner) became a victim of an online fraud. Online fraudsters used his image to publish a large number of fake advertisements on Facebook. The advertisements invited people to click on links which were leading to malicious websites that stole personal and financial data from the victims, many of whom suffered financial losses. Despite multiple complaints from the victims and Martin Lewis, Facebook allegedly failed to swiftly remove the fraudulent advertisements. As a result, defamation charges were brought against Facebook by Martin Lewis and his brand. In January 2019, Lewis reached a settlement agreement with Facebook. Apart from paying Lewis's legal fees, the social media giant has agreed to make a £3 million donation to Citizens Advice towards a new UK Scams Action Project. Facebook has also pledged to develop a new scam ads reporting tool and to create a dedicated team which would monitor ad scams.

Apart from the social aspects of cybersecurity, ethical consideration became a topic for the heated debates. For example, there is a popular view that since we expect that the government should keep us safe in the physical spaces, it is also their responsibility to keep us safe in the digital space. This, however, may not be feasible. The nature of issues which we face in the cybersecurity space can only be solved co-operatively. As we saw earlier,

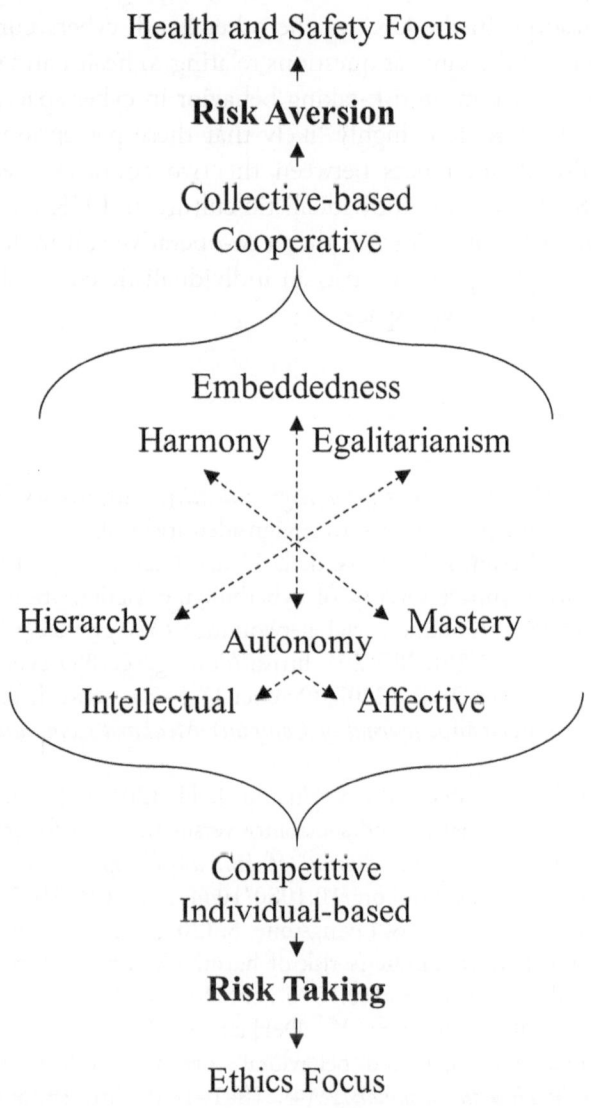

Fig. 10.1   Cybersecurity, culture, and risk attitudes

effective communication and information sharing is necessary in order for us to be able to succeed against cybercriminals. And in this sense, cybersecurity is not only a matter of public and corporate responsibility, it is also a matter of personal responsibility (Fig. 10.1).

We have conducted many cross-cultural tests and discovered that countries with different cultural systems perceive cybersecurity issues differently. For example, in the USA, people view cybersecurity issues as issues of personal ethics. In other words, for a US citizen, staying safe in digital spaces is an ethical question. In the UK, on the other hand, cybersecurity questions are perceived to be the same as questions relating to health and safety [12].

This is why we see more risk-taking behavior in cyber spaces in the USA compared to the UK. It is highly likely that these perceptions are directly related to cultural differences between the two countries (see Fig. 10.1), where the USA has a more individualistic culture and UK has more co-operative culture [12]. Our hunch is that a co-operative culture leads to higher risk aversion in cyberspace, whereas an individualistic culture leads to more risk-taking behavior in cyberspace.

References

1. Allen, C. *The path to self-sovereign identity.* http://www.lifewithalacrity. com/2016/04/the-path-to-self-soverereign-identity.html.
2. Dredge, R., Gleeson, J. F. M., & de la Piedad Garcia, X. (2014). Risk factors associated with impact severity of cyberbullying victimization: A qualitative study of adolescent online social networking. *Cyberpsychology, Behavior, and Social Networking, 17*(5), 287–291. https://doi.org/10.1089/cyber.2013.0541.
3. Boyd, D., & Ellison, N. B. (2007, October 1). Social network sites: Definition, history, and scholarship. *Journal of Computer-Mediated Communication, 13*(1), 210–230.
4. Brandtzæg, P. B., Lüders, M., & Skjetne, J. H. (2010). Too many Facebook "friends"? Content sharing and sociability versus the need for privacy in social network sites. *International Journal of Human–Computer Interaction, 26*(11–12), 1006–1030. https://doi.org/10.1080/10447318.2010.516719.
5. Staksrud, E., ILafsson, K., & Livingstone, S. (2013). Does the use of social networking sites increase children's risk of harm? *Computers in Human Behavior, 29*(1), 40–50. https://doi.org/10.1016/j.chb.2012.05.026.
6. Przybylski, A. K., Murayama, K., DeHaan, C. R., & Gladwell, V. (2013). Motivational, emotional, and behavioral correlates of fear of missing out. *Computers in Human Behavior, 29*(4), 1841–1848. https://doi.org/10.1016/j. chb.2013.02.014.

7. Buglass, S. L., Binder, J. F., Betts, L. R., & Underwood, J. D. M. (2016). When 'friends' collide: Social heterogeneity and user vulnerability on social network sites. *Computers in Human Behavior, 54*, 62–72. https://doi.org/10.1016/j.chb.2015.07.039.

8. Livingstone, S., & Smith, P. K. (2014). Annual research review: Harms experienced by child users of online and mobile technologies: The nature, prevalence and management of sexual and aggressive risks in the digital age. *Journal of Child Psychology and Psychiatry, 55*(6), 635–654.

9. Hawdon, J., Oksanen, A., & Räsänen, P. (2015). Online extremism and online hate: Exposure among adolescents and young adults in four nations. *Nordicom Information, 37*(3–4), 29–37.

10. Patchin, J. W., & Hinduja, S. (2010). Cyberbullying and self-esteem. *Journal of School Health, 80*(12), 614–621.

11. Buglass, S. L., Binder, J. F., Betts, L. R., & Underwood, J. D. M. (2017). Motivators of online vulnerability: The impact of social network site use and FOMO. *Computers in Human Behavior, 66*, 248–255.

12. Kharlamov, A., & Pogrebna, G. (2018). *Using human values-based approach to understand cross-cultural commitment towards regulation and governance of cybersecurity* (Working Paper).

Part IV

Cybersecurity: The New Frontier

11

The Next-Generation Cybersecurity

Dealing with Uncertainty

Uncertainty is the most difficult problem when we think about cybersecurity of the future. The fact that we often do not have historical data about various types of threats, vulnerabilities, and risks puts us in a situation of having to design measures without knowing much about the type and nature of the cybersecurity risks we are facing. In many ways, considering the level of uncertainty, this situation is similar to the VIP security problem. Imagine that you are a celebrity or a VIP facing various risks, from being caught in an unguarded moment by the paparazzi to being assassinated. How can you deal with all these risks?

First of all, you understand that the risk of being photographed by the paparazzi is higher than, say, the risk of being shot. However, paparazzi are easier to deal with than assassins. To address the paparazzi problem, it is probably enough to build a high fence in front of your property and make your estate a no-flight zone to avoid being caught on camera from a helicopter or a drone. However, no matter how high your fence is, it is unlikely to stop a highly motivated assassin. So what do you do in this case? It is clear that no technical solution will help here. Therefore, you will seek a human-centered solution—i.e., you will recruit a security detail and train your staff to be on the lookout for strangers and things which seem out of the ordinary. There is, of course, no guarantee that an attempt on your life will be discouraged by these measures. However, a combination of fences, bodyguards, and trained staff is probably the best you can do to decrease the risk of assassination.

© The Author(s) 2019
G. Pogrebna and M. Skilton, *Navigating New Cyber Risks*,
https://doi.org/10.1007/978-3-030-13527-0_11

Likewise, cybersecurity of the future should combine technical and human solutions. Technological solutions will help your business in stopping highly probable but relatively minor threats, while humans will be able to tackle the more sophisticated and high-impact threats, which are not easily detectable by algorithms.

The Samurai Approach

It is believed that Alexander the Great once said: "*Conquer your fear and you will conquer death*". By this he meant that if you are not afraid of a particular negative event or consequence, you will be more effective in avoiding it or in making sure that it does not happen to you. You may wonder how could this be done? In this regard, the Japanese culture offers us many useful references. Specifically, the code of samurai implies that the samurai is always prepared to die because he conquers his fear of death through training and, importantly, considers the consequences of his death prior to undertaking a risky activity. Notice, it does not mean that the samurai wants to die—on the contrary, life is very valuable to a samurai warrior. Yet, he understands that his life, as a life of any human being, is short and uncertain. It can end at any point in time. So, the important thing is to be prepared for death by considering it consequences. Many pragmatic VIPs and celebrities have put in place contingency plans for various types of unexpected risks by considering the consequences of adverse effects. They consider the consequences of the publication of compromising materials or photos, and, equally, think of what will happen to their family, business, or community if there is an unsuccessful or successful attempt on their life.

Similarly, in order to tackle cybersecurity risks, it is useful to apply the Samurai approach to risk assessment and think through all the possible (even catastrophic) consequences which may result from adversarial actions. If your business holds large amounts of customer personal data, what is the worst-case scenario of this data being stolen? It is important not to jump into the fatalist mode when conducting this exercise and stay pragmatic while considering such scenarios. For these purposes, business canvas methodology provides a good template. In practice, understanding how business canvas is related to cybersecurity issues is very important as it allows you to map how cybersecurity fits your business model, where it saves you money and where it generates revenue. One approach was proposed by Boris Taratine in 2015 [1]. Taratine proposed, that cybersecurity should not be considered as an organizational

Key Partners:	Key Activities:	Value Proposition:	Customer Relationships:	Customer Segmentation:
Who are your partners? What are the risks associated with partners? Which are the key digital resources exchanged between you and partners? What are the modes of exchange? What are the risks associated with this exchange? What is the contingency plan if one or several partners are compromised?	What key activities depend on digital infrastructures? What key activities are digital?	Is security core to the value proposition? Is privacy core to the value proposition? Is customer data core to the value proposition? Do stability & reliability of service contribute to the value proposition? How sensitive is the customer data that is stored? What are the consequences of compromising datasets and systems crucial to your value proposition?	Is reputation important? Is trust important?	What segments value security? What segments value privacy? What segments value stability & reliability of service? What segments value trust? What segments value reputation?
	Key Resources: What are the key digital resources? What resources depend on digital infrastructures? What resources are controlled digitally?		**Channels:** What are the digital channels used to reach the consumer? What are the digital channels used to reach the suppliers and partners? Channel redundancy?	

Cost Structure:	Revenue Streams:
What are the security costs? What are the privacy costs? What are the recovery costs? Are all costs above justified in the overall cost structure? What are the cyber security insurance costs?	Are customers willing to pay for security? Are customers indifferent to stability of service? What revenue streams depend on digital infrastructures?

Reputational, Social & Environmental Cost:	Reputational, Social & Environmental Benefit:
Can a cybersecurity issue compromise your business reputation? What is the worst reputational outcome you can think of? Can cybersecurity issue in your business harm the society as a whole? Can these issues harm your network and business environment (trusted parties)?	What are the channels in which reputational and social benefits due to high standards in cybersecurity can be turned into reduction of costs? How could sharing information about cybersecurity practices turn into cutting costs/ new revenue streams?

Fig. 11.1 Cybersecurity business canvas risk assessment tool

fixed cost, but needs to be understood within the context of the entire organizational operations. Extending this approach, we have overlaid cybersecurity risk considerations with a business canvas to create a tool which will provide you with a starting point for thinking about the various risks in cyberspace.

Our Cybersecurity Business Canvas Risk Assessment Tool is presented on Fig. 11.1. The tool outlines a set of questions which should be asked to understand how various cybersecurity issues affect your business model. Following the business canvas methodology, the questions are split into 11 major business model categories: Key Partners, Key Activities, Key Resources, Value Proposition, Customer Relationships (Distribution and Impact) Channels, Customer Segmentation, Cost Structure, Revenue Streams, as well as Reputational, Social, and Environmental Costs and Benefits.

Whereas our tool provides a nice starting point for risk assessment and allows you to map major cybersecurity risks important for your business model, it offers little guidance on what to do next. For this, the Cybersecurity Risk Navigation Matrix could be used.

Navigating New Cybersecurity Risks: Cost Versus Measures Considerations

As humans, we are constantly trying to decrease uncertainty [2–6]. However, it might not always be possible [5]. Under these circumstances, the following navigation matrix approach might be useful. The Cybersecurity Business Canvas approach (described above) will provide an organization with a list of possible risks so that, for each risk, you will be able to identify a potential threat as well as assess what amount of information you have about this threat. In other words, by using the Cybersecurity Business Canvas Risk Assessment Tool you will map a set of potential threats and you will have a good idea about the amount of data you have to diagnoze and approximate the risk for each of these threats. For example, for some potential threats (such as e.g., phishing) you might have a lot of data as your organization is likely to face phishing threats on a regular basis; whereas for other potential threats (such as zero-day) you will have no data at all. In general, all threats which your business might be facing could be roughly divided into four types (see Fig. 11.2).

- Those of which you know and have data (Mitigation threats).
- Those of which you know and do not have data (State of Fear threats).
- Those of which you don't know and have no data (Blissful Ignorance threats).
- Those of which you don't know but have data (Under Your Nose threats).

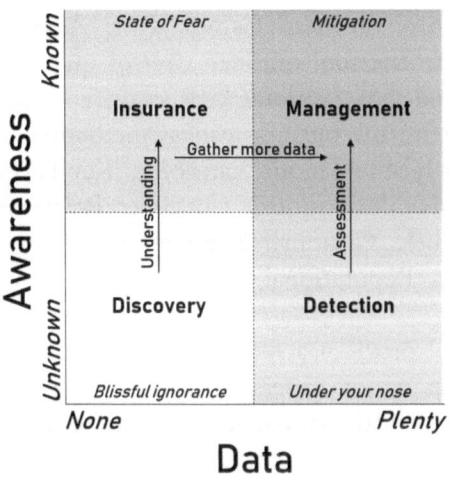

Fig. 11.2 Cybersecurity risk navigation matrix

Now all these threats relate to the corresponding risks, where: Mitigation threats relate to risks which you can *manage* using a set of traditional quantitative risk assessment and risk management tools; State of Fear threats refer to risks which you can *insure* against (i.e., you can purchase insurance if you know of those risks but it is hard or impossible to understand how big or grave those risks are); there is not much you can do about risks related to Blissful Ignorance threats apart from *discovering* them and, equally, about risks related to Under Your Nose threats apart from *detecting* them.

Nevertheless, the goal is to translate all types of risks into those which you can *manage*. This can be achieved in the following way. In order to turn Insurable risks into Manageable risks, you simply need to collect more data about them (via organizational communication or information sharing). Risks which are Discoverable need to be better understood to become Insurable and then translated into Manageable. Risks which are Detectable could be assessed using available data to become Manageable.

In order to decrease this underlying uncertainty about cybersecurity risks, planning, building, and managing techniques are useful. In what follows, we provide a set of principles which will help you navigate new cybersecurity risks through planning, building, and managing safe and secure digital spaces.

References

1. Taratine, B. (2015). Cybersecurity and business canvas: How to put cybersecurity risk into business models. Limited audience talk materials.
2. Loomes, G., & Pogrebna, G. (2017). Do preference reversals disappear when we allow for probabilistic choice? *Management Science, 63*(1), 166–184.
3. Loomes, G., & Pogrebna, G. (2014). Testing for independence while allowing for probabilistic choice. *Journal of Risk and Uncertainty, 49*(3), 189–211.
4. Loomes, G., & Pogrebna, G. (2014). Measuring individual risk attitudes when preferences are imprecise. *Economic Journal, 124*(576), 569–593.
5. Blavatskyy, P., & Pogrebna, G. (2010). Models of stochastic choice and decision theories: Why both are important for analyzing decisions. *Journal of Applied Econometrics, 25*(6), 963–986.
6. Li, Z., Loomes, G., & Pogrebna, G. (2017). Attitudes to uncertainty in a strategic setting. *Economic Journal, 127*(601), 809–826.

12

Navigating a Safe Space

How to PLAN a Safe Space

In the early 1970s and 1980s, with the advent of what we can describe as modern enterprise computing, organizations used to typically buy their networks and computers at the department level. They all bought different networks and systems and they did not talk to each other in the enterprise.

As a result, we are currently faced with multiple efficiency issues, as we try to centralize everything and have one system. Purchasing power increases when it is centralized; and for ease of maintenance to standard ways of recruiting and training staff. A lack of diversity is brilliant for this, but it does not help resilience.

Look at the characteristics of resilient habitats in the natural world; they tend to have:

- Diversity
- Reserves
- A certain sense of openness

Increasing the complexity of the system through multiple data records can help in building traps for adversaries where some of this data may be a decoy or a "honeypot" to attract attackers to try to get that data. This can help in collecting evidence for a legal case against an adversary who may unwittingly collect or use this data trap. Having multiple data sources can also increase the complexity of the system environment making it more difficult for adversaries to move in the network undetected as they have to deal with more network and data storage features in the system, some of which may

© The Author(s) 2019
G. Pogrebna and M. Skilton, *Navigating New Cyber Risks*,
https://doi.org/10.1007/978-3-030-13527-0_12

be traps. This can create what is called a "signature" of a pattern in the system environment that suggests an anomalous transaction or system behavior suggesting something is not quite right and may indicate the presence of an adversary who might have entered the system. Hence creating more complexity in the system creates more obstacles for the potential, adversaries but it can have challenges for the defenders to monitor a more complex systems environment. This is arguably better than having one central system with all your data and assets ino one place as it presents just one target to the attacker, something that is often referred to as the "Pearl Harbor" problem where most of the American Battle Fleet in World War Two were in one Hawaiian harbor and presented an opportunity of a single attack target to the Japanese Aircraft.

With the immersive and pervasive nature of digital technology connecting personal data, transactions, appliances, building, vehicles and many other things in society, this physical world and the virtual digital worlds are become more intertwined as an attack surface.

In assessing our risk, we typically start with uncertainty and then map from uncertainty to risk, defining the likelihood of the type of risk and the percentage confidence interval in the next, say, twelve months of a cyberattack-for example, an attack through a website to steal our credit card information. We tend to do this very quickly. Because our start point is a very dangerous situation, and uncertainty is not a nice place to be, so we make rapid calculations to try to move to a safer position. This is a critical question about the effectiveness of resilience planning, building, and response because you may not be targeting efforts on the real problem.

Make the Space Hostile to Adversaries

One of the advantages of creating a rich environment with lots of diverse features is that you get a "web of evidence" as a natural consequence. To take a specific example, if somebody wants to hack into a Linux or Unix system and change the configuration in its directory of files, you can change or replace the files and the timestamp. But there are also things called "inode" records, which are created at the time of the file's inception. If a file has been tampered with, you can check this source for any suspicious changes. You can create an environment of overlapping and interleaving strands of information to cross-check and look for changes.

Attackers will go for the weak points in a system. What you can try to do is compose an attack that is a collection of attacks that individually are not devasting but together would be this could be an effective cyber attack strategy in a situation where the cyber defenses have been build in discrete parts of the total company system but have not considered if many or all of the system was attacked. You can fix individual weak points in a system, but the attacker may be composing an attack over the horizon that you cannot see or cannot anticipated from the combination of actions they may take against your system.

It is about the cost to the attacker of a successful attack versus the costs to the defender of protecting a system. Take the example of ransomware that may be used against a modern premium electric car. You can disable the car remotely and demand a payment to release the vehicle controls. The attacker may take several months to develop this, including having to buy several cars to test this out until they know it will work. As a result, the car manufacturer may have to recall all the vehicles for repair, at great cost. What happens if the attacker uses the same system utilized by the automotive supplier to install over-the-air remote updates to the vehicles? The attacker could infect many vehicles remotely with the ransomware software. Alternatively, the vehicle manufacturer might be able to update over-the-air protection to onboard vehicles at the chip level to block new attacks. At some point, it may not be cost-effective for the attacker to plan and mount the attack if the cost to the vehicle manufacturer is lower and the problem easier to fix. It is a continual battle between the cost of attack and the cost of defense. There are, however, practical ways in which the landscape can be made economically hostile to attackers.

Recruiting Cybersecurity People with the Right Motivations

Hackers are not concerned about organizational department boundaries or what type of operating systems they prefer. They will do what they want and work with who they want.

On the company's side, even if you have the right level of skills, you need to ensure your employees are correctly motivated, and they care. This is one of the key issues in cybersecurity recruitment. Traditional recruiting may identify motivations, but it may not translate into job performance later. It can be beneficial to get to know potential new recruits before they become part of the organization. The use of recruitment fares, internships, and pre-screening are often useful in this regard.

Even after recruitment, the characteristics of personal resilience and perseverance may not become evident until a few weeks later when, in the middle of an attack, they are able to think clearly under stress and pursue actions to try to respond to these threats. These are the real tests. Such people are key to cybersecurity, but they must also be able to work as team players to co-ordinate actions as a group. Creativity as well technical skill, a healthy hunger to learn and motivation are also key. Having different experiences and qualifications in the cybersecurity group also helps enrich the team dynamics for creativity and thought-pattern approaches.

Quantify the Consequences of Potential Cyberattacks

If an adversarial agent from the outside wants to effect maximum disruption, we need to ask how can we defend the most vulnerable parts of the company (the attack surface) and sources attack entry (the attack vectors)—for example, an employee, subcontractor or customer personal activity, key company products and services and their channels to market, key enterprise assets and buildings, or key transport roads or utility and hospital services of a city depending on your scope of planning?

Many scenarios of this kind can be mapped out in planning cyberdefense. From examining vulnerabilities, consequences, threads, and defense options, you can prioritize where you want to put your resources. You defend the points of weakness and exploits that have the highest index of vulnerability combined with the consequences. This requires a quantification of the impact of the consequences if this point of vulnerability is attacked. So, high vulnerability to attack may not be a priority if we know the consequences. You need to model all these factor when planning cyber responses. You can work out the level of optimal allocation of the defensive resources you have available based on the conceptual and intellectual framework models to calculate the costs of security and its level of predicted adequacy. This is a formal mathematical problem; it does not necessarily look at all issues but at least it provides a conceptual framework to think about it.

Some events may not be initially a cyber risks issue. For example, in regions that are vulnerable to earthquakes such as the West Coast of the USA and Silicon Valley, there are potentially many vulnerable people. A major cybersecurity attack on infrastructure is in many ways similar to an earthquake: you may have to evacuate a city and restore infrastructure, recover homes, businesses, and people's lives. Can you get people out fast enough? The answer is you may not be able to, as transport routes are not designed for mass evacuation, and the transport controls may be down. Similar issues are faced on a different scale in the evacuation of a football stadium or large buildings. It is just applied at the city level. How do you do this securely and safety? Following the triple disaster of the Great East Japan earthquake in 2011, and the resulting devastating tsunami and nuclear crisis at the Fukushima nuclear power plant [1, 2], swift decisions had to be taken at government level without waiting for reports from areas where communications had broken down.

AI Changes Your Cybersecurity Planning Approach

The field of cybersecurity is increasingly working together with other fields, including, for example, ML automation, the legal profession, ethicists, social science and social media specialists. Yet these fields are also being impacted and disrupted by automation.

Cybersecurity may be one of the most protected professions in the world right now, in that it is in increasingly high demand as threat vectors multiply and the volume of cyberattacks spreads into all corporate, social, and government spheres.

Automation is still useful in assisting and replacing some cybersecurity tasks, but creativity and experience remain the key factors when it comes to tackling things that cannot necessarily be programmed and automated.

Some cybersecurity attack vectors can be anticipated. Other areas of increasingly complex behaviors and patterns across many system end-points in, for example, thousands of ATM-attached networks, may be better monitored by automation that can work continuously, 24 hours a day all year without rest.

New forms cybersecurity AI automation are now being discovered that are being used by hackers to monitor and mimic human activity in a new phase of cyberattacks.

But in other situations, such as fake news, which is a different kind of attack vector, it may be difficult to employ automation fully due to the semantic nuances involved. Automation progress will be able to work through these complex challenges, but it remains an issue of equilibrium between constantly evolving threats and responses. This is the struggle.

The Dangers of a Machine Making Decisions in Cybersecurity

From a defender's perspective, if you invest in AI for defense but after a time it blocks access to customers as part of an automated action, causing significant financial losses for customers and millions to resolve, but may have saved hundreds of millions up to that point, how do the company executive board members respond to this? Often, at that moment, they will look at each individual incident rather than the overall picture as the potential reputational risk takes precedence over other considerations. These may include such operational issues as fixing the algorithmic rules, but in other cases may be part of an underlying weakness in the use of AI. This is a repeated issue of using statistical methods to "learn" automated rules in AI. You need to train the machine learning algorithms but sometimes these can develop rules that may evolve over time to do things that are not in value alignment with the original policies that were being automated. A well reporting example is the training of self-driving automobiles where the algorithms may not be fit for purpose in all scenarios resulting in damage or loss of life. This may be a combination of poorly defined data dimensions of the learning algorithm not being able to response safety to achieve its objective function (such as "do not hit an object"), or a feature of learning from training data that fails to recognise a state change in its environment, a failure in its ability to automate sensory feedback-control appropriately for the given objective function. These examples, and many others are new phenomena that is emerging as part of the field of machine learning and artificial intelligence that create new risks that can also include cyber attacks and cyber defense where the machine learning data or algorithms may be compromised or the technology may itself be used to carry out a cyber attack. This is a subject outside the scope of this book.

Internet of Things Changes Your Cybersecurity Planning Approach

Today, most organizations treat cybersecurity as a cost, a daunting proposition that they will only implement as a last resort because where is the benefit? But business models are changing because of the impact of cybersecurity. To cite one example, Philips Lighting, now called Signify [3], are moving from selling "light bulbs" to smart cities to selling "lighting-as-a-service". It is this "as-a-service" that is the key issue, if your revenues are moving from manufacturing goods to selling updates and support in the longer term. So, employment and employees will change to support this. But also, cybersecurity becomes the fundamental platform in enabling "everything-as-a-service" because you must be able to talk to these devices through their total lifecyle that includes management, updates, and billing for device use.

What the IoT offers compared to the earlier machine-to-machine (M2M) connections is these new business models that sit on top. This is evolving across all industry sectors—it becomes health-as-a-service, lighting-as-a-service, cars-as-a-service, and so on. Uber, Zipcar, and others, for example, developed other as-a-service models, called the uberization effect, a concept from the online taxi company Uber, which pioneered this business model. This opened up assets and services with direct contact between buyers and the owners of these objects, facilities, or work services. The physicality of the object has a different dimension in the cyberspace digital world. The ability to interact with different people, different public and private networks, different multiple vendors to deliver different services is the next wave. With the IoT era, this is the reality.

- How do you validate who you are working with?
- How do you isolate data so that it is harder to identify the person?
- How do you build entire systems from different vendors who may not talk with each other, may be competitors, and will not share critical information with other people in the system?
- How do you build a secure system that may connect to 3rd party technology or external networks and systems that you may not know the configuration of, or have access to, but have access to your enterprise system as part of connection services such as supply chain business to business (B2B) or Business to customer (B2C) service connected to many suppliers and other external companies; or in the case of bring your own device (BYOD) mobile services.
- How do you build a framework where these different vendors and systems inter-work, inter-operate securely?
- How do I formally prove that this device or system is trustworthy to receive my data?
- How do I know that this device or system is able to manage my data without having to know everything about me or the information context behind my data?

Build Appropriate Tracking into Spaces, Things, and People

Rather than just design systems to prevent hackers from getting in, we want to let them in and observe and learn what they are doing without, of course, allowing them to steal information or impact service levels. "Honeypots" are computer security techniques [4] that may be a dedicated server on a network to attract, deflect and detect, acting as a decoy to potential hackers as part of an intrusion detection system (IDS) [4, 5].

How to trace events when things are gone—the example of flight MH370.

We need to add markers to objects, so we can track them if they are moved or stolen. Take the example of Malaysian Airlines flight MH370 that disappeared on 8 March 2014 in the southern Indian Ocean [6]. Despite an extensive air and sea search, the location of the aircraft and occupants remains unknown. However, some debris has been recovered consistent with having drifted over nearly two years from the area in which impact is thought to have occurred? [7].

There was no easy, distinct way of tracking the aircraft parts.

How to BUILD Safe Spaces

In cybersecurity, following an incident, we need to find out what happened, but this is often not easy to establish. A lack of organizational disclosure regarding cyber incidents is not helpful in understanding events from the perspective of knowledge sharing and analysis. This problem is compounded by people not reporting or understanding when they have been attacked and are victims of cybercrime. Appropriate levels of investment and resources need to be available to build effective investigation and defenses against cyberattacks. Just using fines as a mechanism to change company behavior who fail to respond adequately to cyber-attacks can be an incomplete answer when enforcing new government regulation such as the European GDPR. This needs to be balanced with encouraging companies to invest in cyber-defense and training to prevent attacks. Not just more fines. Many companies, particularly small to medium size enterprises (SMEs), do not have the resources to handle cyberattacks.

People experience fear and desire in relation to cyberattacks. Fear that they will not be able to secure themselves, so they avoid it. The image of cybersecurity as too daunting and complicated drives this behavior. Human behavior has a tendency in threatening situations to de-sensitize themselves to stressful emotions by imagining they will not be attacked. A positive fear appeal would promote a 'danger control process' which can lead to a successful outcome as the message recipient undertakes a cognitive process to avert a threat. But fear appeals in isolation do not provide effective or adequate assurance, as per its definition, and organizations should not rely upon this mechanism. Neuroscience suggests these fear and desire behaviors are part of the nervous system function to reduce surprise and optimize actions [8–11].

Use Deception Technologies

New developments in cyber defense are emerging as a consequence of realizing that attacks will happen and that not all vulnerabilities will be discovered in time. One key development has been the use of deception through technologies that create decoys and other misdirection techniques as part of a cyber-deception solution. In effect creating a "maze of deception" to slow down, deflect or collect evidence to identify stealthy attackers or entrap them.

Currently, general thinking today is geared towards building cyberdefenses to stop hackers getting into the systems; this is called a defense-in-depth strategy. But is this the right approach? Maybe you want to let them in, you want to collect data on them and you want to make it hard so that the effort and cost involved for the attack makes them want to stop and give up trying to attack. Given the complexity of systems and the ever-present vulnerabilities and exploits that you may not have discovered yet to zero-day and polymorphic code attack, this is a better strategy than trying to second-guess everything.

There is a lot of cybersecurity deception technology, from honeypots and automated traps and decoys that imitate target systems such as cash machines (ATMs), to medical devices and internal network switches and routers. Firewalls and the end-point security of devices, from mobile cellphones to IoT devices, cannot defend a perimeter with 100% certainty. Neither can communications networks and database servers with encryption be protected from access that may have be compromised. Hackers seek to gain backdoor entry into a corporate network with the typical aim of exploiting and navigating networks to identify and exfiltrate data.

Backdoor is a method, often secret, of bypassing normal authentication or encryption in a computer system, a product, or an embedded device, such as a home router, or its embodiment as part of a cryptosystem, an algorithm, a chipset, or a "homunculus computer"—a tiny computer-within-a-computer, such as that found in Intel's AMT technology [12]. Backdoors are often used for securing remote access to a computer or obtaining access to plaintext in cryptographic systems. The concept of a homunculus computer is a system within a system that mirrors what that system does and monitors its function. It is a concept drawn from human neuro-biology representing the brain and the way it functions as representing and processing collections of sensory inputs and output feedback, that are interpreted with the "mind" and its ability to perceive, think, and reason about the external world.

Deception technologies are part of Security Information and Event Management (SIEM) tools, in that they differ from IDS but allow automated static and dynamic analysis of this injected malware and provide these reports through automation to the security operations personnel. Deception technology may also identify, through indicators of compromise (IoC), suspect end-points that are part of the compromise cycle. Automation also allows for an automated memory analysis of the suspect end-point, and then automatically isolates the suspect end-point.

TrapX is is one vendor of deception technology that was effective at deceiving TeslaCrypt, Locky, and 7ev3n ransomware families known as advanced persistent threats (APTs), luring hackers away from valuable data assets [13]. These deception technologies are able, for example, to engage a ransomware attack with decoy resources, while isolating the infection points and alerting cyberdefense blue teams.

Fidelis Cybersecurity was another example of a deception technology vendor made public by First Midwest Bank, a financial institution that used this technology to set up decoy solutions to identify patterns of anomalies in their networks and end-points. This is particularly relevant when operating in a highly regulated industry: the bank is subject to the Federal Financial Institution Examination Council's uniform principles and standards for financial institutions and its processes are periodically tested for compliance with a litany of laws and regulations [14]. Examples of deception technologies vendors include [15]:

- Rapid7
- Hexi cybersecurity
- Smokescreen Technologies
- TrapX

- Fidelis Cybersecurity
- Attivo Networks
- Illusive Networks

Deception is one technology that can significantly reduce dwell time. On top of this, it is easy to install, does not require a lot of resources to manage, and increases the effectiveness and efficiency of security teams [16].

Kill Chain Concept

Deception technologies are typically based around a set of strategies that were developed in 2011 by Lockheed Martin's kill chain concept to categorize different phases of a cyberattack they describe as Adversary Campaigns and Intrusion Kill Chains. It includes the following steps [17]:

(1) Reconnaissance,
(2) Weaponization,
(3) Delivery,
(4) Exploitation,
(5) Installation,
(6) Command, and
(7) Action on objectives.

This work by Lockheed Martin determined that conventional network defense tools, such as IDS and antivirus, focus on the vulnerability component of risk, and traditional incident response methodology presupposes a successful intrusion. An evolution in the goals and sophistication of computer network intrusions has rendered these approaches insufficient for certain actors. A new class of threats, appropriately dubbed the "advanced persistent threat" (APT), represents well-resourced and trained adversaries that conduct multiyear intrusion campaigns targeting highly sensitive economic, proprietary, or national security information. The evolution of APTs necessitates an intelligence-based model because in this model the defenders mitigate not just vulnerability, but also the threat component of risk.

A key issue is how far to advertise the existence of deception technologies; it is one thing to track and trace what is going on to establish who is attacking, the attribution, followed by understanding the motives. But there is a fine line between that and entrapment, which may result in tricking someone into committing a crime to secure their prosecution. From a legal standpoint, this is questionable. This could also create a burden of work in a company that may seek information on attackers that might not necessarily add a great deal to the security of the company. From a learning point of view, deception technologies are excellent planning approaches to cybersecurity, but the issue is, how far do you pursue this strategy? In financial services, enticing the adversary to commit a financial theft or transaction, or to reveal their location and identity, is useful but very rarely done as it would lead to a prosecution in the law courts, assuming they were caught.

Individual and Class-Level Attacks

The chip is the basic level of digital technology. It is a fast-evolving area but its very nature means that you make billions of them. If one sustains an attack, it will potentially work on billions. If you have an attack on one, it will potentially work on billions. It is a class-level attack, in that its target is a whole group of technologies. A small design flaw on a chip can have a major impact if this is also a cybersecurity vulnerability and an exploit point for an attack vector.

One case study from 2017 was the Spanish identity smart card that incorporated a chip developed by the German company Infineon. It was found that Infineon's key pair-generation algorithm had the "ROCA" flaw, which made it possible for someone to discover a target's private key just by knowing what their public key was. Dan Cvrcek, CEO at the security firm Enigma Bridge, which was co-founded by researchers who identified the ROCA flaw, told ZDNet that exploitation of the flaw could allow attackers to revert or invalidate contracts that people had signed, in part because the Spanish don't use timestamps for very important signatures. The card, known as a DNIe, had a chip that contained two certificates, one for identification and one for electronically signing documents etc. The cryptography used for identity cards is high-level keys, to save money in the development costs of the system, the security encryption keys for the crypto algorithm were physically stored on the card. Once you knew the factors, the theoretical breakage time goes from the lifetime of the universe to 20,000 computer hours, which is trivial considering today's computing power, making a potential attack economically viable.

A fix would require all affected cards to be updated. On Infineon's disclosure of the vulnerability, the Spanish authorities revoked all certificates and stopped letting people sign documents with the card at the self-service terminals found at many police stations. That decision affected every card, not only those that had the flaw. However, people could still digitally sign documents online, using a small card reader that connects to their PCs [18].

Securing the Billions of Connected Things

Sensors, phones, or PCs are subject to injection attacks that can pull back critical information. Individually, it may not matter to you if someone can see emails on your phone, but if they can see it when you and a million people or more are doing their online banking, then that is the challenge. The solution to this type of class attack is to make every chip truly unique. This can be done through cryptography, frameworks, changes at the silicon physical level, creating islands of isolation.

On a PC, the attacker can come in through the USB port and get to the main computer processor, but you can have a separate security domain that this is not connected to—an island with integrity. The rest of the PC might be attacked but this area can be maintained in isolation. You can then identify, remediate, and recover.

You can also plan to improve the security against class-level attacks:

- Make the chip set unique
- Give things identity
- Give things a level of robustness
- Manage ownership

Blockchain technology (BCT) can play an important part in this.

The typical purchase of a PC laptop by a person, they will always be the only user of that PC laptop. They will never sell or get rid of it, and the data remains on that PC laptop. This "one-person-only" ownership paradigm simply does not work in the world of the internet of things (IoT) that involves many assets and devices connected together sharing data and services, many of which you do not own but will use and provide your personal data and transactions to these systems. This is the case of the web enabled heating system in a house that you may then sell the house, or with the aftermarket for cars that are resold to new vehicle owners.

- How do you manage identity when ownership is changing hands?
- How do you manage identity in cars?

In the case of Jaguar Land Rover cars, if you privately sell your vehicle, the person who buys it cannot take control of the car until it has been zeroed at the dealership. If you buy it through the car dealership, they will blank it. It is about clear asset ownership and exchange of goods and services.

In IoT ownership and data privacy, who owns the data?

- Is it the OEM who sold the heater?
- Is it my utility service provider?
- Is it the third-party service company with whom I may have a contract?
- Is it the insurance company with whom I may have a contract?

The question of who owns the data can be very obscure, involving multiple levels of a system that may have many actors and corporations involved directly or indirectly.

You put your personal data and behavior out on Facebook who are mining your data to sell you services or sell on to 3rd parties who may in turn sell you services or use it for other reasons which may be discloses or hard to trace to identify what it is used for. This involves an inherent transaction in which you have use of the platform for free, but agree to their terms and conditions, which include permission to mine your data and provide you with advertising that you may or may not want. You may be fine with this until you realize that enough data has been gathered that they can start to nudge your perspectives. This can work in unintended ways, from the reported generation of fake news to influence political elections [19, 20], to the misuse of data that third-party companies obtain from Facebook without direct user consent, as seen in the Cambridge Analytica case in 2017 [21]. This is similarly the case for other major search engines and social media platforms. Our digital footprints are huge and this online data can be out there for another decade or more, the consequences of which we will never know.

In a New Zealand Auckland University study, it was reported that an average New Zealand citizen may appear in about 40 different databases, while a US citizen is in about 200—and these include information such as your age, date of birth, marital status, and where you live [6]. Then there are the business models that come out of this. Take the example of a heating system: the utility service provider can look after it and gather data, so they can bill customers for the service they use. They might be able to offer additional services such as automated energy savings to turn things on and off in a more ecological and economic way. Or they can suggest added-value services such as insurance cover. There is a lot that can be deduced from an analysis of the electrical load signal of a house, right down to which TV channel you are watching.

We Are Building a Very Powerful Cage Around Ourselves

The interesting thing, though, is the data: if I own that data, then a whole range of services may become available. This is the potential of the IoT business model. If I am selling lighting-as-a-service, do I want the lights to come on when I walk into the house? And AI based on my data in my house is great, if it is under my control. But what I don't want is for all this data to go back to a cloud third party. I may be quite happy to share parts of that data with my utility provider. I may want to send data back to my insurance company about are my habits, so long as it is obfuscated. And I may have services such as my alarm system that might use my behavior data. If an intruder has entered the house and is behaving in a different way (i.e., they have not switched on any lights), then this might be used to deduce a break-in alert. For police and security services, the IoT is very powerful, but for warranted surveillance we need to be able to switch everything off, so they can gain entry to bug the house.

IoT is the ultimate two-edge sword. It offers huge new revenues and a whole new way for individuals to interact with the world around them, but only if we can trust it, and trust is a very delicate thing.

- Monetization of data
- Monetization of software
- Selling solutions.

We will likely move to a service-oriented economy in the years ahead. But the challenges are:

- Who owns the data?
- How do I protect the data?
- How do I ensure the operation of a system is correct against the conditions of use that was agreed or intended by the providers of the data that were input into that system, and the actions and consequences resulting from that system's action?
- What predictive solutions could you implement?
- What completely new things can you imagine doing in this hyperconnected, embedded world that you cannot do today?

Say, for example, you have meetings in London, followed by one in Bristol, so your calendar lines up an Uber taxi for you and books your train ticket; it also knows the sort of food you like and is monitoring your blood pressure, along with much more. All of these things are predictive around you, so you don't even have to think about many of them. It could de-risk these scenarios, it could make you safer or help you avoid situations that may be less optimal based on criteria. It could improve your quality of life and enhance more healthy living, potentially increasing your life expectancy. There are, however, ethical issues in this relating to bias and the way decisions are made in these scenarios. How does it arbitrate if there are risky decisions that may affect you and others; how does it affect choices that may be bad for your health or impact your experience in other ways regarding who you meet or the things that you consume or do? These are questions that ethicists and legislators will have to consider. Development of these issues must establish frameworks and policies to develop best practices and legislation to ensure the future of effective cybersecurity and safe spaces.

How to MANAGE Safe Spaces

The "business logic" which represented the highest level of a system activity, the business activities, trading and commercial behavior, is perhaps the hardest to understand when trying to map where the paths through this business are to vulnerabilities that may exist in that business logic. It may be that even after all the internal investment, testing, and monitoring, external security researchers, members of the public, or routine investigations into the organization can find things that all the other layers may have missed.

Towards Self-Healing Systems

The future of cybersecurity management needs to augment these layers to include and integrate all the threat and vulnerability information from:

- intelligence sources
- vendor communities
- academic communities
- user communities
- hacker communities.

In the first instance, there is automation of detection for protection such as firewall rule updates. Then there are more complex issues, such as a code library vulnerability that needs fixing through vendor and/or internal and external actions. These libraries are subsequently updated to ensure that any developers are using improved code. This reperesents a move towards the concept of self-healing systems, which may include using ML techniques to fix applications based on inputs from threat sources, information gathered from human interactions and other models that look at business logic as rule-based logic. The aim is to develop insights and prevent common errors in the design of coding libraries.

But You Never Can Be Secure for Certain

You cannot know for certain whether a system is secure, though there are mathematical algorithms that can prove a set of rules are secure. A cryptographic set of rules, then, can be used to determine whether an encryption is secure. Theoretically speaking, however, it is still vulnerable from a cybersecurity practitioner perspective and they must decide if the level of security is sufficient. If a system is broken, then clearly it is insecure; but if it is functioning, then it is secure to some degree that may or may not be acceptable.

Utilizing all the SIEM[1] tools, for example, can demonstrate that nothing anomalous has been detected but you can never know with absolute certainty. Factors may include:

- Insufficient time to check all system areas
- Lack of investment in tools to protect the system
- Lack of cybersecurity technical skills
- Lack of risk management skills
- Lack of leadership skills to validate and respond to risks
- Human error in design of the system
- Human error in configuration, support, monitoring, and response to attack
- Zero-day events that are new vulnerabilities/exploits
- Fake information manipulation, clandestine or cyberwarfare agenda attacks
- Proximity to use of other networks and vendors who are attacked.

---

[1]Security information and event management (SIEM) https://searchsecurity.techtarget.com/definition/security-information-and-event-management-SIEM.

Leveraging Domain Knowledge

In complex systems where you cannot anticipate every interaction, the use of subject experts in their field, as well as non-experts with experience, can enable a broader evaluation of this complexity similar to the concepts of crowdsourcing ideas and solutions. A key part of this is domain knowledge who can facilitate this than just the use of experts.

Any application that is compromised could lead to catastrophic financial losses. The immediate risk approach would be to ask how secure the network is, then use a VPN, where are the APIs, and how can we secure them with secure HTTPS and secure API protocols and so on. But the question of just fixing the API may be insufficient from the viewpoint of complete security. The question can be reframed from: "How do we fix secure APIs?" to "How can we run insecure APIs?" This assumes that despite a secure system, there may be vulnerabilities and attacks; the question is how the system can be managed to respond to these threats. This typically generates many more ideas and potential solutions to what-if scenarios than just a focus on a fix. This can introduce other levels of security to improve the resilience of the system overall. Making a system architecture that is robust enough for certain failures is one thing; but a better approach would be to make the system more flexible, such that it can adjust itself and resolve issues and recover from attacks. Instead of patching everything, we should have more responsive support systems that can investigate and fix attacks in a more flexible way that is adaptive and learning all the time. This might also enable better investment decisions regarding cyber security tools and processes, which may not necessarily be just technical but also involve organizational awareness, culture, and leadership.

The right question is: How can an insecure system in a hostile environment stay secure?

References

1. *Japan: Legal responses to the Great East Japan Earthquake of 2011, Law.gov the Law Library of Congress.* Accessed September 2018. https://www.loc.gov/law/help/japan-earthquake/index.php.
2. Kaufmann, D., & Penciakova, V. (2011, March). *Japan's Triple Disaster: Governance and the Earthquake, Tsunami and Nuclear Crises.* Brookings Institute. https://www.brookings.edu/opinions/japans-triple-disaster-governance-and-the-earthquake-tsunami-and-nuclear-crises/.

3. *Philips Lighting is now Signify*. Press Release 16 May 2018. https://www.signify. com/en-us/about/news/press-releases/2018/20180516-philips-lighting-is-now-signify.
4. Honeypot. https://searchsecurity.techtarget.com/definition/honey-pot.
5. Cole, E., & Northcutt, S. *Honeypots: A Security manager's guide to Honeypots*. V1.1 SANS Technology Institute, Security Laboratory. https://www.sans.edu/ cyber-research/security-laboratory/article/honeypots-guide.
6. Hatton, E. *Life online: How big is your digital footprint?* 12 February 2018 RNZ. https://www.radionz.co.nz/news/national/350224/life-online-how-big-is-your-digital-footprint.
7. Lyons, K., Ellis-Petersen, H., Kuo, L., & Zhou, N. Malaysian investigators release 1,500-page report into disappearance of MH370, *The Guardian*, 30 July 2018. https://www.theguardian.com/world/live/2018/jul/30/mh370-final-report-released-by-malaysian-government-live.
8. Johnston, A., & Warkentin, M. (2010, September). Fear appeals and information security behaviours: An empirical study. *MIS Quarterly, 34*(3). http://www. uab.edu/cas.
9. Evans, M., Maglaras, L. A., He, Y., & Janicke Jan, H. (2016). *Human behavior as an aspect of cyber security assurance*. arXiv:1601.03921v1[cs.CR].
10. Aytes, K., Connolly, T., Ovelgonne, M., Dumitras, T., Prakash, A., Subrahmanian, V. S., & Wany, B. (2017, July). Understanding the relationship, between human behavior and susceptibility to cyber-attacks: A data-driven approach. *ACM Transactions on Intelligent Systems and Technology (TIST)— Special Issue: Cyber Security and Regular Papers, 8*(4), Article no. 51.
11. Gross, M. L. Canetti, D., & Vashdi, D. R. (2016). The psychological effects of cyber terrorism. PMC US National Library of Medicine. *Bulletin of the Atomic Scientists, 72*(5), 284–291. Published online 4 August 2016. https://doi.org/10. 1080/00963402.2016.1216502.
12. Hoffman, C. (2017, November). *Intel management engine, explained: The Tiny computer inside your CPU*. How-To Geek. https://www.howtogeek. com/334013/intel-management-engine-explained-the-tiny-computer-inside-your-cpu/.
13. Davis, J. TrapX launches ransomware deception tool, CryptoTrap. *HealthITNews*, August 2016. https://www.healthcareitnews.com/news/trapx-launches-ransomware-deception-tool-cryptotrap.
14. First Midwest Bank Uses Fidelis Deception™ to Detect and Respond to Security Anomalies, case study. Accessed October 2018. https://www.fidelissecurity. com/case-study-first-midwest-bank.
15. 20 Deception Technology Companies: In-depth Guide [2018] Applied AI blog. https://blog.appliedai.com/deception-tech-companies/.
16. 5 ways deception tech is disrupting cybersecurity, Doron Kolton, TNW, May 2018. https://thenextweb.com/contributors/2018/05/26/5-ways-deception-technology-is-changing-cybersecurity/.

17. Hutchins, E. M., Cloppert, M. J., & Amin, R. M. (2011, January). *Intelligence-driven computer network defense informed by analysis of adversary campaigns and intrusion Kill Chains.* https://www.lockheedmartin.com/content/dam/lockheed-martin/rms/documents/cyber/LM-White-Paper-Intel-Driven-Defense.pdf.
18. Myer, D. ID card security: Spain is facing chaos over chip crypto flaws. ZDNet, 17 November 2017. https://www.zdnet.com/article/id-card-security-spain-is-facing-chaos-over-chip-crypto-flaws/.
19. Lapowsky, I. *How Russian Facebook ads divided and targeted US voters before the 2016 election*, 18 April 2018 Wired. https://www.wired.com/story/russian-facebook-ads-targeted-us-voters-before-2016-election/.
20. Stewart, E. *Facebook has already detected suspicious activity trying to influence the 2018 elections*, 31 July Vox. https://www.vox.com/2018/7/31/17635592/facebook-elections-russia-2018-midterms.
21. *Facebook-Cambridge Analytica data scandal, BBC.* Accessed October 2018. https://www.bbc.co.uk/news/topics/c81zyn0888lt/facebook-cambridge-analytica-data-scandal.

13

The Twelve Principles of Safe Places

In this chapter, we explore several best practice principles from experts and practitioners[1]

- Principle 1: Develop effective information-sharing communications
- Principle 2: Identify who your real experts are in fact-checking
- Principle 3: Empower people to appropriately pursue cyber issues
- Principle 4: Manage the balance between commercial and ethical concerns
- Principle 5: Manage the collection of data to assess risk effectively
- Principle 6: Run red teams, blue teams, and purple teams
- Principle 7: Manage an effective portfolio of cyberdefense tools
- Principle 8: Manage organizational discipline and fix knowledge gaps
- Principle 9: Manage your existential threats
- Principle 10: Manage your intellectual property (IP)
- Principle 11: Manage the legal liabilities of the board of directors
- Principle 12: Manage losing control of your company operation.

---

[1]Many of the ideas communicated in this chapter came out of interviews with our consultants, to whom we are really grateful for sharing their thoughts and ideas with us. We are particularly grateful to Boris Taratine for many insightful comments and suggestions, which helped to significantly improve this chapter.

© The Author(s) 2019
G. Pogrebna and M. Skilton, *Navigating New Cyber Risks*,
https://doi.org/10.1007/978-3-030-13527-0_13

Principle 1: Develop Effective Information-sharing Communications

Often, a key problem is access and sharing of information between the organization and affected or interested parties (stakeholders). Organizations are required to report cybersecurity attacks. For example, the Securities and Exchange Commission (SEC) issued guidance on disclosure obligations for cyber incidents a decade ago; this guidance was updated in February 2018 [1, 2]. A similar obligation to report cybersecurity breaches is also contained in the recent EU GDPR legislation, which came into effect in 2018.

As the cybersecurity industry matures, we have special interest groups (SIGs), industrial bodies, compliance standards, and regulation, but we are draining the creativity and innovation out of this space. We need to build this back by looking *outside the box*, beyond what we currently do.

Principle 2: Identify Who Your Real Experts Are in Fact-Checking

It is impossible to protect against all cyberattacks. Phishing emails may sometimes get through and you will inadvertently give away your email address to a fake account that you thought was owned by a friend. A key issue is to understand is the severity of these risks and build solutions that are appropriate to the potential risk. A crucial factor in this approach to risk is the level of appetite for risk-taking. This may vary from culture to culture and from individual to individual.

Safety is often well funded in regulatory industries and corporations. Safety assessments are conducted and safety training and organizational responsibilities for safety defined, involving the whole workforce. But in security training, this cannot be a one-off exercise as the nature of cyber security risks are different. You can only do it that way if nothing changes, but this is never the case. Security is a long-term game; it is not like safety where you can provide the right equipment such as fire extinguishers, fire sensors, and sprinklers in buildings and then conduct regular safety checks of apparatus and procedures. You can get safety right and it is stable because the risks do not change that much in that context. Security is not like that, yet organizations are still trying to delivery cybersecurity training without explanation and appropriate methods. Organizations have failed to understand the fluid nature of the cyberthreats. Security is a long-term game, the technology and threats are changing and evolving all the time.

Research conducted by Professor Karen Renault of Abertay University took 12 groups of project managers and studied how they were selected for jobs. Just matching job requirements with perceived job competency on a CV alone is not enough.

The study also looked at autonomy and relatedness as well as competency (self–autonomy is the degree of personal ability to carry out specific tasks; relatedness is the social ability to relate and communicate with others in influencing and getting tasks done). Professor Renaud found that autonomy and relatedness, and not just competence, are very important in meeting job needs. This may be due to the particular type of role, but the observations were that the intrinsic needs were increasingly met when all three abilities were combined and effective.

With the World Wide Web, social media, and on YouTube channels, the perception is that "everyone is an expert", but this clearly is not the case, and no measure of intrinsic competence. Identifying true expertise is important, but this becomes more difficult and can be undermined if purported authoritative research is fraudulent, as was the case in the UK in 1998 when Dr Andrew Wakefield published research into the MMR vaccine, in which he asserted that it caused autism [3]. This was refuted as fraudulent following clear evidence of the falsification of data reported by the General Medical Council (GMA) and the British Medical Association (BMA). Child vaccinations in the UK plummeted, falling to their lowest in 2003/2004, only returning to their previous levels in 2012 [4, 5].

This remains a contentious case, in that the information is still available on the Internet, over time stoking conspiracy theories and perceptions-Pandora's jar is open. A consequence of these events is the erosion of trust in authority and expertise. More contentious is the exposure of the cost of care and the complexities of regulation and meeting public health needs. Both the GMC, BMA, and the NHS had to make extensive public communications to redress the perception of the event.

This highlights a more fundamental issue in fact-checking and the ability to validate the fact or message as true and that it comes from a trusted source. This is a key aspect of non-repudiation. In law, non-repudiation refers to the ability to ensure that a party to a contract or a communication cannot deny the authenticity of their signature on a document or the sending of a message they originated.

Principle 3: Empower People to Appropriately Pursue Cyber Issues

It is hard to use rules to control people. We can state that we want to be secure—we want to prevent hackers from stealing information—but how do we develop a culture that motivates people to believe in these values? How do we change people's behavior and the organizational perception?

One way is to stop treating people as enemies.

When a person dies in hospital from unexpected causes, the clinicians will carry out a mortician's conference to discuss how could they have saved this person's life. It is not about finger pointing, but about learning lessons. This is set out in Regulation 20: Duty of Candor of the Health and Social Care Act 2008 (Regulated Activities) Regulations 2014 [6]. Regulated by the Care Quality Commission, an independent regulator of health and social care in England, it sets out some specific requirements that providers must follow when things go wrong with care and treatment.

The issue of blame versus a process for learning is key. This impacts human behavior, in that an individual may resist telling the truth when something goes wrong to avoid blame. This potentially becomes an issue in ensuring the wider context of a safe living environment.

In computing, we are often concerned with accountability—who does what, who pressed this button. It is not a matter of accountability when it concerns malicious acts. Some acts may be unintentional mistakes. We should not treat everyone as if they were Edward Snowden.

These are controversial issues. We do not just talk about people dying in hospital but also where people were saved as well. You need some flexibility to allow people to break rules if they feel there is an issue that needs to be resolved in a cyberattack.

The "Gimli Glider" Case

Air Canada Flight 143 was a scheduled domestic passenger flight between Montreal and Edmonton that ran out of fuel on July 23, 1983, at an altitude of 12,500 meters (41,000 feet), midway through the flight due to a metric conversion error [7]. The crew was able to glide the Boeing 767 aircraft safely to an emergency landing at a former Royal Canadian Air Force base in Gimli, Manitoba. One interesting aspect was the creative way in which Captain Bob

Pearson, an experienced glider pilot, and his First Officer, Maurice Quintal, in extreme adversity, managed to glide the plane to the landing site having guessed the optimal glide speed of a 767 traveling at 220 knots [7]. In the absence of power, the pilots also employed another technique, a gravity drop, harnessing the force of gravity to lower the landing gear and lock it into place [8, 9]. There was nothing in the manual about how to deal with such an event. The subsequent investigation revealed that a combination of company failures, human errors, and confusion over unit measures had led to the aircraft being refueled with insufficient fuel for the planned flight.

We should avoid creating a blame culture where people are blamed for making honest mistakes. This is also an organizational and societal culture issue. In different parts of the world, the culture may require different forms of communication and compliance to senior roles. You must deal with the issues of culture and not just the person. Rigid organizational control systems can undermine trust in the very organization they are designed to control and keep safe.

Principle 4: Manage the Balance Between Commercial and Ethical Concerns

Organizational commercial interest will often motivate the organization to corporate governance, including cybersecurity, if it is in their self-interest.

Ethics Versus Legal Requirements

The problem with ethics is that there is no institutional reporting mechanisms demanding compliance to ethical privacy; whereas the law has institutions through which we enforce violations of our rights. It is possible to do everything legally but still act unethically. One example of this, known as the "Herod Clause", illustrated people's total disregard for security. Backed by the European law enforcement agency Europol, this 2014 experiment involved a group of security researchers setting up a free Wi-Fi spot in London [10]. In return for accessing the free Wi-Fi, customers had to agree to give up their first-born child! The so-called "Herod clause" stated: "the recipient agreed to assign their first-born child to us for the duration of eternity". Six people signed up!

Principle 5: Manage the Collection of Data to Assess Risks Effectively

The National Cyber Security Centre (NCSC) in the UK has computing issue response teams staffed with expert cybersecurity specialists who investigate malware and other reported attacks. These are highly confidential. They do not publish them. Qualifying the risk needs more data.

The Open Source Versus Proprietary Code Cyber Risk Debate

In a paper on open-source versus propriety code [11] published in 2002, Ross Anderson and others showed that proprietary programs should mathematically be as secure as those developed under the open-source model. Anderson argued that, other things being equal, he expected that open and closed systems will exhibit similar growth in reliability and in security assurance. The assumption was that using open-source solutions such as Linux's open-source operating system that are freely available could also be accessed by hackers, who could find vulnerabilities in the code; whereas closed-source code such as Microsoft Windows operating system has limited access to only selected employees of the company or that require the purchase of expense source code to gain access. The ability to reverse engineer a vulnerability to attack this type of code is harder and a much higher level of skill is required by the hacker. The open-source community claimed that for every hacker, there are many more good coders who on balance can find and fix bugs better and quicker than the rate of attacks and vulnerabilities. In closed-source systems, it takes much longer for hackers to devise an attack, but the code owners like Microsoft have far fewer coders to fix the problem.

The question over open-source and closed-source software has been hotly debated in terms of the level of risk and vulnerability in sharing code with a public group. Anderson argued that the implementation of the code was typically sufficiently different. Supporters in the Linux community have maintained that open-source programs are more secure; others such as Jim Allchin, a Microsoft executive at the time, argued in a court case that same year that opening Windows code would undermine security. He suggested that the more creators of viruses know about how antivirus mechanisms in Windows operating systems work, the easier it will be to create viruses or disable or destroy those mechanisms [12].

Today, this may not be the case as companies use many versions of the open-source code that are changed often enough to make it more difficult to attack, and in that respect resemble the closed-source systems. In addition, many systems are a mix of open-source and closed-source, combining Linux or other open-source code with proprietary systems from Apple, Microsoft, Amazon, Google, and others which may also use some variants of open-source.

The problem of trying to develop a good statistical risk model is difficult when the source of data is from rates of attack that are highly variable across many systems. This can involve many use cases of hundreds to thousands of different types of attack rates and different rates of fixing these problems. Trying to make sense of this in statistical risk model is challenging. This variation is evident both within an organization and between many organizations, making cyber risk models complex. The costs of a successful cyberattack also vary widely because of the diversity of backup processes used to restore data and recover the business operation. Comparing the impact cost of a cyber attack to the cost of fixing the cyber defense to prevent this attack in the first place can be difficult in identifying the right dimensions of comparison. For example, the cost of the impact to the number of people affected by a cyber attack to considering the costs of fixing the systems with the costs of security people and the patching and systems security investment needed.

The Problem of Low Diversity

Organizations can create problems with their IT Systems by only using a small range of types of hardware and software making everything the same standard equipment resulting in a low diversity. Essentially if there is a vulnerability in the equipment then potentially it may affect all of them to be attacked as there is less variation in configuration, less heterogeneity to create more complexity for the attackers to deal with.

Diversity is particularly important when it comes to the cost of a cyberattack and looking at the risks. If the attack hits all of your systems and they are a critical resource, then this potentially represents a significant cost to the business. Diversity helps reduce the attack surface through heterogeneity of the types of systems in use. In the healthcare area, for example, the large hospital operations utilize big computer servers for critical systems such as appointments and patient records, but may have separate systems for x-rays, MRIs, etc., along with many different PCs. If the call center of an insurance company, operating 10,000 machines on the same system, succumbs to a cyberattack, then potentially everything fails and customers will not be able to access the sevices for a day or more, with the potential consequences to the business' reputation and income. Cloud operators such as Google, Amazon, and Microsoft deliberately run diversity in their architectures, with multiple versions of components at any given time. This is partly due to the size and scale of their operations will have different versions of hardware and software accumulated over time but also for better resilience design. The reason is that updating to a new version may not work so rather then affecting all systems, to minimise the impact risk, different versions are upgraded and tested incrementally from what is called different "grandfather systems". This is good resilience design. There can be millions of machines in these large cloud data centers, and the upgrade paths can be much faster, so the management of this is controlled.

Installing a mix of systems for cybersecurity reasons rather than just end-user preference is quite costly and often depends on an organization's available resources. One well-known case was the successful transfer of the UK vehicle driving license system to an online computer version. It replaces many old features of the system, from printed card licenses to various registration documents, all combined electronically into one system. But subsequently, there was a problem with an upgrade which did not work and only had one version of the complete system. Even with essential maintenance downtime, these service disruptions can lead to complaints from customers unable to use critical systems [13]. Other concerns were raised about the installation reliability of the system [14]. It is a critical system with thousands of users visiting the site every day to register vehicle licenses, get insurance, and request identity verifications, etc. The lesson to be learned here is that running multiple versions for diversity and designing resilience in the system, with multiple access to backups if possible, is good practice.

Costs of Cybercrime

A study by a group led by Ross Anderson in 2012 found that as far as direct costs are concerned traditional offenses such as tax and welfare fraud cost the typical citizen in the low hundreds of pounds/euros/dollars a year; transitional frauds cost a few pounds/euros/dollars; while the new computer crimes cost in the tens of pence/cents. However, the indirect costs and defense costs are much higher for transitional and new crimes. For the former, they may be roughly comparable to what the criminals earn; whereas for the latter, they may be of a different order of magnitude. As a striking example, the botnet behind a third of the spam sent in 2010 earned its owners around US$2.7 million, while worldwide expenditures on spam prevention probably exceeded a billion dollars [15].

A member of this study, Richard Clayton, described several surveys made by commercial cybersecurity companies that were potentially exaggerated or dubious sources of data [16]. The point illustrated that reliable sources of cyberattack and fix data are difficult to obtain.

It is possible to measure the diversity of systems as most organizations keep inventories of computing assets. In software engineering, the bug discovery dates in system testing will have similar characteristics to the rate of cyberattacks and fixes statistically. Bugs are caused by program errors. More difficult are design mistakes—one example is HTTPS and SSL as a secure web protocol for identify verification and encryption. A few years ago, some flaws were found but the impact affects everyone who uses this standard protocol [17]. Some were programming mistakes, but some were design mistakes in the actual protocol. In February 2018, the biggest DDoS attack ever to date was an exploit of a misconfiguration on GitHub [18]. The first portion of the attack against the developer platform peaked at 1.35Tbps, and there was a second 400Gbps spike later [19]. Cloud service providers use a service called Memcached [20] and distributed an in-memory object caching system for file systems that should not be visible from outside the data center, but for some reason a default configuration was used which meant it was globally reachable. In what is called a triangulation attack used often in fraud [21], the Memcached system was not directly attacked but used to attack other targets by mimicking the memory block so that it appeared to be from the originating data center.

Principle 6: Run Red Teams, Blue Teams, Purple Teams

In terms of monetary investment, a company can spend millions on cybersecurity tools to monitor the technology infrastructure of applications, networks, operating systems, and traffic data. Examples of common cybersecurity defense tools include:

- Code reviews
- Static code analysis
- Dynamic code analysis testing
- Functional testing
- Non-functional testing
- Red teaming
- Blue teaming
- Purple teaming
- Automatic vulnerability scans
- Manual scans
- Threat detection and security incident response systems (SIEM)
- Incident log management and analysis, incident response.

Red Teams, Blue Teams, and Purple Teams in Cybersecurity

Red Teams

A red team is an internal group that explicitly challenges a company' s strategy, products, and preconceived notions. It frames a problem from the perspective of an adversary or a sceptic, to find gaps in plans, and to avoid blunders [22]. The term *red team* comes from the cold war practice of in which US officers adopted a Soviet, "red" perspective (Moscow did the same thing and called it a "blue team"). US officers would "think red" to attempt to defeat US plans and systems, rather than mirror-image US thinking onto the Soviets. For example, the US navy used a red team to try to defeat its own submarine force using Soviet concepts and technology. Today, red teams are used to double-check important assumptions and overcome groupthink, a term referring to the practice of thinking or making decisions as a group, resulting typically in unchallenged, poor-quality decision-making.

Blue Teams

A blue team is a group of individuals who perform an analysis of information systems to ensure security, identify security flaws, verify the effectiveness of each security measure, and to make certain all security measures will continue to be effective after implementation [23]. In preparation for a computer security incident, the blue team will perform hardening techniques on all operating systems throughout the organization [24]. If an incident does occur within the organization, the blue team will perform actions to identify, contain, eradicate, and recover from the incident, seeking to learn lessons from the event for future response management [25].

Purple Teams

Purple teams are ideally superfluous groups that exist to ensure and maximize the effectiveness of the red and blue teams. They do this by integrating the defensive tactics and controls from the blue team with the threats and vulnerabilities found by the red team into a single narrative that ensures the efforts of each are utilized to their maximum. When done properly, 1 + 1 will equal 3, but this should be happening naturally as the benefit of having a red and blue team. The purpose of a red team is to find ways to improve the blue team, so purple teams should not be needed in organizations where the red team/blue team interaction is functioning properly [26].

Principle 7: Manage an Effective Portfolio of Cyberdefense Tools

SIM, SEM, and SIEM: Security Information and Event Management Technology

SEM provides real-time monitoring and event management to support IT security operations. SEM requires several capabilities: event and data collection, aggregation and correlation in near real time; a dynamic monitoring/ security event console for viewing and managing events; and automated response generation for security events.

SIM delivers more historical analysis and reporting for security event data. This requires event and data collection/correlation (but not in real time), an indexed repository for log data and flexible query and reporting capabilities. When SEM and SIM are combined, they become Security Information and Event Management (SIEM) [27].

SIEM software supports threat detection and security incident response by performing real-time data collection and analysis of security events. This type of software also uses data sources outside of the network, including IoC threat intelligence. Vendors sell SIEM as software, as appliances, or as managed services; these products are also used to log security data and generate reports for compliance purposes. Examples of the types of SIEM functions include:

Type of vulnerability/exploit detection	SIEM tool function
Logging events	Parsing, log normalization, and categorization
Security events and log failures	
Detect zero-days	
Detect polymorphic code (computer virus)	Visualization of pattern anomalies
Protocol anomalies which can indicate a misconfiguration or a security issue	Pattern detection, alerting, baseline, and dashboards
Detect covert, malicious communications and encrypted channels	Network traffic pattern anomalies

(continued)

Type of vulnerability/exploit detection	SIEM tool function
Detect cyberwarfare acts	Identify evidence of attackers and victims
Trigger early warning of cyberattack	Set policy thresholds for alerts

Adapted from Chris Kubecka hacking conference 28C3 (Chaos Communication Congress) 2011 [28]

Examples of SIEM alerts:

Type of vulnerability/exploit detection	SIEM tool alert rule
Early warning for brute force attacks, password guessing, and misconfigured applications	Repeat attack-login source
Early warning for scans, worm propagation	Repeat attack-firewall
	Repeat attack-network intrusion prevention system
Find hosts that may be infected or compromised (exhibiting infection behaviors)	Repeat attack-host intrusion prevention system
Alert when a virus, spyware, or other malware is detected on a host	Virus detection/removal
Alert when > 1 h has passed since malware was detected on a source, with no corresponding virus successfully removed	Virus or spyware detected but failed to clean

Adapted from David Swift, SANS Institute 2010 [29]

Principle 8: Manage Organizational Discipline and Fix Knowledge Gaps

IoT Cyberattacks—the Case Study of the Philips Hue "Smart" Lightbulb Cyberattack

The Philips Hue "smart" lightbulb cyberattack in 2016 was an example of an IoT attack, which in this case was developed as a demonstration by Israeli and Canadian university researchers. A malware program "worm" was able to be inserted remotely through a wireless connection into a vulnerability in the device [30, 31]. The attack exploited hardcoded symmetric encryption keys to control devices over Zigbee wireless networks. They were all symmetric keys instead of asymmetric keys that may have contributed to a more comprehensive protection [32]. Apart from using just symmetric keys and hiding them with differential power measures only, they were very vulnerable to cyberattack.

This allowed the malware to compromise a single light globe from up to 400 meters away. The worm spread by jumping directly from one light to its neighbors, using only their built-in Zigbee wireless connectivity and their physical proximity. The attack could be initiated by plugging in a single infected bulb anywhere in the city, which then catastrophically spread everywhere within minutes, enabling the attacker to turn all the city lights on or off, permanently brick them, or exploit them in a massive DDoS attack.

The worm could also then spread from a single smart bulb to other smart bulbs due to them using the same symmetric encryption keys duplicated on each device using the same base keys. It was a classic asymmetric attack, but there was no proper public-key infrastructure (PKI) system in place that could have defined the policies and procedures needed to create, manage, distribute, use, store, and revoke digital certificates and manage public-key encryption [33]. The bulb device did have differential power analysis (DPA) attack countermeasures to the side-channel attack [34–36], but these can typically be broken in a cyber attack; it just depends how much effort, time, and resources are involved. (The embedded device code symmetric keys could in fact be discovered by examining the firmware code.) A side-channel is an unintentional channel providing information about the internal activity of the chip—for example, power consumption or EM emissions. These low-cost, non-invasive methods enable attackers to stealthily extract secret cryptographic keys used during normal device operations [37].

Several lessons can be learned from this case:

- Poor cybersecurity disciplines in firmware controls of public key management on IoT embedded code can result in the same symmetric keys on all devices; meaning if one is infected, then they all can be simultaneously infected.
- This was amplified by the wireless connectivity between the devices themselves, further facilitating the spread of the attack vector and attack surface vulnerabilities. The attack is a worm and can jump from connected device to connected device through the air. It could potentially knock out an entire city with just one infected bulb at the root "within minutes".
- Furthermore, there was a design fault in sending patches to the firmware to fix this; the malicious firmware could disable additional downloads,

and thus any effect caused by the worm (such as blackout, constant flickering, etc.) would be permanent. There is no other method of reprogramming these devices without fully disassembling them (which is not feasible). Any old stock would also need to be recalled, as any devices with vulnerable firmware can be infected as soon as the power is applied [37].

Philips were early to market with the new smart lightbulbs, but the limits this inevitably placed on time and costs meant that they had only used on symmetric keys and hidden them with differential power analysis (DPA) countermeasures. DPA refers to the reality that actual computers and microchips leak information about the operations they process. Cyber attackers can use methods for analyzing power consumption measurements to find secret keys from tamper-resistant devices. The attack exploits biases varying the power consumption of microprocessors or other hardware while performing operations using secret keys. Once the keys have been extracted, attackers can easily gain unauthorized access to a device, decrypt or forge messages, steal identities, clone devices, create unauthorized signatures, and perform additional unauthorized transactions. DPA countermeasures are implemented in layers to include hardware (DPA resistant cores), software (DPA resistant libraries) or both, with the aim of preventing access to EM data leakages.

Organizations need to implement proper countermeasures across the whole organization, from the embedded hardware and software to policies and procedures for effective firmware and encryption management. In Philips Lighting, Philips Medical Systems (now Philips Healthcare) and other divisions, this was done across the whole organization.

Principle 9: Manage Your Existential Threats

Control System Hacks with Physical Damage—the Case Study of the German Steel Mill Attack

The German Steel Mill case study of 2015 was the second instance of a cyberattack that caused physical damage [38]. The control system was hacked. The attack impacted the IT systems, breaking their crucible, and the steel they had produced for the last six months had to be completely reworked, including buildings that had been constructed with the metal [39]. The first case involved Stuxnet, the sophisticated digital weapon the USA and Israel launched against control systems in Iran in late 2007 and early 2008 to sabotage centrifuges at a uranium enrichment plant. The attack destroyed 1000 machines and Iran reportedly decommissioned around 20% of its centrifuges in the Natanz plant during the attack [40].

If You Can Make It, Somebody Can Break It

We are in a full-on asymmetric war, you can be 99.9999% correct but if the bad guys can find one way in, they have won. You can drive yourself to paranoia trying to close off all the points of entry; you can spend large amounts of money in selecting from different vendors who may offer different types of protection. How is this measured? And from what attacks?

How much you invest is a commercial decision. The reality is a pathological one, however—you are always going to lose. Your devices are always going to get "owned" at some level if there is an intent to break through. Like a house, you can install the most sophisticated locks on every door, but someone can still smash a window. I have evidence that someone has broken in. This is a similar analogy to be found in zero-trust strategy that is seeking to find patterns of intrusion through anomalous behavior akin to "smashed glass from the window" leaving behind a sign someone who may be an adversary has entered.

Critical National Infrastructure (CNI) Attacks

In a recent poll of UK MPs by the NCC Group, nearly two-thirds cited attacks on CNI as the biggest cybersecurity threat facing the UK [41]. For each organization, this can have a different level of impact. For an energy company, energy going offline could have a serious impact on people's safety. If an IT company is subject to a CNI type of attack, then there is a duty, a cost, and a process that needs to be undertaken.

Existential Threats

Existential threats to a company include, for example:

- Losing your intellectual property (IP breach).
- Losing control and value of your brand, ethics (brand theft, brand reputation).

- Legal charges directed at company owners and directors, loss of director employment.
- Losing control of your company operation, becoming a takeover target—the nudging of data and data manipulation.

Such threats could cause the company to collapse.

The Nature of Threats Has Multiplied

It used to be that denial of service, Trojans, and similar attacks represented the bleeding edge of technology, but today you can buy them off the Dark Web and deploy them easily; to some extent, we have been desensitized to these types of threats. But new types of threats have evolved; they are all existential threats to some extent but in different ways. DoS can bring your telecommunications down, but there are ways of dealing with this. This requires resilience in the system: when your primary network has stopped, you bring up a second connection backup so you have a secondary network IP address. These are transitory attacks and we are somewhat used to them, but then there are the more insidious attacks.

In a 2016 interview to *Raconteur* magazine, Johnny Hornby, founder of WPP-backed communications group The&Partnership, described how the situation has changed: "Today's environment is radically different from that of just five years ago, when businesses were only targeted if they held a large and substantial prize. Nowadays, opportunists armed with the digital equivalent of a set of lock picks and a crowbar may attempt an attack. So, it's critical that businesses of all sizes continually review the locks on their doors and the transparency of their windows." [42]

In 2018, a *Telegraph* article on director liabilities and insurance quoted Nigel Peters, managing partner at resourcing firm Alium Partners: "It is an extra dimension now (for Corporate Board Strategy) and cyberattacks are now affecting firms of all descriptions, from SMEs to the NHS. Companies now usually hold vast amounts of data that can be vulnerable to attack from anywhere in the world" [43].

To best sum up the continual debate about the effectiveness of cybersecurity standards, certification, and accreditation, we can say that cybersecurity standards are involved in measuring security planning rather than measuring information security. That said, standards and guideline frameworks are critical to best practices and are continually evolving, while areas such as zero-trust strategies, continuous threat monitoring and response readiness are necessary in the face of the increasing volume and changing nature of new cyberattacks.

Principle 10: Manage Your Intellectual Property (IP)

Losing your intellectual property (IP breach)—the case study of the Australian Metal Detector Company.

In 2011, an Australian metal detector company, Codan, suffered an IP breach in which Chinese hackers stole the company's metal detector designs. Sales and prices of the firm's metal detectors collapsed as the Chinese hackers sold cheap imitations into Africa, and Codan was forced to slash prices to compete with the counterfeits. The company only began to realize it had a problem when its services center started receiving faulty metal detectors. Those products, stamped with the Codan logo, had unrecognizable, inferior parts. The company spent "significant sums" on private investigators, who worked with the Chinese police to track down operatives involved in the supply chain of the counterfeit metal detectors, leading to subsequent fines and convictions [44].

Losing Control of Your Brand

In the cyberattack on telecommunications company TalkTalk in October 2015, personal information belonging to more than 150,000 customers was compromised, and almost one in ten of those customers had their bank account numbers and sort codes accessed. TalkTalk profits more than halved following the attack, and pre-tax profits fell to £14 million in the year to March 31, from £32 million a year earlier. After losing 95,000 customers in the third quarter as a direct result of the hacking, the company share price did eventually recover over time. Although the breach was not as bad as it initially feared, the telecoms firm's reputation took a pounding as it emerged that teenage hackers had breached the website with ease [45].

Legal Charges Directed at Company Owners and Directors, Loss of Director Employment

These attacks can create follow-on problems and legal claims that may have a serious impact on the directors of the company. The 2015 cyberattack by the activist hacker team calling itself "The Impact Team" threatened to expose the identities of 37.5 million users of the notorious Canadian-based extramarital dating website Ashley Madison. On August 18 and 20, the group leaked more than 25 gigabytes of company data, including user details [46].

The attack was allegedly instigated by the activists to demonstrate the claim that customers of Ashley Madison could use a "full delete function" for $19 that could remove their personal identity permanently was false. The attack came just two months after another relationship site, AdultFriendFinder, was hacked, and as Ashley Madison was considering a $200 million initial public offering on the London exchange later that year [47].

The cyberattack forced its chief executive Noel Biderman to resign in August 2015. Already under pressure after details of the website's 37 million users had been stolen and dumped online, his personal integrity also came under fire when leaked emails raised questions about his own marital behavior. The share price of parent company, Avid Life Media at the time saw its share price halved since the data breaches emerged and were facing the prospect of multiple legal cases of class-action lawsuits against Avid Dating Life and Avid Life Media, the owners of Ashley Madison [48].

The attack also exposed ethical issue impacts. Several suicides were reported, including in Toronto, where two unconfirmed suicides were linked to the data breach, in addition to "reports of hate crimes connected to the hack". And there was also an unconfirmed report of a man committing suicided in the USA [49, 50].

The Rise of Intellectual Property as the Source of Value and the Target of Threats

Denial of services, data breaches, and ransomware are insidious attacks; but they are also theoretical.

I may or may not suffer from a DoS attack; I may or may not be the victim of ransomware—this is how businesses think: they try to deal with real risks as opposed to assumed risk. However, there is another aspect to this—Intellectual property. As businesses move from selling a device to selling a service, the software on that product, the intellectual property, becomes the sole point of value. The container, device, vehicle, building, or location is just a means by which an organization can hold or generate that IP and its associated experiences. So, the protection of intellectual property is becoming increasingly important. This includes [51]:

- Inhibiting cloning
- Preventing counterfeiting
- Preventing overproduction
- Using strong non-disclosure agreements

- Due care when filing for patent to avoid copying
- Working rapidly to develop innovations to remain competitive
- Using separate teams to de-risk the possibility of employees, ex-employees, or contractors walking away from the company with IP
- Using strong access control to store manuscripts, creations, and ideas in a safe place that is protected by an identity and access-management solution. The majority of all data breaches start with the theft of credentials
- Using open-source
- Using organizational separation
- Avoiding joint ventures to reduce later risks of shared ownership and legal issues.

To cite one example, a door opener locksmith company in Japan discovered that an ex-employee has stolen all their intellectual property and set up his own company in Iran to make the same products. In another case, the Massachusetts based robot vacuum cleaning iRobot Roomba produced 600,000 robots in 2016 but 1.2 million were sold in China, a case of grand larceny. Interestingly, the software was identical, utilizing commercial-off-the-shelf chips, and the plastics were indistinguishable. iRobot also filed legal cases of IP violations against Hoover and Black and Decker, including misuse of its obstacle-detection system, brush designs and navigation controls [52].

In a third case, an industrial controls company learned that people were overproducing or cloning their products, injecting them into the distribution channel, they are great at mixing these counterfeit products into the existing market supply chain. The initial impact was a loss of sales. Then they started receiving support calls from customers who had bought the cheap knock-offs, complaining that the products had stopped working. People think they have bought an authentic product, but the end the customer is laboring under a misapprehension. The company then had to incur the costs of sending out repair vehicles to the industrial control systems to establish why they were not working. Unable to locate the problem, they had to install a replacement. So, not only had they not sold the first one but had had to replace it, thus incurring two losses. They have not even sold the first one and having to replace it with a proper one. It was only when they subsequently carried out an investigation that they realized it was a clone. This fundamentally undermined the organizational finances and well as the brand's reputation. It was a potentially existential threat to the company. One solution to this problem could have been to replace with a product and to then through a connected online connected system, use this for condition monitoring. This would mean that customers who bought the product could know it was authentic and verified by the original legal company.

It is not the components and the materials but the software and the brand that is the value. Software can be stolen, and brand can be damaged. This an issue for large OEMs: they can work out all possible scenarios, but how much are they prepared to spend to protect themselves? They don't know if these attacks will happen and it is hard to communicate the potential risks to the company board. On the other hand, they may spend a hundred million or more on R&D; then the question is "would you like to protect that hundred million?" and stop being ripped off. Paying a bit extra per device to protect it is good investment. It is like a second amendment for the digital world—the ability to protect the freedoms of the spaces and things we use and the rights we hold.

Principle 11: Manage the Legal Liabilities of the Board of Directors

In the USA, directors and officers insurance (D&O) was created following years of class acts and litigations. Cyber data and security breaches, if they are material to the firm and the business of the organization, can result in D&O claims brought by shareholders and potentially regulators [53]. The US Federal Trade Commission (FTC) sets cybersecurity enforcement regulations which rely on a cost–benefit analysis, weighing harm to consumers against the benefits to consumers and their own ability to avoid the harm [54]. There have also been proposals for enhanced rules by the US Office of the Comptroller of the Currency, the Federal Reserve System, and the Federal Deposit Insurance Corporation relating to cyber risk management standards for large banks. These include requirements for the boards of banks to develop cyber risk management strategies and have adequate expertise on cybersecurity matters [55].

The main US cybersecurity regulations include the 1996 Health Insurance Portability and Accountability Act (HIPAA), which covers data management in healthcare; the 1999 Gramm-Leach-Bliley Act (GLBA), which provides due diligence for financial institutions. Following the September 11, 2001 attacks, the 2002 Homeland Security Act (HSA) covers provisions for counterterrorism, information and intelligence, and includes the Critical Infrastructure Information Act 2002 (CIIA) and the Cyber Security Enhancement Act 2002 (CSEA). The CSEA covers sentencing laws for cybercrimes and legal rules for cybersecurity violations. The HSA also includes the 2002 Federal Information Security Management Act (FISMA) that contains a compliance framework covering information systems classification, security and risk controls, systems security plans, continuous monitoring, and certification and accreditation [56].

In the UK, if a loss occurs and the executive board of a company is found to be negligent in its duties, then each director potentially faces unlimited personal liability [57]. Under the Companies Act 2006, the board of directors must:

- Keep up to date about issues in cybersecurity risks—cybersecurity should definitely be a priority.
- Take professional or expert advice. You can be held personally negligent if you fail to take appropriate advice in areas you don't have enough expertise in yourself.

The board also retains a residual duty when they rely on external experts to manage functions like cybersecurity. In this scenario, the board has a duty to ensure that they are monitoring the performance of these outside companies effectively and acting on their advice.

Directors and Officers Insurance (D&O), Cyber Insurance, and Vicarious Liability

D&O was invented in the USA, where many huge claims have been paid out, fueled by class actions. In the UK, there is a different legal framework, but there have been claims against directors and the numbers are rising. Although not as frequent in the UK, claims by shareholders/debt holders do occur, but in addition to these there are an increasing number of criminal prosecutions or investigations arising from incidents such as deaths or injuries in the workplace, food contamination, and breaches of consumer protection laws.

D&O sees an insurer stepping in to provide guidance at the first sign of a problem and ensuring legal costs and damages are met. A typical D&O policy covers individual directors for all acts, errors, and omissions arising from their conduct as directors, which could include matters relating to a cyber incident. However, there is no cyber exclusion on the policy which may invalidate cover.

The coming years, however, could see data issues as a further reason to put directors in the dock and a spur for this is likely to be the impending General Data Protection Regulation (GDPR). In the case of a cyberattack in the UK, GDPR, and the Data Protection Act 2018 that implements this, requires the company to report the attack to the ICO—Information

Commissioner's Office within 72 hours. The ICO will take an increasingly tough stance against firms with lax standards and, equally, directors could be in the line of fire if they fail to act diligently.

The ICO wants directors to take responsibility and we are likely to see more criminal prosecutions. The Data Protection Act (updated in 2018) has a specific section relating to criminal offenses and directors' liability. Directors should also be aware of "vicarious liability" where an employee is guilty of wrongdoing and if this could have been prevented. There is a partial role for D&O here as directors may be blamed in the event of a breach that results in a financial impact on the business due to a large fine or reputational damage—or it may be that the affected business simply needs to put things right and shore up its systems again. In this case, cover should be provided by cyber insurance. Separate standalone cybersecurity insurance policies will generally provide cyber breach response services, the cost of which is met under the policy [43].

Principle 12: Manage Losing Control of Your Company Operation

The Nudging of Data

This refers to driving a change in company behavior to effect an end goal. This may be something that will break a system in the event of a more nuanced financial attack. For example, an energy company might suspect they are being hacked—their systems are dumping energy and they have to overproduce, so they are making a loss on energy production. As a result, they have to sell bonds to raise capital. The Chinese are buying the bonds and consequently acquire the company cheaply. This is a form of stealth attack that needs new forms of pattern recognition and real-time detection of hybrid and stealthy cyberattacks in a smart grid [58, 59].

Data Manipulation

Another example is data manipulation that weakens the data integrity of an organization or person. This is the practice of altering digital documents and other information that could seriously undermine corporations and critical infrastructure services providers, health care providers, national security agencies, and individuals around the world. The hackers can infiltrate networks via any attack vector, find their way into databases and applications, with the aim of just changing the information contained in those systems, rather than stealing data and holding it for ransom [60]. The severity of this attack is increased by the modified data making it more difficult to determine what is the original version of the true data and "the truth" if this is not immediately available or has been destroyed in the attack.

References

1. *CF disclosure guidance: Topic No. 2 2011 cyber security.* https://www.sec.gov/divisions/corpfin/guidance/cfguidance-topic2.htm.
2. Updated SEC guidance February 2018 17 CFR Parts 229 and 249 [Release Nos. 33-10459; 34-82746]. *Commission statement and guidance on public company cybersecurity disclosures.* https://www.sec.gov/rules/interp/2018/33 10459.pdf.
3. Godlee, F., Smith, J., & Marcovitch, H. Wakefield's article linking MMR vaccine and autism was fraudulent. *British Medical Journal* 342, doi:https://doi.org/10.1136/bmj.c7452 (Published 6 January 2011) *British Medical Journal* 342: c7452. https://www.bmj.com/content/342/bmj.c7452.
4. Ruling on doctor in MMR scare. (2010, January). NHS. https://www.nhs.uk/news/medical-practice/ruling-on-doctor-in-mmr-scare/.
5. Smith, R. (2012, November). MMR uptake rates finally recovered from Wakefield scandal figures show. *The Telegraph.* https://www.telegraph.co.uk/news/health/news/9705374/MMR-uptake-rates-finally-recovered-from-Wakefield-scandal-figures-show.html.
6. Health and Social Care Act 2008 (Regulated activities) Regulations 2014. *Regulation 20: Duty of candour.* https://www.cqc.org.uk/guidance-providers/regulations-enforcement/regulation-20-duty-candour.
7. Witkin, R. (1983, July). Jet's fuel ran out after metric conversion errors. *New York Times.* https://www.nytimes.com/1983/07/30/us/jet-s-fuel-ran-out-after-metric-conversion-errors.html.
8. Aviation Safety Network. July 1983 Report. https://aviation-safety.net/database/record.php?id=19830723-0.
9. Great miscalculations: The French railway error and 10 others (2014, May). BBC. https://www.bbc.co.uk/news/magazine 27509559.
10. Fox-Brewster, T. (2014, September). Londoners give up eldest children in public Wi-Fi security horror show. *The Guardian.* https://www.theguardian.com/technology/2014/sep/29/londoners-wi-fi-security-herod-clause.
11. Ross Anderson. (2002, June 20–21). Security in open versus closed systems—The dance of Boltzmann, Coase and Moore. Open source software: Economics, law and policy, Toulouse, France.
12. Lemos, R. (2002, June). Open, closed source security about equal? Zdnet. https://www.zdnet.com/article/open-closed-source-security-about-equal-5000296876/.

13. Smith, Luke J. (2018, August). Why buying a car or trying to tax your car this weekend could see you land a £1,000 fine. *The Express*. https://www.express.co.uk/life-style/cars/1004805/DVLA-car-tax-website-down-fine-buying-car-UK.

14. John, L. (2018, March). DVLA denies driving license processing site is a security 'car crash'. The Register. https://www.theregister.co.uk/2018/03/09/dvla_insecure_site_dispute/.

15. *Measuring the cost of cybercrime*, WES2012 Conference. https://www.econinfosec.org/archive/weis2012/papers/Anderson_WEIS2012.pdf.

16. Clayton, R. *Measuring Cybercrime*, University of Cambridge, Computer laboratory. October 2012. https://www.cl.cam.ac.uk/~rnc1/talks/121019-cybercrime.pdf.

17. Hoffman, C. (2014, February). *5 serious problems with HTTPS and SSL security on the web*. How-To Geek. https://www.howtogeek.com/182425/5-serious-problems-with-https-and-ssl-security-on-the-web/.

18. February 28th DDoS incident report. (2018, March). GitHub Engineering, skottler. https://githubengineering.com/ddos-incident-report/.

19. Ranger, S. (2018, March). *GitHub hit with the largest DDoS attack ever seen*. ZDNet. https://www.zdnet.com/article/github-was-hit-with-the-largest-ddos-attack-ever-seen/.

20. Memcached. https://memcached.org/.

21. Understanding Triangulation fraud. (October 2015). Radial. https://www.radial.com/insights/understanding-triangulation-fraud.

22. *Red Team Definition from Financial Times Lexicon*. http://lexicon.ft.com/term?term=red-team.

23. "DoDD 8570.1: Blue Team". ADI (formerly Sypris Electronics). https://www.sypriselectronics.com/information-security/cyber-security-solutions/computer-network-defense/.

24. *Cyber guardian: Blue team*, SANS Institute https://www.sans.org/cyber-guardian/blue-team.

25. Murdoch, D. (2014). *Blue team handbook*. Incident Response Edition (2nd ed.). Scotts Valley: CreateSpace Independent Publishing Platform. ISBN 978-1500734756.

26. Miessler, D. (February, 2016). *The difference between red, blue, and purple teams*. https://danielmiessler.com/study/red-blue-purple-teams/.

27. Jamil, A., Sectier. (2010, March 29). *The difference between SEM, SIM and SIEM*. https://www.gmdit.com/NewsView.aspx?ID=9IfB2Axzeew=.

28. Kubecka, C. (2011, December 29). *28c3: Security log visualization with a correlation engine*. https://www.youtube.com/watch?v=j4pF9VUdphc&feature=youtu.be https://events.ccc.de/congress/2011/Fahrplan/events/4767.en.html.

29. Swift, D. (2010). *Successful SIEM and log management strategies for audit and compliance*. SANS Institute. https://www.sans.org/reading-room/whitepapers/auditing/paper/33528.

30. Pauli, D. (2016, November). IoT worm can hack Philips Hue lightbulbs, spread across cities. The Register. https://www.theregister.co.uk/2016/11/10/iot_worm_can_hack_philips_hue_lightbulbs_spread_across_cities/.

31. Ronen, E., O'Flynn, C., Shamir, A., Weingarten, A.-O. *IoT Goes nuclear: Creating a ZigBee chain reaction.* IoT IEEE Security & Privacy. https://doi.org/10.1109/msp.2018.1331033.

32. *Symmetric vs. asymmetric encryption—What are differences?*, SSL2Buy. Accessed October 2018. https://www.ssl2buy.com/wiki/symmetric-vs-asymmetric-encryption-what-are-differences.

33. *An overview of public key infrastructures (PKI).* Accessed October 2018. https://www.techotopia.com/index.php/An_Overview_of_Public_Key_Infrastructures_(PKI).

34. Kocher, P., Jae, J., & Benjamin, J. *Differential Power Analysis (DPA).* Cryptography Research, Inc. https://www.paulkocher.com/doc/DifferentialPowerAnalysis.pdf.

35. Introduction to side-channel attacks, Rambus. Accessed October 2018. http://info.rambus.com/hubfs/rambus.com/Gated-Content/Cryptography/Introduction-to-Side-Channel-Attacks-eBook.pdf?hsCtaTracking=c476fb62-8de1-44e8-b7c9-9607f0cb447e%7Cafdca38a-dd94-44ba-a18c-a7eb8ad70d5d.

36. *DPA Countermeasures.* Rambus. Accessed October 2018. https://www.rambus.com/security/dpa-countermeasures/.

37. Seppala, T. J. (2016, November). Hackers hijack Philips Hue lights with a drone. Engadget. https://www.engadget.com/2016/11/03/hackers-hijack-a-philips-hue-lights-with-a-drone/.

38. Kim Zetter. (2015, January). *A cyberattack has caused confirmed physical damage for the second time ever.* Wired. https://www.wired.com/2015/01/german-steel-mill-hack-destruction/.

39. *Die Lage der IT-Sicherheit in Deutschland 2014 German.* Steel Mill Hack Report. https://www.wired.com/wp-content/uploads/2015/01/Lagebericht2014.pdf.

40. Timeline: How Stuxnet attacked a nuclear plant. BBC, Iwonder. https://www.bbc.com/timelines/zc6fbk7.

41. Phil Muncaster. (2018, June). MPs: CNI attacks are UK's biggest cyber-threat. *Infosecurity Magazine.* https://www.infosecurity-magazine.com/news/mps-cni-attacks-are-uks-biggest/.

42. Spanier, G. (2016, March 8). *Protecting brand reputation in the wake of a cyber-attack.* Raconteur. https://www.raconteur.net/risk-management/protecting-brand-reputation-in-the-wake-of-a-cyber-attack.

43. Why digital-age directors need directors and officers (D&O) cover. (2018, February 28). *The Telegraph.* https://www.telegraph.co.uk/business/risk-insights/directors-need-d-and-o-insurance/.

44. Australian metal detector company counts cost of Chinese hacking. (2015, June). Reuters. https://www.reuters.com/article/china-cybersecurity-australia/

australian-metal-detector-company-counts-cost-of-chinese-hacking-idUSL3N-0YX2OX20150624.

45. Monaghan, A. (2016, May 12). TalkTalk profits halve after cyber-attack. *The Guardian*. https://www.theguardian.com/business/2016/may/12/talktalk-profits-halve-hack-cyber-attack.

46. Ashley Madison data breach. Wikipedia. Accessed October 2018. https://en.wikipedia.org/wiki/Ashley_Madison_data_breach.

47. Thomsen, S. (2015, July 20). Extramarital affair website Ashley Madison has been hacked and attackers are threatening to leak data online. Business Insider. http://uk.businessinsider.com/cheating-affair-website-ashley-madison-hacked-user-data-leaked-2015-7?r=US&IR=T.

48. Ashley Madison hack threatens to expose 37 m adulterers, Sophie Curtis, *The Telegraph*. https://www.telegraph.co.uk/technology/internet-security/11750432/Adultery-website-Ashley-Madison-hack-threatens-to-expose-37.5m-cheaters.html.

49. Ashley Madison hack: 2 unconfirmed suicides linked to breach, Toronto police say. (2015, August 24). CBC Canada. https://www.cbc.ca/news/canada/toronto/ashley-madison-hack-2-unconfirmed-suicides-linked-to-breach-toronto-police-say-1.3201432.

50. Richard Chirgwin, Ashley Madison spam starts, as leak linked to first suicide. (2015, August 23). The Register. https://www.theregister.co.uk/2015/08/23/ashley_madison_spam_starts_as_leak_linked_to_first_suicide/.

51. 10 Effective ways to protect your intellectual property. (2018, July 23). Forbes Technology Council. https://www.forbes.com/sites/forbestechcouncil/2018/07/23/10-effective-ways-to-protect-your-intellectual-property/#254c7f5732e1.

52. iRobot sues Hoover and Black & Decker over robo-vacuums. (2017, April 18). BBC. https://www.bbc.co.uk/news/technology-39629339.

53. D&O liability in data privacy and cyber security situations in the US. (2014, January). *Financier Worldwide*. https://www.financierworldwide.com/do-liability-in-data-privacy-and-cyber-security-situations-in-the-us/#.W9V-GtP7QdU.

54. 15 U.S.C.A. § 45(n) (West). In assessing the reasonableness of cybersecurity practices, courts have considered the sensitivity of data, the size and complexity of the company's network, and the cost of additional security measures. See F.T.C. v. Wyndham Worldwide Corp., 799 F.3d 236, 255 (3d Cir. 2015).

55. *Enhanced cyber risk management standards*, 81 Fed. Reg. 74315 (proposed 26 October 2016) (to be codified at 12 C.F.R. pt. 30). https://www.federalregister.gov/documents/2016/10/26/2016-25871/enhanced-cyber-risk-management-standards.

56. *Cyber-security regulation*, Wikipedia. Accessed October 2018. https://en.wikipedia.org/wiki/Cyber-security_regulation.

57. Cyber-attack: Your legal responsibilities as a company director. (2017, September). Finch. https://www.finchib.co.uk/cyber-attack-legal-responsibilities-company-director/.

58. Kurt, M. N., Yılmaz, Y., & Wang, X. (2018, June 28). Real-time detection of hybrid and stealthy cyber-attacks in smart grid. IEEE arXiv:1803.00128v2 [cs. IT]. https://arxiv.org/pdf/1803.00128.

59. Cazorla, L., Alcaraz, C., & Lopez, J. (2018 June). Cyber stealth attacks in critical information infrastructures. *IEEE Systems Journal, 12* (2). https://ieeexplore. ieee.org/document/7445136.

60. Is data manipulation the next step in cybercrime? Cloudmask. Accessed October 2018. https://www.cloudmask.com/blog/is-data-manipulation-the-next-step-in-cybercrime.

61. David M. (2017, November 17). ID card security: Spain is facing chaos over chip crypto flaws. ZDNet. https://www.zdnet.com/article/ id-card-security-spain-is-facing-chaos-over-chip-crypto-flaws/.

62. Leyden, J. (2017, November 3). Estonia government locks down ID smartcards: Refresh or else. The Register. https://www.theregister.co.uk/2017/11/03/ estonian_e_id_lockdown/.

63. Meltdown and spectre. Accessed October 2018. https://meltdownattack.com/.

64. WikiLeaks dumps docs on CIA's hacking tools. Krebsonsecurity. Accessed October 2018. https://krebsonsecurity.com/tag/weeping-angel/.

65. Friedmann, S. (2017, March 13). What is the weeping angel program? John Oliver debunked the rumors. March 2017. https://www.bustle.com/p/ what-is-the-weeping-angel-program-john-oliver-debunked-the-rumors-43861.

66. Lee, D. (2016, February 18). *Apple v the FBI—A plain English guide*. BBC. https://www.bbc.co.uk/news/technology-35601035.

67. Lapowsky, I. (2018, April 18). How Russian Facebook ads divided and targeted US voters before the 2016 election. *Wired*. https://www.wired.com/story/ russian-facebook-ads-targeted-us-voters-before-2016-election/.

68. Stewart, E. (2018, July 31). Facebook has already detected suspicious activity trying to influence the 2018 elections. Vox. https://www.vox. com/2018/7/31/17635592/facebook-elections-russia-2018-midterms.

69. Facebook-Cambridge Analytica data scandal. BBC. Accessed October 2018. https://www.bbc.co.uk/news/topics/c81zyn0888lt/facebook-cambridge-analytica-data-scandal.

70. Hatton, E. (2018, February 12). Life online: How big is your digital footprint?, RNZ. https://www.radionz.co.nz/news/national/350224/life-online-how-big-is-your-digital-footprint.

14

In Place of a Conclusion

Most books end with conclusions. However, at the beginning of our story we told you that this is a story about trust. And any trustworthy relationships are based on reputation, which is a continuous and dynamic phenomenon. Trust is the reason why most companies successfully tackle cyber risks and, at the same time, it is also the reason many of us get in trouble when adversaries are tricking us into something we would not otherwise do.

So, we cannot conclude this story just yet because, whether we like it or not, it will live beyond the passages of this book. We simply do not know yet how this story ends …

We are yet to see how cybersecurity threats will evolve in the next few years and what solutions will be designed to counteract those threats. Will we be able to algorithmically model adversarial behavior and cyberattacks in such a way that our algorithms will stand a tough test not only in identifying cybercriminals, but also in a court of law? To what extent will the cybersecurity measures of the future be based on human values? Will we be able to ensure that cybersecurity is achieved without limiting and violating human rights and freedoms? Will we learn how to effectively share information between businesses and customers, within organizations, between businesses, and between businesses and regulators? Will we understand cybersecurity risks better in the next ten years or will the digital spaces become even less structured and more confusing? How will cybercriminal ecosystems and business models evolve in the future? Will we succeed in training humans to successfully detect potential risks and vulnerabilities in

© The Author(s) 2019
G. Pogrebna and M. Skilton, *Navigating New Cyber Risks*,
https://doi.org/10.1007/978-3-030-13527-0_14

cyber spaces? Will we learn to use human psychology to our benefit rather than design measures to stop adversaries exploiting our psychological traits? Will we find optimal ways to manage cybersecurity issues at a country, city, organizational, and individual level? What will the active cyberdefense of the future look like? How will it be affected by the Industrial Revolution 4.0 with the development of AI and quantum computing?

All these questions remain unanswered. Therefore, to all our readers we are saying—"thank you!" But we are not saying "good bye" … We are saying "good luck!" (Figure 14.1).

Fig. 14.1   Good luck!

References

1. *Edward Snowden Biography*. Accessed September 2018. https://www.biography.com/people/edward-snowden-21262897.
2. Greenwald, G. (2013, June 6). NSA collecting phone records of millions of Verizon customers daily. *The Guardian*. https://www.theguardian.com/world/2013/jun/06/nsa-phone-records-verizon-court-order.
3. Greenwald, G., MacAskill, E., & Poitras, L. (2013, June 11). Edward Snowden: The whistleblower behind the NSA surveillance reveltions. *The Guardian*. https://www.theguardian.com/world/2013/jun/09/edward-snowden-nsa-whistleblower-surveillance.
4. Franceschi-Bicchierai, L. (2014, June 5). The 10 biggest revelations from Edward Snowden's leaks. *MashablesUK*. https://mashable.com/2014/06/05/edward-snowden-revelations/?europe=true#E9W_W2HdFPqV.
5. Assange, J., & Rusbridger, A. (2011, January). WikiLeaks: The Guardian's role in the biggest leak in the history of the world. *The Guardian*. https://www.theguardian.com/media/2011/jan/28/wikileaks-julian-assange-alan-rusbridger.
6. *Chelsea Manning Biography*. Accessed September 2018. https://www.biography.com/people/chelsea-manning-21299995.
7. Ellison, S. (2011, February). The man who spilled the secrets. *Vanity Fair*. https://www.vanityfair.com/news/2011/02/the-guardian-201102.
8. Stempel, J., & Finkle, J. (2017, October). Yahoo says all three billion accounts hacked in 2013 data theft. *Reuters*. https://www.reuters.com/article/us-yahoo-cyber/yahoo-says-all-three-billion-accounts-hacked-in-2013-data-theft-idUSKCN1C82O1.
9. Perlroth, N. (2016, September). Yahoo says hackers stole data on 500 million users in 2014. *New York Times*. https://www.nytimes.com/2016/09/23/technology/yahoo-hackers.html.

© The Editor(s) (if applicable) and The Author(s), under exclusive
licence to Springer Nature Switzerland AG 2019
G. Pogrebna and M. Skilton, *Navigating New Cyber Risks*,
https://doi.org/10.1007/978-3-030-13527-0

10. Evens, M. (2015, February). Hackers steal £650 million in world's biggest bank raid. *The Telegraph.* https://www.telegraph.co.uk/news/uknews/crime/11414191/Hackers-steal-650-million-in-worlds-biggest-bank-raid.html.

11. Palmer, D. (2018, May). WannaCry ransomware crisis, one year on: Are we ready for the next global cyber attack? *zdnet.* https://www.zdnet.com/article/wannacry-ransomware-crisis-one-year-on-are-we-ready-for-the-next-global-cyber-attack/.

12. Ghena, B., Beyer, W., Hillaker, A., Pevarnek, J., & Halderman, J. A. (2014, August) Green lights forever: Analyzing the security of traffic infrastructure. In *Proceedings of the 8th USENIX Workshop on Offensive Technologies (WOOT'14).*

13. Greenberg, A. (2015, July). Hackers remotely kill a jeep on the highway—With me in it. *Wired.* https://www.wired.com/2015/07/hackers-remotely-kill-jeep-highway/.

14. Perez, E. (2015, May 19). FBI: Hacker claimed to have taken over flight's engine controls. *CNN.* https://edition.cnn.com/2015/05/17/us/fbi-hacker-flight-computer-systems/index.html.

15. Valero, J. (2016, July). Hackers bombard aviation sector with over 1000 attacks per month. *EuroActiv.* https://www.euractiv.com/section/justice-home-affairs/news/hackers-bombard-aviation-sector-with-more-than-1000-attacks-per-month/.

16. Jay J. (2018, May). Healthcare sector suffered more than half of all cyber-attacks in 2017. *SC Media.* https://www.scmagazineuk.com/healthcare-sector-suffered-half-cyber-attacks-2017/article/1472744.

17. 2017 Cylance Threat Report. Accessed September 2018. https://pages.cylance.com/2018-03CylanceThreatReport2017.html.

18. Hern, A. (2017, August 31). Hacking risk leads to recall of 500,000 pacemakers due to patient death fears. *The Guardian.* https://www.theguardian.com/technology/2017/aug/31/hacking-risk-recall-pacemakers-patient-death-fears-fda-firmware-update.

19. Smith, R. (2018, July 23). Russian hackers reach U.S. utility control rooms, Homeland security officials say. *Wall Street Journal.* https://www.wsj.com/articles/russian-hackers-reach-u-s-utility-control-rooms-homeland-security-officials-say-1532388110.

20. Rosenbush, S. (2017, November 16). The morning download: First AI-powered cyberattacks are detected. *CIO Journal, Wall Street Journal.* https://blogs.wsj.com/cio/2017/11/16/the-morning-download-first-ai-powered-cyberattacks-are-detected/.

21. Giles, M. (2018, January). Six cyberthreats to really worry about in 2018. *MIT Technology Review.* https://www.technologyreview.com/s/609641/six-cyber-threats-to-really-worry-about-in-2018/.

22. Ukraine power cut "was cyber-attack". (2017, January 11). *BBC.* https://www.bbc.co.uk/news/technology-38573074.

23. Dickinson, B. (2017, May 3). This is what fraud looks like in the age of artificial intelligence. *The NextWeb*. https://thenextweb.com/contributors/2017/05/03/what-fraud-looks-like-in-the-age-of-artificial-intelligence/.

24. AI and ML curbing financial fraud. (2018, March 6). *Fintech Futures*. https://www.bankingtech.com/2018/03/ai-and-ml-curbing-financial-fraud/.

25. Williams, S. (2017, May 12). Inside China's phoney "click farm": Tiny office uses 10,000 handsets to send fake ratings and "likes" for boosting clients' online popularity. *The Daily Mail*. https://www.dailymail.co.uk/news/article-4499730/click-farm-10-000-phones-boost-product-ratings.html.

26. Tackling the challenges of securing a trillion connected devices at Arm TechCon 2017. (2017, September 6). *ARM TechCon2017*. https://www.arm.com/company/news/2017/09/tackling-the-challenges-of-securing-a-trillion-connected-devices-at-arm-techcon-2017.

27. UK Government. (2018, March 7). *Secure-by-design*. https://www.gov.uk/government/publications/secure-by-design.

28. Pratt, M. K. (2018, January 16). What is Zero Trust? A model for more effective security. *CSO*. https://www.csoonline.com/article/3247848/network-security/what-is-zero-trust-a-model-for-more-effective-security.html.

29. Bird, J. (2018, September 26). AI is not a "silver bullet" against cyber attacks. *Financial Times*. https://www.ft.com/content/14cd2608-869d-11e8-9199-c2a4754b5a0e.

30. The White House just issued a Defcon scale for cyber attacks. (2016, August 3). *The Fanatical Futurist*. https://www.fanaticalfuturist.com/2016/08/the-white-house-issued-a-defcon-scale-for-cyber-attacks/.

31. Lee, D. (2018, September). Facebook security breach: Up to 50m accounts attacked. *BBC News*. https://www.bbc.co.uk/news/technology-45686890.

32. Kuckler, H. (2018, September 28). Facebook reveals cyber attack affecting up to 50m users. *Financial Times*. https://www.ft.com/content/c5f13f30-c33f-11e8-8d55-54197280d3f7.

33. Gross, M. L., Canetti, D., & Vashdi, D. R. (2016). The psychological effects of cyber terrorism. *Bulletin of the Atomic Scientists, 72*(5), 284–291.

34. Vatis, M. A. (2000). *Statement on cybercrime before the Senate Judiciary Committee, Criminal Justice Oversight Subcommittee and House Judiciary Committee, Crime Subcommittee*. Washington, DC: US Department of Justice, 29.

35. Denning, D. (2001). Is cyber terror next? *Understanding September, 11*, 191–197.

36. Denning, D. E. (2001). Activism, hacktivism, and cyberterrorism: The Internet as a tool for influencing foreign policy. *Networks and netwars: The future of terror, crime, and militancy* (pp. 239, 288). Santa Monica: RAND Corporation.

37. Coleman, G. (2014, November 4). *Hacker, hoaxer, whistleblower, spy: The many faces of anonymous*. London and New York: Verso Books.

38. Denning, D. (2000, Autumn). Cyberterrorism: The logic bomb versus the truck bomb. *Global Dialogue, 2*(4). Archived from the original on 27 June 2013. Retrieved 20 August 2014.

39. Holt, T. J., & Schell, B. H. (2010). *Corporate hacking and technology-driven crime: Social dynamics and implications* (p. 146). Hershey: IGI Global.

40. Parikka, J. (2007). *Digital contagions: A media archaeology of computer viruses* (p. 145). New York: Peter Lang.

41. Salomon, D. (2005). *Foundations of computer security* (p. 43). https://doi.org/10.1007/1-84628-341-8.

42. Bocij, P. (2006). *The dark side of the internet* (p. 57). Westport, CT: Praeger.

43. Szor, P. (2005). *The art of computer virus research and defense*. Reading: Addison-Wesley.

44. Holt, T. J., & Schell, B. H. (2013). *Hackers and hacking: A reference handbook* (p. 31). Santa Barbara: ABC-CLIO.

45. Indictment. *United States of America v. Victor Netyksho, Boris Antonov, Dmitriy Badin, Ivan Yermakov, Aleksey Lukashev, Sergey Morgachev, Nikolay Kozachek, Pavel Yershov, Artem Mayshev, Aleksandr Osadcguk, Aleksey Potemkin, and Alatoliy Kovalev.* Accessed at https://int.nyt.com/data/documenthelper/80-netyksho-et-al-indictment/ba0521c1eef869deecbe/optimized/full.pdf?action=click&module=Intentional&pgtype=Article.

46. *Frank Abagnale: "Catch me if you can" | Talks at Google.* https://www.youtube.com/watch?v=vsMydMDi3rI.

47. Digital Catapult UK. (2015). *Trust in personal data: The UK review* (The Digital Catapult Report).

48. Ashenden, D., & Lawrence, D. (2013, December). Can we sell security like soap? A new approach to behaviour change. In *Proceedings of the 2013 Workshop on New Security Paradigms Workshop* (pp. 87–94). ACM.

49. Ashenden, D., & Sasse, A. (2013). CISOs and organisational change: Their own worst enemy? *Computers & Security, 39*, 396–405.

50. Friedman, S. E., Musliner, D. J., & Rye, J. M. (2014). Improving automated cybersecurity by generalizing faults and quantifying patch performance. *International Journal on Advances in Security, 7*(3–4), 121–130.

51. Jenkins, D., Arnaud, J., Thompson, S., Yau, M., & Wright, J. (2014). *Version control and patch management of protection and automation systems.* Paper Presented at the 2014 12th International Conference on Developments in Power System Protection (DPSP), Copenhagen, Denmark, 31 March–3 April.

52. Boris Taratine on "Robustness, Resilience, and Agility". *LinkedIn article.*

53. Snowden, D. (2011). *Risk and resilience.* https://www.youtube.com/watch?v=2Hhu0ihG3kY.

54. Wolff, J. (2006). Risk, fear, blame, shame and the regulation of public safety. *Economics and Philosophy, 22*, 409–427.

55. Ralston, P. A., Graham, J. H., & Hieb, J. L. (2007). Cyber security risk assessment for SCADA and DCS networks. *ISA Transactions, 46*(4), 583–594.

56. Cherdantseva, Y., Burnap, P., Blyth, A., Eden, P., Jones, K., Soulsby, H., & Stoddart, K. (2016). A review of cyber security risk assessment methods for SCADA systems. *Computers & Security, 56*, 1–27.

57. Hughes, J., & Cybenko, G. (2013). Quantitative metrics and risk assessment: The three tenets model of cybersecurity. *Technology Innovation Management Review, 3*(8), 15–24.

58. Cooper, P. (2016). *Cognitive active cyber defence: Finding value through hacking human nature* (MSc dissertation). Cranfield University.

59. Kilber, J., Barclay, A., & Ohmer, D. (2014). Seven tips for managing Generation Y. *Journal of Management Policy and Practice, 15*(4), 80.

60. Morgan, T. (2002). *Business rules and information systems: Aligning IT with business goals.* New York: Addison-Wesley.

61. Tobin, D. R. (1998). *The knowledge-enabled organization: Moving from "training" to "learning" to meet business goals.* Amacom.

62. Chmielecki, T., Cholda, P., Pacyna, P., Potrawka, P., Rapacz, N., Stankiewicz, R., et al. (2014, September). Enterprise-oriented cybersecurity management. In *2014 Federated Conference on Computer Science and Information Systems (FedCSIS)* (pp. 863–870). IEEE.

63. Aviram, A., & Tor, A. (2003) Overcoming Impediments to Information Sharing. *Alabama Law Review, 55*, 231.

64. Dressler, J., Bowen, C. L., Moody, W., & Koepke, J. (2014). Operational data classes for establishing situational awareness in cyberspace. In *2014 6th International Conference on Cyber Conflict (CyCon 2014)* (pp. 175–186). IEEE.

65. Koepke, P. (2017). *Cybersecurity information sharing incentives and barriers* (Working Paper CISL# 2017-13). MIT. Available from http://web.mit.edu/smadnick/www/wp/2017-13.pdf.

66. Kadobayashi, Y. (2010). Cybersecurity information exchange framework. *Computer Communication Review, 40*(5), 59–64.

67. Kharlamov, A., Jaiswal, A., Parry, G., & Pogrebna, G. (2018a). *A cyber domain-specific risk attitudes scale to address security issues in the digital space.* British Academy of Management Award-Winning Paper. Available from https://bit.ly/2P9o990.

68. Kharlamov, A., Jaiswal, A., Parry, G., & Pogrebna, G. (2018b). *Heavy regulation and excessive information about cybersecurity makes people risk taking in cyberspace* (Alan Turing Institute Working Paper).

69. Loomes, G. & Pogrebna, G. (2017). Do preference reversals disappear when we allow for probabilistic choice? *Management Science, 63*(1), 166–184.

70. Loomes, G. & Pogrebna, G. (2014). Testing for independence while allowing for probabilistic choice. *Journal of Risk and Uncertainty, 49*(3), 189–211.

71. Loomes, G. & Pogrebna, G. (2014). Measuring individual risk attitudes when preferences are imprecise. *Economic Journal, 124*(576), 569–593.

72. Blavatskyy, P. & Pogrebna, G. (2010). Models of stochastic choice and decision theories: Why both are important for analyzing decisions. *Journal of Applied Econometrics, 25*(6), 963–986.

73. Li, Z., Loomes, G. & Pogrebna, G. (2017). Attitudes to uncertainty in a strategic setting. *Economic Journal, 127*(601), 809–826.

74. Brenner, S. W. (2007). History of computer crime. In *The history of information security* (pp. 705–721). Amsterdam: Elsevier.

75. DeNardis, L. (2007). A history of internet security. In *The History of Information Security* (pp. 681–704). Amsterdam: Elsevier.

76. May, R. (2018). *The human firewall: Cybersecurity is not just an IT problem* (Kindle Edition).

77. Evans, K., & Reeder, F. (2010). *A human capital crisis in cybersecurity: Technical proficiency matters.* Washington, DC: CSIS.

78. Nakamoto, S. (2009, May 24). *Bitcoin: A peer-to-peer electronic cash system* (PDF). Archived (PDF) from the original on 20 March 2014. Retrieved 5 March 2014.

79. Nakamoto, S. (2008, October 31). *Bitcoin P2P e-cash paper.* Archived from the original on 28 December 2012. Retrieved 5 March 2014.

80. Kharlamov, A., Parry, G., & Pogrebna, G. (2018). *Measuring vulnerability towards cybersecurity risks* (Working Paper).

81. Penrose, L. S., & Penrose, R. (1958). Impossible objects: A special type of visual illusion. *British Journal of Psychology, 49,* 31–33. https://doi.org/10.1111/j.2044-8295.1958.tb00634.x. (pmid13536303).

82. Druga, S., Williams, R., Breazeal, C., & Resnick, M. (2017, June). Hey Google is it OK if I eat you?: Initial explorations in child-agent interaction. In *Proceedings of the 2017 Conference on Interaction Design and Children* (pp. 595–600). ACM.

83. Augello, A., Gentile, M., Weideveld, L., & Dignum, F. (2016). A model of a social chatbot. In *Intelligent interactive multimedia systems and services 2016* (pp. 637–647). Cham: Springer.

84. Janarthanam, S. (2017). *Hands-on chatbots and conversational UI development: Build chatbots and voice user interfaces with Chatfuel, Dialogflow, Microsoft Bot Framework, Twilio, and Alexa Skills.* Birmingham: Packt.

85. *Jane Jacobs biography.* https://www.biography.com/people/jane-jacobs-9351679.

86. Yeung, S., Downing, N. L., Fei-Fei, L., & Milstein, A. (2018, April 5). Bedside computer vision—Moving artificial intelligence from driver assistance to patient safety. *The New England Journal of Medicine, 378*(14). https://www.nejm.org/doi/full/10.1056/NEJMp1716891.

87. Evers, J. (2006, August 7). Vista hacked at Black Hat. *CNET.* https://www.cnet.com/news/vista-hacked-at-black-hat/.

88. Adams, J. (1995 [2002]). *Risk*. London: Routledge.
89. *Taking account of societal concerns about risk: Framing the problem*. (2002). Professor John Adams UCL, Professor Michael Thompson University of Bergen, Health and Safety Executive HSE. http://www.hse.gov.uk/research/rrpdf/rr035.pdf.
90. The risk of freedom: Individual liberty and the modern world. (1999). *Institute of United States Studies*. http://john-adams.co.uk/wpcontent/uploads/2006/risk,%20freedom%20&%20responsibility.pdf.
91. *What is gamification?* https://www.bunchball.com/gamification.
92. Ashford, W. (2018, April 3). Automation and gamification key to cyber security. *Computer Weekly*. https://www.computerweekly.com/news/252437833/Automation-and-gamification-key-to-cyber-security.
93. *Using gamification to transform security awareness—SANS Security Awareness Summit*, London 2016, Masha Sedova, Senior Director of Trust Engagement, Salesforce. https://www.sans.org/summit-archives/file/summit-archive-1493221150.pdf.
94. *6 reasons gamification improves cybersecurity training*. *TechRepublic*. Michael Kassner | August 19, 2018, https://www.techrepublic.com/article/6-reasons-gamification-improves-cybersecurity-training/.
95. *Attribution theory*. https://www.simplypsychology.org/attribution-theory.html.
96. *Fundamental attribution error*. https://ethicsunwrapped.utexas.edu/glossary/fundamental-attribution-error.
97. *Secure by design*, Policy Paper, UK Government, March 2018 relating to Consumer Internet of Things (IoT). https://www.gov.uk/government/publications/secure-by-design.
98. Security by design principles. *OWASP*. https://www.owasp.org/index.php/Security_by_Design_Principles.
99. Bada, M. & Sasse, A. (2014, July). *Cyber security awareness campaigns—Why do they fail to change behavior?* (Draft Working Paper). Global Cyber Security Capacity Center. http://discovery.ucl.ac.uk/1468954/1/Awareness%20CampaignsDraftWorkingPaper.pdf.
100. Lohrmann, D. (2017, June). The trouble if security awareness training is mainly a punishment. *Government Technology*. http://www.govtech.com/blogs/lohrmann-on-cybersecurity/the-trouble-if-security-awareness-training-is-only-a-penalty.html.
101. Jackson, W. (2007, March). Culture of security, Dan Lohrmann. *GCN*. https://gcn.com/articles/2007/03/01/dan-lohrmann--culture-of-security.aspx.
102. *10 steps: User education and awareness* (2016, August). National Cyber Security Centre, UK Gov. https://www.ncsc.gov.uk/guidance/10-steps-user-education-and-awareness.
103. Condon, R. (2009, May). *NHS imposes USB stick security*. https://www.computerweekly.com/news/1356428/NHS-imposes-USB-stick-security.

104. Heathcote, A. (2017, May). *Secure configuration, Good Practice Guide*. NHS Digital. file://mac/Home/Downloads/secure_configuration_-_good_practice_guide_230517.pdf.

105. *Honeypot* https://searchsecurity.techtarget.com/definition/honey-pot.

106. Cole, E., & Northcutt, S. *Honeypots: A security manager's guide to honeypots*. V1.1 SANS Technology Institute, Security Laboratory. https://www.sans.edu/cyber-research/security-laboratory/article/honeypots-guide.

107. Lyons, K., Ellis-Petersen, H., Kuo, L., & Zhou, N. (2018, July 30). Malaysian investigators release 1,500-page report into disappearance of MH370. *The Guardian*. https://www.theguardian.com/world/live/2018/jul/30/mh370-final-report-released-by-malaysian-government-live.

108. *Safety Investigation Report, Malaysia Airlines Boeing B777-200ER (9 M-MRO)*, 8 March 2014. The Malaysian ICAO Annex 13 Safety Investigation Team for MH370. Issued 2 July 2018 MH370/01/2018. http://mh370.mot.gov.my/MH370SafetyInvestigationReport.pdf.

109. Scruton, P., Phipps, C., & Levett, C. (2017, January). Missing flight MH370—A visual guide to the parts and debris found so far. *The Guardian*. https://www.theguardian.com/world/ng-interactive/2017/jan/17/missing-flight-mh370-a-visual-guide-to-the-parts-and-debris-found-so-far.

110. Lawler, J. (2017, May). Nutrition and biomarkers—New ways to track food intake? *Irish Tech News*. https://irishtechnews.ie/nutrition-and-biomarkers-new-ways-to-track-food-intake/.

111. Combs, G. F., Trumbo, P. R., McKinley, M. C., Milner, J., Studenski, S., Kimura, T. et al. (2013, March). Biomarkers in nutrition: New frontiers in research and application. *Annals of the New York Academy of Sciences, 1278*(1), 1–10. https://doi.org/10.1111/nyas.12069.

112. Blood, DNA and Lifestyle habits test biotrackers for wellness. *InsideTracker*. Accessed September 2018. https://www.insidetracker.com/ https://www.insidetracker.com/customer/onboarding/choose-plan/.

113. Johnston, A., & Warkentin, M. (2010, September). Fear appeals and information security, behaviours: An empirical study. *MIS Quarterly, 34*(3). http://www.uab.edu/cas.

114. Evans, M., Maglaras, L. A., He, Y. & Janicke, H. (2016, January). Human behavior as an aspect of cyber security assurance (arXiv:1601.03921v1 [cs.CR]).

115. Aytes, K., Connolly, T., Ovelgonne, M., Dumitras, T., Prakash, A., Subrahmanian, V. S., & Wany, B. (2017, July). Understanding the relationship, between human behavior and susceptibility to cyber-attacks: A data-driven approach. *ACM Transactions on Intelligent Systems and Technology (TIST)—Special Issue: Cyber Security and Regular Papers, 8*(4), Article no. 51.

116. Gross, M. L. Canetti, D., & Vashdi, D. R. (2016). The psychological effects of cyber terrorism. PMC US National Library of Medicine. *Bulletin of the Atomic Scientists, 72*(5), 284–291. Published online 4 August, 2016. https://doi.org/10.1080/00963402.2016.1216502.

117. Whipple, A. (2016, May). The hacker psychology plays on these human fears and misperceptions. *Hacker psychology: Understanding the 4 emotions of social engineering.* Network World. Accessed September 2018. https://www.net-workworld.com/article/3070455/cloud-security/hacker-psychology-under-standing-the-4-emotions-of-social-engineering.html.

118. Paulie "Gloves" Gavoni. (2018, February). *Fight Science: Overcoming fear and anxiety through ACTion.* Bloody Elbow, for MMA and UFC news. https://www.bloodyelbow.com/2018/2/13/17006696/fight-science-overcoming-fear-anxiety-through-action.

119. Mobbs, D., Hagan, C. C., Dalgleish, T., Silston, B. & Prévost, C. (2015). The ecology of human fear: Survival optimization and the nervous system. *Frontiers in Neuroscience, 9,* 55. https://doi.org/10.3389/fnins.2015.00055.

120. Liu, C., Marchewka, J. T., Lu, J., & Yu, C. S. (2004, December). Beyond concern—A privacy-trust-behavioral intention model of electronic commerce. *Information & Management, 42*(2), 289–304. https://doi.org/10.1016/j.im.2004.01.003.

121. Ferrara, E. (2015, Spring). Manipulation and abuse on social media. *ACM SIGWEB Newsletter.* Article 4. https://arxiv.org/pdf/1503.03752.pdf.

122. van Deursen, A. & Helsper, E. (2015). A nuanced understanding of Internet use and non-use amongst older adults. *European Journal of Communication,* ISSN 0267-3231 https://doi.org/10.1177/0267323115578059.

123. *Children's online privacy and freedom of expression.* (2018, May). ©United Nations Children's Fund (UNICEF). https://www.unicef.org/csr/files/UNICEF_Childrens_Online_Privacy_and_Freedom_of_Expression(1).pdf.

124. *Online abuse, facts and figures.* NSPCC. https://www.nspcc.org.uk/preventing-abuse/child-abuse-and-neglect/online-abuse/facts-statistics/.

125. Global alliance against child sexual abuse online—Report—December 2013. *EU.* https://ec.europa.eu/home-affairs/sites/homeaffairs/files/what-we-do/policies/organized-crime-and-human-trafficking/global-alliance-against-child-abuse/docs/global_alliance_report_201312_en.pdf.

126. *Child sexual abuse—National children's advocacy center.* (2018). http://www.nationalcac.org/wp-content/uploads/2018/02/CSA-Perpetrators.pdf.

127. Neumann, P. R. (2013). Options and strategies for countering online radicalization in the United States. *Journal, Studies in Conflict and Terrorism, 36*(6). https://doi.org/10.1080/1057610X.2013.784568.

128. Malcher, A. (2016, August). Psychological manipulation via social media and self-identity. *Security news desk.* http://www.securitynewsdesk.com/psychological-manipulation-via-social-media-concept-self-identity/.

129. Palos-Sanchez, P. R., Hernandez-Mogollon, J.M., & Campon-Cerro, A. M. (2017). The behavioral response to location based services: An examination of the influence of social and environmental benefits, and privacy. *Sustainability, 9*(11) (1988). https://doi.org/10.3390/su9111988, https://www.mdpi.com/2071-1050/9/11/1988/pdf.

130. The "basketball" awareness study. *YouTube*. Accessed September 2018. https://www.youtube.com/watch?v=47LCLoidJh4.

131. The "door" study. *YouTube*. Accessed september 2018. https://www.youtube.com/watch?v=FWSxSQsspiQ.

132. Cromwell, H.C. (2008). Sensory gating: A translational effort from basic to clinical science. *Clinical EEG and Neuroscience*. https://doi.org/10.1177/155005940803900209.

133. 31 psychological defense mechanisms explained. *Psychologist World*. Accessed September 2018. https://www.psychologistworld.com/freud/defence-mechanisms-list.

134. Whitbourne, S. K. (2016, October). *Your 9 top defense mechanisms, revisited*. https://www.psychologytoday.com/us/blog/fulfillment-any-age/201610/your-9-top-defense-mechanisms-revisited.

135. Ziegler, D. J. (2016). Defense mechanisms in rational emotive cognitive behavior therapy personality theory. *Journal of Rational-Emotive & Cognitive-Behavior Therapy, 34*, 135–148. https://doi.org/10.1007/s10942-016-0234-2.

136. Field, T. A., Beeson, E. T., & Jones, L. K. (2015). The new ABCs: A practitioner's guide to neuroscience-informed cognitive-behavior therapy (PDF). *Journal of Mental Health Counseling, 37*(3), 206–220. https://doi.org/10.17744/1040-2861-37.3.206.

137. Cognitive behavioral therapy (CBT). *Mind*. Accessed September 2018. https://www.mind.org.uk/information-support/drugs-and-treatments/cognitive-behavioural-therapy-cbt/#.W6n7LNNKgdU.

138. *The ethics of manipulation*. (2018, March). Stanford Encyclopedia of Philosophy. https://plato.stanford.edu/entries/ethics-manipulation/.

139. Ienca, M. & Vayena, E. (2018, March). Cambridge analytica and online manipulation. *Scientific American*. https://blogs.scientificamerican.com/observations/cambridge-analytica-and-online-manipulation/.

140. *Microsoft security servicing commitments to windows bulletin*. (2018, June). https://msdnshared.blob.core.windows.net/media/2018/06/Microsoft-Security-Servicing-Commitments_SRD.pdf.

141. Sheyner, O., & Wing, J. (2003). Tools for generating and analyzing attack graphs. Carnegie Mellon University, USA. *International Symposium on Formal Methods for Components and Objects. FMCO 2003: Formal Methods for Components and Objects* (pp 344–371). http://www.cs.cmu.edu/afs/cs/project/svc/projects/security/fmco04.pdf.

142. Durkota, K., Lisý, V., Bošanský, B., & Kiekintveld, C. (2015). Optimal network security hardening using attack graph games. In *Proceedings of the Twenty-Fourth International Joint Conference on Artificial Intelligence (IJCAI)*.

143. Ingols, K., Lippmann, R., & Piwowarski, K. Practical attack graph generation for network defense. In *Proceedings of the 22nd Annual Computer Security Applications Conference (ACSAC'06)* (pp. 121–130). https://doi.org/10.1109/acsac.2006.39.

144. Zhang, S., Ou, X., Singhal, A., & Homer, J. An empirical study of a vulnerability metric aggregation method. *NIST Website*. https://ws680.nist.gov/publication/get_pdf.cfm?pub_id=908558.

145. Homer, J., Varikuti, A., Ou, X., & McQueen, M. A. (2008). Improving attack graph visualization through data reduction and attack grouping. In J. R. Goodall, G. Conti, K. L. Ma (eds.), *Visualization for Computer Security*. VizSec 2008. Lecture Notes in Computer Science, vol. 5210. Berlin and Heidelberg: Springer.

146. Ou, X., Govindavajhala, S., & Appel, A. W. MulVAL: A logic-based network security analyzer. *SSYM 2005 Proceedings of the 14th conference on USENIX Security Symposium—Volume 14* (p. 8).

147. *OVAL website*. https://oval.cisecurity.org/.

148. *PC mag definition of root level access*. https://www.pcmag.com/encyclopedia/term/63338/root-level.

149. Desjardins, J. (2017, February). Here's how many millions of lines of code it takes to run different software. *Business Insider*. http://uk.businessinsider.com/how-many-lines-of-code-it-takes-to-run-different-software-2017-2?r=US&IR=T.

150. McCandless, D. (2015). *Information is beautiful*. https://informationisbeautiful.net/visualizations/million-lines-of-code/.

151. Lloyd, S. (2001, September). Measures of complexity: A nonexhaustive list. *IEEE Control Systems Magazine, 21*(4) (MIT), 7–8. https://doi.org/10.1109/mcs.2001.939938.

152. Hoffman, C. (2017, November). Intel management engine, explained: The tiny computer inside your CPU. *How-To Geek*. https://www.howtogeek.com/334013/intel-management-engine-explained-the-tiny-computer-inside-your-cpu/.

153. Davis, J. (2016, August). TrapX launches ransomware deception tool, CryptoTrap. *HealthITNews*. https://www.healthcareitnews.com/news/trapx-launches-ransomware-deception-tool-cryptotrap.

154. *First midwest bank uses Fidelis Deception™ to detect and respond to security anomalies, case study*. Accessed October 2018. https://www.fidelissecurity.com/case-study-first-midwest-bank.

155. 20 deception technology companies: In-depth guide [2018]. *Applied AI blog*. https://blog.appliedai.com/deception-tech-companies/.

156. Kolton, D. (2018, May). 5 ways deception tech is disrupting cybersecurity. *TNW*. https://thenextweb.com/contributors/2018/05/26/5-ways-deception-technology-is-changing-cybersecurity/.

157. Hutchins, E. M., Cloppert, M. J., & Amin, R. M. (2011, January). *Intelligence-driven computer network defense informed by analysis of adversary campaigns and intrusion kill chains*. https://www.lockheedmartin.com/content/dam/lockheed-martin/rms/documents/cyber/LM-White-Paper-Intel-Driven-Defense.pdf.

158. Goldwasser, S., Micali, S., & Rackoff, C. (1989, February). The knowledge complexity of interactive proof systems. MIT. *Society for Industrial and Applied Mathematics, 18*(1), 186–208. http://people.csail.mit.edu/silvio/Selected%20Scientific%20Papers/Proof%20Systems/The_Knowledge_Complexity_Of_Interactive_Proof_Systems.pdf.

159. Lexie. (2017, November). Zero-knowledge proofs explained: Part 1. *ExpressVPN.* https://www.expressvpn.com/blog/zero-knowledge-proofs-explained/.

160. Quisquater, J. J., Guillou, L. C., & Berson, T. A. (1990). How to explain zero-knowledge protocols to your children. *Advances in Cryptology—CRYPTO'89: Proceedings, 435,* 628–631. http://pages.cs.wisc.edu/~mkowalcz/628.pdf.

161. Zero-knowledge proof. *Wikipedia.* https://en.wikipedia.org/wiki/Zero-knowledge_proof.

162. Lukas S. "On zero-knowledge proofs in blockchains", May, The Argon Group, *Medium.* https://medium.com/@argongroup/on-zero-knowledge-proofs-in-blockchains-14c48cfd1ddl.

163. Blum, M., Feldman, P., & Micali, S. (1988). Non-interactive zero-knowledge and its applications. In *Proceedings of the twentieth annual ACM symposium on Theory of computing (STOC 1988)* (pp. 103–112).

164. Goldreich, O., & Oren, Y. (1994). Definitions and properties of zero-knowledge proof systems. *Journal of Cryptology, 7*(1), 1–32.

165. Bitansky, N., Canetti, R., Chiesa, A., & Tromer, E. From extractable collision resistance to succinct non-interactive arguments of knowledge, and back again. (*Proceeding ITCS'12*) *Proceedings of the 3rd Innovations in Theoretical Computer Science Conference* (pp. 326–349). https://eprint.iacr.org/2011/443.pdf.

166. Sasson, E. B., Chiesa, A., Garman, C., Green, M., Miers, I., Tromer, E., & Virza, M. (2014, May 18). *Zerocash: Decentralized anonymous payments from bitcoin* (PDF). IEEE.

167. Orcutt, M. (2017, November). A mind-bending cryptographic trick promises to take blockchains mainstream. *MIT Technology Review.* https://www.technologyreview.com/s/609448/a-mind-bending-cryptographic-trick-promises-to-take-blockchains-mainstream/.

168. Greenwald, J. (2016, September). *PPPL and Princeton demonstrate novel technique that may have applicability to future nuclear disarmament talks.* Princeton Plasma Physics Laboratory. https://www.pppl.gov/news/2016/09/pppl-and-princeton-demonstrate-novel-technique-may-have-applicability-future-nuclear.

169. Cameron-Huff, A. (2017, March). How tokenization is putting real-world assets on blockchains. *Nasdaq.* https://www.nasdaq.com/article/how-tokenization-is-putting-real-world-assets-on-blockchains-cm767952.

170. Cosset, D. (2018, January). Blockchain: What is mining? *Dev.to.* https://dev.to/damcosset/blockchain-what-is-mining-2eod.

171. Khatwani, S. (2018, October). What is double spending & how does bitcoin handle it? *coinsutra*. https://coinsutra.com/bitcoin-double-spending/.

172. *How bitcoin mining works*. Accessed October 2018. https://www.bitcoinmining.com/.

173. Eremenko, K. (May). How does bitcoin/blockchain mining work? *Medium*. https://medium.com/swlh/how-does-bitcoin-blockchain-mining-work-36db1c5cb55d.

174. Dwork, C., & Naor, M. (1993). *Pricing via processing, or, combatting junk mail*. Advances in Cryptology. CRYPTO'92: Lecture Notes in Computer Science No. 740. Springer: 139–147.

175. Jakobsson, M., & Juels, A. (1999). Proofs of work and bread pudding protocols. *Communications and Multimedia Security*. Kluwer Academic Publishers: 258–272.

176. Cecin, F. (2016, June). Digital money with proof-of-useful-work. *Medium*. https://medium.com/money-games/digital-money-with-proof-of-useful-work-81ff547695e4.

177. *What is zero trust? Centrify zero trust security*. Accessed October 2018. https://www.centrify.com/education/what-is-zero-trust/.

178. BeyondCorp. *Google Cloud*. https://cloud.google.com/beyondcorp/.

179. *Operation Aurora Cyberattack 2009*. https://en.wikipedia.org/wiki/Operation_Aurora.

180. *BeyondCorp.com*. https://beyondcorp.com/.

181. *Aruba perspective with Gartner Report seven imperatives to adopt a CARTA approach*. https://www.gartner.com/imagesrv/media-products/pdf/hpe/hpe-1-504080P.pdf.

182. *Ronald Reagan: Trust but verify; watch closely and don't be afraid to see what you see*. Accessed October 2018. https://www.youtube.com/watch?v=yfZ5fa5bPJU.

183. Robertson, J., & Riley, M. (2018, October 4). The big hack: How China used a tiny chip to infiltrate U.S. companies. *Bloomberg Businessweek*. https://www.bloomberg.com/news/features/2018-10-04/the-big-hack-how-china-used-a-tiny-chip-to-infiltrate-america-s-top-companies.

184. *The Guardian*. (2018, June 7). China's ZTE to pay US $1bn fine in new deal to save company. https://www.theguardian.com/business/2018/jun/07/us-china-zte-deal-fine-sanctions.

185. Wolfe, H. B. (2018). Australia should reverse its Huawei 5G ban. *Huawei paid post New York Times*. https://www.nytimes.com/paidpost/huawei/australia-should-reverse-its-huawei-5g-ban.html?cpv_dsm_id=191241192&tbs_nyt=2018-oct-nytnative_hp.

186. *The link between perceived comfort and perceived safety, VTI Swedish Transport Administration*. Accessed September 2018. https://www.vti.se/en/Research-areas/driving-simulation1/Application/Perceived-comfort-and-perceived-safety/.

187. *CF disclosure guidance: Topic No. 2.* (2011). Cyber Security. https://www.sec.gov/divisions/corpfin/guidance/cfguidance-topic2.htm.

188. Updated SEC guidance February 2018 17 CFR Parts 229 and 249 [Release Nos. 33-10459; 34-82746]. *Commission statement and guidance on public company cybersecurity disclosures.* https://www.sec.gov/rules/interp/2018/33-10459.pdf.

189. Godlee, F., Smith, J., & Marcovitch, H. (2011). *Wakefield's article linking MMR vaccine and autism was fraudulent.* https://doi.org/10.1136/bmj.c7452 (Published 6 January 2011) *BMJ,* 342, c7452 https://www.bmj.com/content/342/bmj.c7452.

190. *Ruling on doctor in MMR scare.* (2010, January). *NHS.* https://www.nhs.uk/news/medical-practice/ruling-on-doctor-in-mmr-scare/.

191. Smith, R. (2012, November). MMR uptake rates finally recovered from Wakefield scandal figures show. *The Telegraph.* https://www.telegraph.co.uk/news/health/news/9705374/MMR-uptake-rates-finally-recovered-from-Wakefield-scandal-figures-show.html.

192. *Health and Social Care Act 2008 (Regulated Activities) Regulations 2014: Regulation 20: Duty of candor.* https://www.cqc.org.uk/guidance-providers/regulations-enforcement/regulation-20-duty-candour.

193. Witkin, R. (1983, July). Jet's fuel ran out after metric conversion errors. *New York Times.* https://www.nytimes.com/1983/07/30/us/jet-s-fuel-ran-out-after-metric-conversion-errors.html.

194. *AviationSafetyNetwork. July 1983 Report.* https://aviation-safety.net/database/record.php?id=19830723-0.

195. Great miscalculations: The French railway error and 10 others. (2014, May). *BBC.* https://www.bbc.co.uk/news/magazine-27509559.

196. Fox-Brewster, T. (2014, September). Londoners give up eldest children in public Wi-Fi security horror show. *The Guardian.* https://www.theguardian.com/technology/2014/sep/29/londoners-wi-fi-security-herod-clause.

197. Anderson, R. (2002, June 20–21). *Security in open versus closed systems—The dance of Boltzmann, Coase and Moore.* Open Source Software: Economics, Law and Policy, Toulouse, France.

198. Lemos, R. (2002, June). Open, closed source security about equal? *Zdnet.* https://www.zdnet.com/article/open-closed-source-security-about-equal-5000296876/.

199. Smith, L. J. (2018, August). Why buying a car or trying to tax your car this weekend could see you land a £1,000 fine. *The Express.* https://www.express.co.uk/life-style/cars/1004805/DVLA-car-tax-website-down-fine-buying-car-UK.

200. Leyden, J. (2018, March). DVLA denies driving license processing site is a security 'car crash'. *The Register.* https://www.theregister.co.uk/2018/03/09/dvla_insecure_site_dispute/.

201. Measuring the cost of cybercrime, *WES2012 Conference*. https://www.econ-infosec.org/archive/weis2012/papers/Anderson_WEIS2012.pdf.

202. Clayton, R. (2012, October). *Measuring Cybercrime*. University of Cambridge, Computer laboratory. https://www.cl.cam.ac.uk/~rnc1/talks/121019-cybercrime.pdf.

203. Hoffman, C. (2014, February). 5 serious problems with HTTPS and SSL security on the web. *How-To Geek*. https://www.howtogeek.com/182425/5-serious-problems-with-https-and-ssl-security-on-the-web/.

204. *February 28th DDoS Incident Report*. (2018, March). GitHub Engineering. SKottler. https://githubengineering.com/ddos-incident-report/.

205. Ranger, S. (2018, March). GitHub hit with the largest DDoS attack ever seen. *zdnet*. https://www.zdnet.com/article/github-was-hit-with-the-largest-ddos-attack-ever-seen/.

206. *Memcached*. https://memcached.org/.

207. Understanding triangulation fraud. (2015, October). *Radial*. https://www.radial.com/insights/understanding-triangulation-fraud.

208. *Red team definition from Financial Times Lexicon*. http://lexicon.ft.com/term?term=red-team.

209. DoDD 8570.1: Blue team. ADI (formerly Sypris Electronics). https://www.sypriselectronics.com/information-security/cyber-security-solutions/computer-network-defense/.

210. Cyber guardian: Blue team. *SANS Institute*. https://www.sans.org/cyber-guardian/blue-team.

211. Murdoch, D. (2014). *Blue team handbook*. Incident Response Edition (2nd ed.). CreateSpace Independent Publishing Platform. ISBN 978-1500734756.

212. Miessler, D. (2016, February). *The difference between red, blue, and purple teams*. https://danielmiessler.com/study/red-blue-purple-teams/.

213. Jamil, A. (2010, March 29). *The difference between SEM, SIM and SIEM*. Sectier. https://www.gmdit.com/NewsView.aspx?ID=9IfB2Axzeew=.

214. Kubecka, C. (2011, December 29). *28c3: Security log visualization with a correlation engine*. https://www.youtube.com/watch?v=j4pF9VUdphc&feature=youtu.be, https://events.ccc.de/congress/2011/Fahrplan/events/4767.en.html.

215. Swift, D. (2010). Successful SIEM and log management strategies for audit and compliance. *SANS Institute*. https://www.sans.org/reading-room/whitepapers/auditing/paper/33528.

216. Pauli, D. (2016, November). IoT worm can hack Philips Hue lightbulbs, spread across cities. *The Register*. https://www.theregister.co.uk/2016/11/10/iot_worm_can_hack_philips_hue_lightbulbs_spread_across_cities/.

217. Ronen, E., O'Flynn, C., Shamir, A., & Weingarten, A. O. Goes nuclear: Creating a zigbee chain reaction. *IoT IEEE Security & Privacy*. https://doi.org/10.1109/msp.2018.1331033.

218. Symmetric vs. Asymmetric encryption—What are differences? *SSL2Buy*. Accessed October 2018. https://www.ssl2buy.com/wiki/symmetric-vs-asymmetric-encryption-what-are-differences.

219. *An overview of public key infrastructures (PKI)*. Accessed October 2018. https://www.techotopia.com/index.php/An_Overview_of_Public_Key_Infrastructures_(PKI).

220. Kocher, P., Jaffe, J., & Jun, B. *Differential power analysis (DPA)*. Cryptography Research, Inc. https://www.paulkocher.com/doc/DifferentialPowerAnalysis.pdf.

221. Introduction to side-channel attacks. *Rambus*. Accessed October 2018. http://info.rambus.com/hubfs/rambus.com/Gated-Content/Cryptography/Introduction-to-Side-Channel-Attacks-eBook.pdf?hsCtaTracking=c476fb62-8de1-44e8-b7c9-9607f0cb447e%7Cafdca38a-dd94-44ba-a18c-a7eb8ad70d5d.

222. DPA Countermeasures. *Rambus*. Accessed October 2018. https://www.rambus.com/security/dpa-countermeasures/.

223. Seppala, T. J. (2016, November). Hackers hijack Philips Hue lights with a drone. *Engadget*. https://www.engadget.com/2016/11/03/hackers-hijack-a-philips-hue-lights-with-a-drone/.

224. Zetter, K. (2015, January). A cyberattack has caused confirmed physical damage for the second time ever. *Wired*. https://www.wired.com/2015/01/german-steel-mill-hack-destruction/.

225. *Die Lage der IT-Sicherheit in Deutschland 2014 German* (Steel Mill Hack Report). https://www.wired.com/wp-content/uploads/2015/01/Lagebericht2014.pdf.

226. Timeline: How Stuxnet attacked a nuclear plant. *BBC iwonder*. https://www.bbc.com/timelines/zc6fbk7.

227. Muncaster, P. (2018, June). MPs: CNI attacks are UK's biggest cyber-threat. *Infosecurity Magazine*. https://www.infosecurity-magazine.com/news/mps-cni-attacks-are-uks-biggest/.

228. Spanier, G. (2016, March 8). Protecting brand reputation in the wake of a cyber-attack. *Raconteur*. https://www.raconteur.net/risk-management/protecting-brand-reputation-in-the-wake-of-a-cyber-attack.

229. *The Telegraph*. (2018, February 28). Why digital-age directors need directors and officers (D&O) cover. https://www.telegraph.co.uk/business/risk-insights/directors-need-d-and-o-insurance/.

230. Australian metal detector company counts cost of Chinese hacking. (2015, June). *Reuters*. https://www.reuters.com/article/china-cybersecurity-australia/australian-metal-detector-company-counts-cost-of-chinese-hacking-idUSL3N0YX2OX20150624.

231. Monaghan, A. (2016, May 12). TalkTalk profits halve after cyber-attack. *The Guardian*. https://www.theguardian.com/business/2016/may/12/talktalk-profits-halve-hack-cyber-attack.

232. Ashley Adison data breach. *Wikipedia*. Accessed October 2018. https://en.wikipedia.org/wiki/Ashley_Madison_data_breach.

233. Thomsen, S. (2015, July 20). Extramarital affair website Ashley Madison has been hacked and attackers are threatening to leak data online. *Business Insider.* http://uk.businessinsider.com/cheating-affair-website-ashley-madison-hacked-user-data-leaked-2015-7?r=US&IR=T.

234. Curtis, S. Ashley Madison hack threatens to expose 37m adulterers. *The Telegraph.* https://www.telegraph.co.uk/technology/internet-security/11750432/Adultery-website-Ashley-Madison-hack-threatens-to-expose-37.5m-cheaters.html.

235. Ashley Madison hack: 2 unconfirmed suicides linked to breach, Toronto police say. (2015, August 24). *CBC Canada.* https://www.cbc.ca/news/canada/toronto/ashley-madison-hack-2-unconfirmed-suicides-linked-to-breach-toronto-police-say-1.3201432.

236. Chirgwin, R. (2015, August 23). Ashley Madison spam starts, as leak linked to first suicide. *The Register.* https://www.theregister.co.uk/2015/08/23/ashley_madison_spam_starts_as_leak_linked_to_first_suicide/.

237. 10 effective ways to protect your intellectual property. (2018, July 23). *Forbes Technology Council.* https://www.forbes.com/sites/forbestechcouncil/2018/07/23/10-effective-ways-to-protect-your-intellectual-property/#254c7f5732e1.

238. iRobot sues Hoover and Black & Decker over robo-vacuums. (2017, April 18). *BBC.* https://www.bbc.co.uk/news/technology-39629339.

239. D&O liability in data privacy and cyber security situations in the US. (2014, January). *Financier Worldwide.* https://www.financierworldwide.com/do-liability-in-data-privacy-and-cyber-security-situations-in-the-us/#.W9V-GtP7QdU.

240. 15 U.S.C.A. § 45(n) (West). In assessing the reasonableness of cybersecurity practices, courts have considered the sensitivity of data, the size and complexity of the company's network, and the cost of additional security measures. See F.T.C. v. Wyndham Worldwide Corp., 799 F.3d 236, 255 (3d Cir. 2015).

241. *Enhanced cyber risk management standards*, 81 Fed. Reg. 74315 (proposed October 26, 2016) (to be codified at 12 C.F.R. pt. 30). https://www.federalregister.gov/documents/2016/10/26/2016-25871/enhanced-cyber-risk-management-standards.

242. Cyber-security regulation. *Wikipedia.* Accessed October 2018. https://en.wikipedia.org/wiki/Cyber-security_regulation.

243. Cyber-attack: Your legal responsibilities as a company director. (2017, September). *Finch.* https://www.finchib.co.uk/cyber-attack-legal-responsibilities-company-director/.

244. *The Telegraph.* (2018, February 28). Why digital-age directors need directors and officers (D&O) cover. https://www.telegraph.co.uk/business/risk-insights/directors-need-d-and-o-insurance/.

245. Kurt, M. N., Yılmaz, Y., & Wang, X. (2018, June 28). *Real-time detection of hybrid and stealthy cyber-attacks in smart grid.* IEEE (arXiv:1803.00128v2 [cs. IT]). https://arxiv.org/pdf/1803.00128.

246. Cazorla, L., Alcaraz, C., & Lopez, J. (2018, June). Cyber stealth attacks in critical information infrastructures. *IEEE Systems Journal, 12*(2). https://iee-explore.ieee.org/document/7445136.

247. Is data manipulation the next step in cybercrime? *Cloudmask*. Accessed October 2018. https://www.cloudmask.com/blog/is-data-manipulation-the-next-step-in-cybercrime.

248. Myer, D. (2017, November 17). ID card security: Spain is facing chaos over chip crypto flaws. *ZDNet*. https://www.zdnet.com/article/id-card-security-spain-is-facing-chaos-over-chip-crypto-flaws/.

249. Leyden, J. (2017, November 3). Estonia government locks down ID smartcards: Refresh or else. *The Register*. https://www.theregister.co.uk/2017/11/03/estonian_e_id_lockdown/.

250. *Meltdown and spectre*. Accessed October 2018. https://meltdownattack.com/.

251. WikiLeaks dumps docs on CIA's hacking tools. *Krebsonsecurity*. Accessed October 2018. https://krebsonsecurity.com/tag/weeping-angel/.

252. Friedmann, S. (2017, March 13). What is the weeping angel program? John Oliver debunked the rumors. *Bustle*. https://www.bustle.com/p/what-is-the-weeping-angel-program-john-oliver-debunked-the-rumors-43861.

253. Lee, D. (2016, February 18). Apple v the FBI—A plain English guide. *BBC*. https://www.bbc.co.uk/news/technology-35601035.

254. Lapowsky, I. (2018, April 18). How Russian Facebook ads divided and targeted US voters before the 2016 election. *Wired*. https://www.wired.com/story/russian-facebook-ads-targeted-us-voters-before-2016-election/.

255. Stewart, E. (2018, July 31). Facebook has already detected suspicious activity trying to influence the 2018 elections. *Vox*. https://www.vox.com/2018/7/31/17635592/facebook-elections-russia-2018-midterms.

256. Facebook-Cambridge Analytica data scandal. *BBC*. Accessed October 2018. https://www.bbc.co.uk/news/topics/c81zyn08881t/facebook-cambridge-analytica-data-scandal.

257. Hatton, E. (2018, February 12). Life online: How big is your digital footprint? *RNZ*. https://www.radionz.co.nz/news/national/350224/life-online-how-big-is-your-digital-footprint.

258. ISO/IEC 27032:2012—Information technology—Security techniques—Guidelines for cybersecurity. http://www.iso27001security.com/html/27032.html.

259. *Cost of Cyber Crime Report 2017*. Ponemon Institute LLC. https://www.accenture.com/t20171006T095146Z__w__/us-en/_acnmedia/PDF-62/Accenture-2017CostCybercrime-US-FINAL.pdf#zoom=50.

260. *Bletchley park*. Accessed October 2018. https://en.wikipedia.org/wiki/Bletchley_Park.

261. *How Alan Turing cracked the enigma code*. (2018, January). Imperial War Museum, UK. https://www.iwm.org.uk/history/how-alan-turing-cracked-the-enigma-code.

262. *Case study: Screening out malicious computer hackers*. FAMA. Accessed October 2018. https://static1.squarespace.com/static/58d277cfe6f2e10bb-3d0ea70/t/59026913e6f2e110bafd7b75/1493330195511/Fama+Case+Study+-+Hacking.pdf.

263. *Anonymous hackers' official website*. http://www.anonymoushackers.net/.

264. *The operation newblood super-secret security handbook by anonymous*. https://elusuariofinal.wordpress.com/2011/07/01/the-operation-newblood-super-secret-security-handbook-by-anonymous/.

265. Octave v2.0 (and Octave-S v1.0 for small and medium businesses). https://www.enisa.europa.eu/topics/threat-risk-management/risk-management/current-risk/risk-management-inventory/rm-ra-methods/m_octave.html.

266. Egan, M. (2018, April). What is the dark web and how to access it. *Tech Advisor IDG*. https://www.techadvisor.co.uk/how-to/internet/dark-web-3593569/.

267. Frey, T. (2015, September). The future of the darknet: 9 critically important predictions. *Futurist Speaker*. https://www.futuristspeaker.com/business-trends/the-future-of-the-darknet-9-critically-important-predictions/.

268. Hacker ratings, rating defenses. (2018, September). *NCSC*. https://www.ncsc.gov.uk/blog-post/rating-hackers-rating-defences.

269. Structured Threat Information eXpression (STIX™) 1.x archive website a structured language for cyberthreat intelligence. https://oasis-open.github.io/cti-documentation/.

270. STIX™ TAXII™ documentation. https://oasis-open.github.io/cti-documentation/.

271. *Japan: Legal responses to the Great East Japan Earthquake of 2011, Law.gov The Law Library of Congress*. Accessed September 2018. https://www.loc.gov/law/help/japan-earthquake/index.php.

272. Kaufmann, D., & Penciakova, V. (2011, March). *Japan's triple disaster: Governance and the earthquake, tsunami and nuclear crises*. Brookings Institute. https://www.brookings.edu/opinions/japans-triple-disaster-governance-and-the-earthquake-tsunami-and-nuclear-crises/.

273. Dellinger, A. J. (2017, May). Telefonica WannaCry Ransomware: One of Spain's largest telecom companies hit by cyberattack. *International Business Times*. https://www.ibtimes.com/telefonica-wannacry-ransomware-one-spains-largest-telecom-companies-hit-cyberattack-2538211.

274. *Investigation: WannaCry cyber-attack and the NHS*. (2018, April). (NAO Report) Department of Health. https://www.nao.org.uk/wp-content/uploads/2017/10/Investigation-WannaCry-cyber-attack-and-the-NHS.pdf.

275. Smart, W. (2018, February). *Lessons learned review of the WannaCry Ransomware cyber attack* (NHS Independent Report). Chief Information Officer for Health and Social Care. https://www.england.nhs.uk/wp-content/uploads/2018/02/lessons-learned-review-wannacry-ransomware-cyber-attack-cio-review.pdf.

276. Jones, S. (2017, May). Timeline: How the WannaCry cyber-attack spread. *Financial Times.* https://www.ft.com/content/82b01aca-38b7-11e7-821a-6027b8a20f23.

277. Cyber grand challenge (CGC). *DARPA.* https://www.darpa.mil/program/cyber-grand-challenge.

278. "decidability" and "verifiability". *StackExchange.* https://cs.stackexchange.com/questions/12068/please-explain-decidability-and-verifiability.

279. *NP-hardness.* Accessed September 2018. https://ipfs.io/ipfs/QmXoypizjW3WknFiJnKLwHCnL72vedxjQkDDP1mXWo6uco/wiki/NP-hardness.html.

280. Stepanova, E. (2008). *Terrorism in asymmetrical conflict: Stockholm International Peace Research Institute* (SIPRI Report 23) (PDF). Oxford University.

281. *Asymmetric cyber-attack definition.* Accessed September 2018. https://whatis.techtarget.com/definition/asymmetric-cyber-attack.

282. Solon, O. (2016, August). Hacking group auctions 'cyber weapons' stolen from NSA. *The Guardian.* https://www.theguardian.com/technology/2016/aug/16/shadow-brokers-hack-auction-nsa-malware-equation-group.

283. Megiddo, G. (2018, July). NSO employee 'Stole' classified Israeli cyberweapons to sell on Darknet. *Haaretz.* https://www.haaretz.com/israel-news/nso-employee-stole-classified-israeli-cyber-weapons-to-sell-on-darknet-1.6244589.

284. Zilber, N. (2018, August). The rise of cyber-mercenaries. *Foreign Policy.* https://foreignpolicy.com/2018/08/31/the-rise-of-the-cyber-mercenaries-israel-nso/.

285. Morris Worm, *DDoS attack definitions—DdoSPedia.* https://security.radware.com/ddos-knowledge-center/ddospedia/morris-worm/.

286. *Phone phreaking.* http://www.historyofphonephreaking.org/faq.php.

287. Grey Market. *Wikipedia,* Accessed October 2018. https://en.wikipedia.org/wiki/Grey_market.

288. Pastrana, S., Hutchings, A., Caines, A., & Buttery, P. (2018, September 10–12). Characterizing eve: Analysing cybercrime actors in a large underground forum. *21st International Symposium*, RAID 2018, Heraklion, Crete, Greece. Proceedings. https://www.cl.cam.ac.uk/~sp849/files/RAID_2018.pdf.

289. Leyden, J. (2016, April). Hackers so far ahead of defenders it's not even a game. *The Register.* https://www.theregister.co.uk/2016/04/26/verizon_breach_report/.

290. Gaissmaier, W. (2012, September). *More traffic deaths in wake of 9/11.* Senior Fellow/Harding Center for Risk Literacy, Max Planck Institute for Human Development, Berlin. https://www.mpg.de/6347636/terrorism_traffic-accidents-USA.

291. Jenkins, A. (2017, July). Which is safer: Airplanes or cars? *Fortune.* http://fortune.com/2017/07/20/are-airplanes-safer-than-cars/.

292. *The 6 dimensions of national culture*. Accessed October 2018. https://www. hofstede-insights.com/models/national-culture/.

293. McCarthy, N. (2015, July). America's insane rate of gun homicide in perspective. *Statista*. https://www.statista.com/chart/3672/americas-insane-rate-of-gun-homicide-in-perspective/.

294. Lopez, G. (2018, June). America's unique gun violence problem, explained in 17 maps and charts. *Vox*. https://www.vox.com/policy-and-politics/2017/10/2/16399418/us-gun-violence-statistics-maps-charts.

295. Kahan, D., & Braman, D. (2003, April). More statistics, less persuasion: A cultural issues of gun-risk perceptions. Article. *University of Pennsylvania Law Review, 151*(4). https://scholarship.law.upenn.edu/cgi/viewcontent. cgi?article=3212&context=penn_law_review.

296. Reddy, C. Top 10 pros and cons of hiring hackers to enhance security. *Wisestep*. Accessed October 2018. https://content.wisestep.com/top-pros-cons-hiring-hackers-enhance-security/.

297. Palmer, D. (2018, September). Is hiring a hacker ever a good idea? *ZDNet*. https://www.zdnet.com/article/is-hiring-a-hacker-ever-a-good-idea/.

298. *Global cyberlympics 2018*. https://www.cyberlympics.org/about-the-games/.

299. Hack the world 2017–2018. *HackerOne*. https://www.hackerone.com/hacktheworld/2017.

300. Khandelwal, S. (2016, September). The project zero contest—Google will Pay you $200,000 to hack android OS. *HackerNews*. https://thehackernews. com/2016/09/hacking-android-competition.html.

301. Silvanovich, N. (2017, March). Project zero prize conclusion. Project zero. *Google*. https://googleprojectzero.blogspot.com/2017/03/project-zero-prize-conclusion.html.

302. Giles, M. (2018, August). AI for cybersecurity is a hot new thing—And a dangerous gamble. *MIT Sloane Review*. https://www.technologyreview. com/s/611860/ai-for-cybersecurity-is-a-hot-new-thing-and-a-dangerous-gamble/.

303. Knight, W. (2017, April). The dark secret at the heart of AI. *MIT Sloane Review*. https://www.technologyreview.com/s/604087/the-dark-secret-at-the-heart-of-ai/.

304. *DARPA's explainable artificial intelligence (XAI) program 2018*. https://www. src.org/calendar/e006556/abstract_gunning.pdf.

305. Kenyon, H. S. (2018, February). *AI, Please Explain Yourself.* Signals AFCEA. https://www.afcea.org/content/ai-please-explain-yourself.

306. *AI is changing cybersecurity, but it's not a catch-all solution*. Computing. Accessed October 2018. https://www.computing.co.uk/ctg/sponsored/3063441/ai-is-changing-cybersecurity-but-its-not-a-catch-all-solution.

307. Partnoy, F. (2011, July). The cost of a human life, statistically speaking. *The Globalist.* https://www.theglobalist.com/the-cost-of-a-human-life-statistically-speaking/.

308. *Philips lighting is now Signify.* (2018, May 16). Press Release. https://www.signify.com/en-us/about/news/press-releases/2018/20180516-philips-lighting-is-now-signify.

309. Ram, A., Wisniewska, A., Kao, J. S., Rininsland, Æ., & Nevitt, C. (2018, October 23). How smartphone apps track users and share data. *Financial Times.* https://ig.ft.com/mobile-app-data-trackers/.

310. Binns, R., Lyngs, U., Van Kleek, M., Zhao, J., Libert, T., & Shadbolt, N. (2018). Third party tracking in the mobile ecosystem. *Computers and Society.* https://doi.org/10.1145/3201064.3201089, https://arxiv.org/pdf/1804.03603.pdf.

311. Taylor, V. F., & Martinovic, I. Short paper: A longitudinal study of financial apps in the google play store. *International Conference on Financial Cryptography and Data Security,* FC 2017: December 2017, Financial Cryptography and Data Security (pp 302–309).

312. Lardinois, F. (2018, January). Google says it removed 700K apps from the Play Store in 2017, up 70% from 2016. *Techcrunch.* https://techcrunch.com/2018/01/30/google-says-it-removed-700k-apps-from-the-play-store-in-2017-up-70-from-2016/.

313. Shu, C. (2018, October). Twitter says it has removed several accounts affiliated with Infowars and Alex Jones. *Techcrunch.* https://techcrunch.com/2018/10/22/twitter-says-it-has-removed-several-accounts-affiliated-with-infowars-and-alex-jones/.

314. Wagner, K. & Molla, R. (2018, May). Facebook has disabled almost 1.3 billion fake accounts over the past six months. *Recode.* https://www.recode.net/2018/5/15/17349790/facebook-mark-zuckerberg-fake-accounts-content-policy-update.

315. *Unity3D website.* https://unity3d.com/.

Index

© The Editor(s) (if applicable) and The Author(s), under exclusive licence to Springer Nature Switzerland AG 2019
G. Pogrebna and M. Skilton, *Navigating New Cyber Risks*,
https://doi.org/10.1007/978-3-030-13527-0